Eris
Sacred Feminine Force of Evolutionary Astrology

Daniel Fiverson

THE WESSEX ASTROLOGER

Published in 2025 by The Wessex Astrologer Ltd
PO Box 9307
Swanage
BH19 9BF
England

For a full list of our titles go to www.wessexastrologer.com

Copyright and Confidentiality Statement
All Rights Reserved by the Author

All material shared is the sole intellectual property of Daniel Fiverson. This includes, but is not limited to: personal stories, biographical details, philosophical views, political commentary, creative writing, original research, astrological interpretations, mythological analysis, teaching content, and conceptual frameworks.

The author retains full copyright and creative control over all content, whether composed during a paid subscription period or otherwise. No content is to be shared, published, replicated, archived, distributed, or used by any affiliated entities without the explicit, written consent of the author.

All content is considered private, privileged, and protected, whether it appears as fact, fiction, hyperbole, or creative metaphor. Any breach of this agreement or unauthorized use of the author's material is considered a violation of intellectual property rights.

All rights are reserved by the author.

© 2025 Daniel Fiverson

ISBN 9781916625402

Cover design by Fiona Bowring

Typeset by Kevin Moore

A catalogue record for this book is available at The British Library

No part of this book may be reproduced or used in any form or by any means without the written permission of the publisher. Without limiting the exclusive rights of any author, contributor, or the publisher of this publication, any unauthorised use of this publication to train generative artificial intelligence (AI) technologies is expressly prohibited.

A reviewer may quote brief passages.

Table of Contents

Acknowledgments	vii
The Long Arc of Becoming	1
A Journey to the Heart of the Heavens	5
We are Stardust	9
As Above, So Below	12
Perhaps There Never Was a "Stone Age"	13
The Astronomy of Eris	18
The Mythology of Eris	20
The Judgment of Paris and the Apple of Discord	30
The Ubiquity of Apples in Culture and Mythology	31
Helen of Troy	33
Helen and Eris: Mirrors of Chaos and Revelation	34
Helen: The Reflection of a Greater Illusion	35
Eris and Helen in Evolutionary Astrology	36
Helen as disrupter	37
Aeneas and The Founding of Rome	37
The Astrology of Eris	39
Outer Planet Transits to Eris	39
The Recent Last Quarter Square between Pluto in Capricorn and Eris in Aries	40
Pluto-Eris and Neptune-Eris Cycles	46
Catalysts of Transformation and Ideological Reckoning	46
Perfections of Eris by Aspect and Sign	46

Pluto and Eris: Cycles of Power and Upheaval	48
Neptune and Eris: Cycles of Myth and Revelation	50
The Rise of Authoritarianism and Social Disruptions (2016–Present)	52
Eris and Climate Change – Earth's Reckoning	54
Earth-Based Spiritual Traditions – Reweaving the Sacred Web	56
A Nation at the Crossroads of Power and Discord	57
The Billionaire Class and Plutocracy's Last Stand	62
Eris in Our Charts: Working with Eris	65
Eris Through The Houses	70
1st House ~ How We Meet The World	73
2nd House ~ What do I need to Survive?	88
3rd House ~ Voice in the World	107
4th House ~ Self Awareness	123
5th House ~ Self Actualization	140
6th House ~ Growth Through Crisis	150
7th House ~ The Dating Game	165
8th House ~ The Sacred Commitment	180
9th House ~ What Is Greater Than Self	194
10th House ~ Consensus Reality	205
11th House ~ Liberation from Conditioning	213
12th House ~ The Reconnection	231
From Chaos to Clarity	243
Afterword	246
About the Author	249

She didn't bow.
She didn't plead.
She felt no hunger.
She had no need.
She stood alone, outside the wall,
And threw the golden apple to them all.

Upon its side, a phrase declared:
"To the fairest"
None were spared.

The sky split wide.
The stillness broke.
The goddesses turned.
The heavens spoke.
The gods took sides.
The war began.
A city burned.
So too, man.

And she?
She vanished in the flame.
No glory sought.
No mortal name.

But no one could ignore her thread
The truth she tossed, the lie it shed.

For Eris doesn't storm the gate.
She names the cracks we cultivate.

© Daniel Fiverson

This book is dedicated to Sadie Fiona
and her Pluto in Capricorn generation
that will build the New Earth.

Acknowledgments

To my beloved partner, Susan Waller, whose unwavering love, intuitive insight, and sharp editorial eye have shaped this manuscript and whose daily presence encourages me to live with greater clarity, truth, and vitality. To Kim Marie Weimer, who opened the door to Evolutionary Astrology and guided me through the certification process. To Jason Holley, who bridged astrology and mythology, transforming my engagement with the chart into a living story. To the late Gwen Pointer, whose boundless heart and luminous spirit uplifted me in ways I am still uncovering. To Kepler College and the Kepler Toastmasters, whose steady support continues to strengthen my voice. To the many authors, teachers, and colleagues who have generously shared their time and wisdom, enriching our growing astrological community. To the spiritual currents of Santa Fe, New Mexico, rooted in the sacred lands and cultural lineages of Native American and Hispanic traditions, whose beauty, mystery, and power have nourished me for over thirty years.

My unbounded gratitude to Margaret Cahill and The Wessex Astrologer for seeing the value in this work and making it available to our worldwide community. My thanks also to Pete Bevington for his articulate editing.

This volume is intended for the astrological community, seekers, healers, and all who feel drawn to this fierce, truth-bearing archetype. It explores Eris in Evolutionary Astrology—her mythology, natal expression, transits, and her role in our individual and collective evolution, honoring her complexity, power, and timing. I dedicate this book to the journey that found me—and to those ready to embrace their truth alongside Eris—not as outsiders, but as guides. We are living in a time when Eris will no longer remain on the margins. She is confronting the gates of the empire, demanding accountability—not for destruction, but for renewal. This book stands in affirmation of that call. It offers both a comprehensive exploration and a practical guide for astrologers, seekers, and soul-centered practitioners eager to consciously engage with Eris and the Evolutionary Astrology lineage of Jeffrey Wolf Green.

Welcome to the story behind the story. Welcome to the long arc of becoming.

Daniel Fiverson
Santa Fe, NM Summer 2025

The Long Arc of Becoming

I didn't seek out astrology; it found me. Quietly, yes—but with a strange feeling that my life had just taken a turn it was always meant to take. It started with a book about Leo that I found at a bookstore in New Jersey. Leo is my Sun sign. At the time, I didn't know much about astrology. The book was large, a coffee table edition, with a tawny lion on the cover. Something about that lion—its head turned, looking straight at me—grabbed my attention. I flipped through every page of that modern tome many times, trying to piece together the astrological puzzle that was me.

A few years later, during my first Saturn return, that quiet spark of curiosity ignited into something unmistakable. I signed up for my first astrology class, and everything changed. It felt less like studying and more like remembering—like something ancient and vital had awakened. The language of astrology didn't just make sense to my mind; it resonated deeply within me. When the teacher described Mars as fiery and independent, I didn't just hear it—I knew it. Yet, I also felt restricted by how astrology was often taught: a limited set of keywords used like formulas, as if the soul could be reduced to flashcards. I sensed that astrology wasn't meant to be memorized and regurgitated; it was meant to be felt, lived, and listened to. When the teacher began speaking of planetary archetypes as living forces—dynamic, evolving, multidimensional—I finally felt at home.

But as always, life moved to its own rhythm. I didn't pursue it professionally—yet. I spent two decades in the growing world of technology, trained on two platforms, Windows and Mac—like Ben-Hur in a chariot race, one of the first IT professionals in Santa Fe. I excelled at it, and it paid the bills. However—the deeper call—the one awakened by that Leo book—never fully quieted down. When my second Saturn return arrived, it didn't just stir old longings—it turned the wheel. A friend came to dinner one evening and mentioned an astrology reading she'd had. Something in her words lit a fuse. I asked for the astrologer's name, and that's how I found Kim Marie Weimer, then director of the Jeffrey Wolf Green School of Evolutionary Astrology. Two readings later, I was deep down the rabbit hole. Not just curious—claimed. I began reading and absorbing Jeffrey Wolf Green's work, letting it seep into me like water into dry ground. As my confidence grew, I started offering readings—tentatively at first, then with increasing clarity. The more I practiced, the more the work came alive, as if the charts themselves were speaking through me.

My first public reading took place in 2013 at a psychic fair in Albuquerque, New Mexico. I remember sitting at my table—nervous, yes, but mostly ready. I trusted the charts to open the way, and they did.

The first person who sat across from me listened with quiet, intense focus. Then she paused,

"I am a medical intuitive. I've had many readings," she said, "but no one has ever told me what you just told me."

That moment was unforgettable. It rooted something inside me—not just affirmation but confirmation. It demonstrated that when you trust the chart and allow it to speak without trying to control or perform, it can touch the soul. And when that occurs, something genuine shifts.

Soon after, I started offering spontaneous fifteen-minute Pluto readings at the Santa Fe Artisan Market. The atmosphere was unpredictable—filled with noise, the rhythm of foot traffic, and distractions—but the questions felt raw, urgent, and alive.

It was there that I sharpened my instincts. I learned to follow the thread, speak from the heart, and hold space for the soul's unfolding. Time and again, I saw how what I said about Pluto penetrated the surface and reached deep.

It wasn't about prediction; it was about recognition. Something within them knew it was true.

I continued to immerse myself in the teachings of Jeffrey Wolf Green, supported by Kim Marie, whose clarity and heart-centered guidance helped steady and ground my path.

Alongside that foundation, I began incorporating insights from other voices—absorbing the wisdom of Liz Greene, Howard Sasportas, Mark Jones, Brian Clark, Patricia Walsh, Steven Forrest, and others. Each offered their unique perspective and language for the soul's journey. I wasn't just gathering techniques; I was weaving a tapestry. In 2017, during my second

Saturn square, a mentorship with Jason Holley opened everything wide. Jason helped me connect astrology and mythology—not as mere metaphor, but as living reality. Through him, I realized that the chart was not just a map or diagnostic tool—it was a mythic script, alive with story, memory, and potential; a reflection of the soul's becoming.

And somewhere in the midst of all this, Eris arrived. Not through Jason. Not from a class or a textbook. I was simply, unmistakably drawn in—pulled in by the dramatic effects I noticed around me with increasing regularity.

Eris declares:

"I will not be ignored. I will not be diminished. I will not partake in deception."

She arrived just like she always does: uninvited, unapologetic, and completely undeniable.

What started as a flicker of curiosity turned into a calling. The more I explored—her cycles, her symbolism, her fingerprints across charts and history—the more it became clear: Eris is not just a minor planet. She is a powerful force in the evolution of consciousness.

She reveals what has been denied, distorted, or exiled—especially in the realm of the sacred feminine, both personal and collective. Eris doesn't just stir the pot; she tips it over when it's full of lies. She brings the truth to the surface, even if it shatters everything wide open.

So it was no surprise when I found out that Eris is conjunct my natal Moon in the 8th house—a placement that changed not only how I saw myself but also set me on a hero's journey of descent, confrontation, and transformation.

This book is the result of years spent listening to her—analyzing charts, tracking transits, tracing patterns through myth and history, and observing her influence in the lives of those she touches. It combines astrology, invocation, analysis, and remembrance. Throughout this journey, I have been supported by the steadfast love and encouragement of my partner, Susan Waller, who believed in this path long before I fully embraced it. Her intuition, keen perception, and deep grounding in the metaphysical have shaped this work in ways words cannot fully express. If you've found your way here, perhaps Eris has already begun working in your life. Maybe she's knocking—gently or forcefully. Either way, remember this: you are not alone.

Her myth, discovery, and undeniable presence in the collective consciousness point to a larger cycle of awakening. She began appearing repeatedly in the charts I examined of those challenging systems, speaking uncomfortable truths and standing at the thresholds of transformation. I realized I had to follow the thread; I needed to learn more. This book represents the culmination of a long and transformative journey—one marked by wonder, disruption, devotion, and the courage to confront what most would rather leave unnamed.

These pages intertwine mythology, historical cycles, collective transformation, and astrological methodology to present Eris as a dynamic evolutionary archetype—one who speaks directly to the thresholds we currently face, both personally and globally. Within the framework of Evolutionary Astrology, Eris emerges not just as a disruptor but as a catalytic force—one who reveals hidden truths, challenges conditioned norms, and stimulates individuality and soul evolution.

The upcoming chapters delve into her mythic and astronomical roots, her natal expression by sign, house, and aspect, and her most significant transits—past, present, and future. Particular focus is given to our current era and its unprecedented nine squares to the U.S. Pluto from 2026 to 2030, analyzed through historical resonance and collective karmic dynamics.

Many case studies show how Eris appears across the evolutionary spectrum—from distortion to integration, including angels and devils, saints and sinners. Whether you're sharpening your interpretive skills, expanding your client work, or responding to Eris' call in your own life, this book invites you to see her not as an outlier but as a crucial archetype for these changing times.

A Journey to the Heart of the Heavens

You have opened a book that is more than words. It is a vessel of transmission, a compass for the initiatory path, a mirror that reflects the soul's unrest. Within these pages, we turn our gaze toward a singular celestial force: **Eris**, the slow-moving awakener at the farthest edge of the solar system. She is the truth-teller and disruptor, the exiled outsider whose return shakes foundations so that deeper alignment may rise.

For centuries unseen, unnamed, ignored—yet never silent—Eris has spoken through upheaval, rebellion, and revelation. She has whispered through myth, stirred the waters of history, and now steps fully into the astrological pantheon. She offers no easy solace. Her gift is clarity; her presence is confrontation. She unmasks what has been denied, excluded, or suppressed, insisting we reckon with what lies in shadow.

Eris is no abstraction. She moves palpably through human lives—artists, visionaries, activists, and outcasts who embody her provocations. Through their stories, we will witness how she manifests: wounding and liberating, shattering illusions and reshaping identity. We will follow her as she squares Pluto, opposes Saturn, trines Uranus, and aligns with the Sun and Moon, sparking transformation that arcs from the deeply personal to the collective soul.

Her aspects weave her into the tapestry of cosmic intelligence. With Pluto she intensifies the call to evolution, with Uranus she ignites awakening, with Neptune she tests transcendence, and with Saturn she hammers at structures until only truth remains. Every movement reveals another thread of her design.

This is not merely a study of a distant body; it is a descent into the psyche and an ascent into the heavens. Eris calls us to remember who we are beneath conditioning, compromise, and control. She summons the voice that has been silenced, the truth that has been exiled, the part of ourselves that refuses conformity. Disruption, in her hands, is not destruction—it is awakening.

Her story mirrors our own. Her path, like ours, is a spiral of endless return. Discovered in the early twenty-first century, she appeared as both omen and oracle, her orbit echoing the turbulence of our times. She bridges the ancient and the modern, the scientific and the sacred, the cosmic and the intimate. Eris is not only a planetary body; she is a living myth, a force who unveils truths that must be lived, not merely known.

At the core of this book stands **Evolutionary Astrology**—not as prediction, nor as personality sketch, but as sacred dialogue between sky and soul. Following Eris' celestial arc, we trace her passage through history, collective upheaval, and the landscapes of our lives. Named for the goddess of strife and discord, Eris reveals the essence of our era: a time of reckoning, unveiling, and radical change.

The world trembles. Divides deepen. Systems fracture. The Earth herself cries out. These are not random calamities but sacred mantras of Eris: symptoms of imbalance and signals of potential. She exposes fault lines so they may be healed. She presses us to confront the denied, dismantle the obsolete, and question the inherited.

Yet Eris does not leave us in ruins. Her upheaval clears the way for renewal. The same current that unsettles also awakens insight and resilience. My own journey, like that of many others, has been marked by her cycles—through both dark nights and radiant dawns she has urged me closer to truth, to witness both the wound and the wonder of being human. In this age of uncertainty, her fierce wisdom is our summons: to embody integrity, to claim our rightful voice, to evolve.

This work emerges not in isolation but from a living community—seekers, healers, teachers, wild crafters, and keepers of Earth's memory—those attuned to the sacred pulse of land and sky. By tending both soil and spirit, we remember the old ways of knowing. Eris now speaks through the biosphere itself, inviting us to reimagine what it means to live in harmony—with one another, with the Earth, with the Mystery that holds us all.

I invite you to enter this journey with reverence and curiosity. Whether you come as a seasoned astrologer or a newcomer to these mysteries, may these pages serve as companions and guides.

As we follow Eris' path across the heavens, let us also map the contours of our own becoming. In that reflection, may we remember: we, too, belong to the vast celestial dance—ever turning, ever evolving, ever illuminated.

Fasten your seat belt. We are about to go out beyond Neptune into the Kuiper Belt.

> "We are stardust
> Billion-year-old carbon.
> We are golden
> Caught in the devil's bargain,
> And we've got to get ourselves
> Back to the garden."
>
> —Joni Mitchell, Woodstock

We are Stardust

As we navigate the first quarter-century of a new era, radical technologies, deepening insights, and global upheavals continue to reshape our understanding of reality. Space telescopes like Hubble and Webb have provided breathtaking images of the cosmos—vistas once confined to imagination—now revealed in luminous detail. These glimpses into our celestial neighborhood expand the boundaries of perception and invite us to contemplate existence on entirely new scales.

At the dawn of the 20th century, Percival Lowell's search for Planet X led to the discovery of Pluto in 1930. This turning point expanded astrology's frontiers and symbolized a descent into the underworld of psyche and power. A century later, a new wave of celestial bodies—Trans-Neptunian objects (TNOs)—has emerged from the icy reaches beyond Neptune. With their elongated, elliptical orbits that span hundreds of years, these distant wanderers remain elusive, mystical, and rich in symbolic meaning.

This object, later named Eris, was first captured in a digital image on October 21, 2003. However, its motion across the sky was so slow that it was initially mistaken for a stationary star. It appeared again in images taken ten days later, on October 31, but the movement still went unnoticed. It wasn't until January 5, 2005—during a reanalysis of earlier data that had also revealed the dwarf planet Sedna—that astronomers realized the object had shifted position. Just three days later, on January 8, they confirmed the discovery.

Originally designated 2003 UB313, the object awaited formal classification by the International Astronomical Union (IAU). In the interim, Brown and his team nicknamed it "Xena," after the television character Xena: Warrior Princess—a tongue-in-cheek choice, but also a conscious nod toward incorporating more female figures into the naming of celestial bodies.

Because Eris initially appeared as large as Pluto, many early reports—including those from NASA—heralded it as the "tenth planet." But its discovery raised fundamental questions about how to define a planet. The possibility of more Pluto-sized objects lurking in the Kuiper Belt prompted the IAU to craft a formal definition of "planet" for the first time since the era of Galileo. As a result, Pluto was reclassified as a dwarf planet in 2006, and Eris was placed in the same category.

Orbiting the Sun at nearly twice Pluto's distance and completing one revolution every 557 years, Eris remains the largest known dwarf planet after Pluto in the solar system. Its discovery sent shockwaves through both the astronomical and astrological communities—true to its namesake, Eris, the Greek goddess of discord, who upends order and reveals hidden tensions.

Although unseen until the 21st century, Eris' astrological signature has long been influential, shaping historical waves of unrest, resistance, and radical change. The evolutionary forces she embodies—disruption, confrontation, the fracturing of old paradigms—are interwoven with the upheavals of the modern era. The rising tension and pressure we face today reflect her influence: fierce, relentless, and often uncomfortable, yet profoundly catalytic.

Her discovery sent shockwaves through both astronomy and astrology. She not only challenged the definition of "planet" itself but also catalyzed a planetary reordering that dethroned Pluto, forcing the scientific community to grapple with a deeper truth: our system is far more complex and far less fixed than we had imagined. The debates, conflicts, and reclassifications that followed her emergence echo the very essence of Eris—a force that disrupts to reveal and provokes to awaken.

This book explores Eris' consciousness as it emerges into collective awareness. Her discovery is not a coincidence but a mirror of archetypal necessity—a reflection of the currents already flowing through our cultural, ecological, and personal lives.

In the pages ahead, I will ask and explore several guiding questions:

- Who is Eris, the mythological figure, and what does she symbolize?
- How does her mythology respond to the crises and transformations of our time?

- What historical events illustrate her archetypal pattern, both past and present?
- How does Eris operate in the natal chart, particularly concerning house and aspect?

Through this inquiry we will uncover Eris not merely as a harbinger of chaos, but as a sacred catalyst—an evolutionary force that demands honesty, agency, and awakening. Her influence is not limited to turmoil; it serves as a call to reclaim what has been excluded, to illuminate what lies in shadow, and to forge new ground where the old has crumbled.

By tracing her orbit, we follow the arc of disruption that leads not to destruction, but to possibility.

As Above, So Below

We are woven from the same elemental forces and energetic frequencies as the planets and stars. Though they may seem distant, separated by millions of miles, there is no true "space" between us and the cosmos. We are entangled in the same ethereal matrix—interconnected, inseparable, and alive within the same breath of creation.

The universe is not merely a collection of isolated bodies but a singularity, a pulsing field of paired opposites. Our survival as a species—and the flourishing of life itself—depends on a dynamic balance: masculine and feminine, light and dark, warmth and cold, strength and vulnerability, positive and negative. These polarities are not in conflict; instead, they exist in a relationship that forms the foundation of all existence.

Circadian rhythms ripple through every living organism, orchestrating cycles of rest and activity. The turning of the seasons choreographs the ancient dance of birth, growth, release, and renewal. All life moves in waves, spirals, and cosmic patterns that are reflected within and beyond the body.

The architecture of creation repeats itself, ranging from the minute structures seen under an electron microscope to the spiraling arms of distant galaxies unveiled by space telescopes. This mysterious, synchronous mirroring suggests a living intelligence that connects the micro and the macro. We stand precisely at the intersection, bridging the infinite with the infinitesimal.

Since the earliest markings on stone and clay, humanity has sensed and celebrated its connection to the heavens. The stars and planets above have been viewed not merely as lights in the sky, but as reflections of the soul, symbols of divine order, and active participants in the grand unfolding of human experience.

Perhaps There Never Was a "Stone Age"

Some of the oldest known human habitations, dating back 20,000 to 30,000 years, feature drawings and pictograms of animals that align with the archetypal images we recognize today. The artistic sophistication of these works rivals that of modern art, suggesting that what we refer to as the 'Stone Age" was a time of intelligence and literacy, perhaps even equal to or surpassing our cognitive abilities. We label this era the Stone Age solely because stone artifacts are the only ones that have endured.

What will future generations call our era? Will they label it the Plastic Age, marked by the synthetic remnants of our civilization? Just as we reconstruct the past from what survives, our legacy will likewise be shaped by what endures.

Monuments and structures scattered along ley lines across the Earth challenge our understanding of ancient civilizations, such as the Sphinx, the Pyramids, Machu Picchu, Göbekli Tepe, Chaco Canyon, and Stonehenge. Is it not a presumptuous miscalculation to assume that early societies lacked a profound understanding of the cosmos? Perhaps their knowledge was on a par with ours, and in some respects, even greater.

In this regard, it is essential to look to the past for the foundation of our modern celestial sciences, with astrology being the earliest among them. Evidence of astrology dates back at least to ancient Sumer, a civilization that predates those of Egypt, China, and India. Sumerian writings, preserved on clay tablets, come from at least 3500 BCE, if not earlier. The history of celestial divination is generally understood to have begun with the late Old Babylonian texts (c. 1800 BCE) and continued through the Middle Babylonian and Middle Assyrian periods (c. 1200 BCE).

However, these timelines depend entirely on the remnants of acknowledged civilizations. History, as we understand it, is shaped by what lasts. Recently discovered footprints in White Sands, New Mexico, indicate a human presence dating back at least 23,000 years, challenging our assumptions about the depth of ancient knowledge and the true origins of our connection to the stars.

Egyptian astrology closely relates to its pantheon, featuring deities that embody archetypal meanings linked to the twelve zodiac signs and their modern interpretations.

> *"If not the originator of horoscopic astrology, Egypt developed the craft into an art, having a significant impact on the Roman world and the Roman elite. Zodiacs appear as a new element in the decoration programmes of temples in the Graeco-Roman period."*[1]

The connection between astrology and Egypt was recognized in antiquity, with the Egyptians often credited for its discovery. This conceptual understanding of human nature and its connection to the cosmos was said to have been invented by the upper echelons of Egyptian society. Advisors to royalty or the royals themselves were believed to have revealed this mysterious art in a glorious past. The renowned sage Imhotep, son of Ptah, during the time of Pharaoh Djoser, is among those acknowledged for its discovery.

The Greeks and Romans developed a celestial divination system that serves as the foundation of modern astrology. This system is grounded in archetypes that resonate with contemporary concepts and experiences. The techniques established during the Hellenistic period, which lasted from the death of Alexander the Great in the 3rd century BCE to the rise of the Roman Empire in the 1st century CE, continue to be central to the practices of various modern astrology schools.

Vedanta, and Jyotisha, originated in India during the last centuries BCE. However, their roots reach even further back, particularly to the Vedas and Upanishads, which are the foundational scriptures of Hinduism. Vedanta is the scriptural philosophy. Jyotisha is the astrological and astronomical practice.

Astrology evolved significantly in the late 19th century. However, not all branches of the tradition adapted in the same way. Hellenistic and Vedic astrology exclude planets beyond Saturn, while many Western astrologers

---

[1] Egyptologist Briant Bohleke

consider the discoveries of Uranus, Neptune, and Pluto essential for interpreting both natal and mundane charts.

The discovery of celestial bodies beyond the traditional five planets Mercury, Venus, Mars, Jupiter, and Saturn—reflects an expanding human consciousness. For early civilizations, the deeper, non-temporal aspects of human nature were often obscure and challenging to comprehend. Classical cultures, reaching back to the dawn of recorded history, frequently attributed the cause-and-effect dynamics of human experience to divine forces. The evolutionary mechanisms driving human behavior remain outside direct awareness, understanding, or control.

In these ancient belief systems, immortal pantheons governed the rewards and punishments of mortal life. Gods and goddesses served as spiritual guides, directing the unfolding dramas of human existence.

William Herschel's discovery of Uranus in 1781 took place during the tumultuous period of the American and French Revolutions. In 1848, the German astronomer Johann Gottfried Galle uncovered Neptune, aligning with the rise of Spiritualism across the globe in the 19th century. Finally, in 1930, Clyde Tombaugh discovered Pluto at the Lowell Observatory, completing the modern lineup of traditional planets.

Every discovery of an outer planet has expanded our awareness and deepened our understanding of the universe. Uranus inspired a sense of individuality, breaking away from tradition. Neptune revealed a connection to unseen realms, suggesting that what is visible is merely a fragment of a larger, hidden reality. Meanwhile, Pluto linked the human experience to the deeper, transformative journey of the soul.

Even for us moderns, the gods and goddesses remain elusive. The frequencies of the outer planets—Uranus, Neptune, Pluto, and Eris—along with other recently discovered minor planets like Sedna, Make-Make, and Haumea—are difficult to fully assimilate. These higher frequencies need to be stepped down through aspects to the inner personal planets—Mercury, Venus, and Mars—as well as the luminaries: the Sun and Moon. This process resembles how radio equipment lowers the frequency of broadcast signals or how computer hardware and software convert digital network language into images, text, and sound.

The 21st century is bringing a vast array of planetary data. As of December 2024, there are 756,999 numbered minor planets—confirmed discoveries—out of a total of 1,424,223 observed small solar system bodies.

The remaining bodies include unnumbered minor planets and comets. This century represents a significant influx of new planetary information, reshaping our understanding of the cosmos.

Hubble transmits about 140 gigabits (Gb) of scientific data to Earth each week, which is roughly equivalent to about 17.5 gigabytes (GB) of processed data after compression.

However, the raw data before onboard processing is substantially larger. The transmission rate varies depending on the instrument and observation mode, but the Hubble Space Telescope typically transmits data at a rate of 1 Mbps (megabit per second) via NASA's Tracking and Data Relay Satellite System (TDRSS).

Over 21,000 peer-reviewed scientific papers have been published in professional journals based on Hubble's discoveries. As of 2023, these papers have received over 1,200,000 citations. Additionally, a total of 25,000 astronomers have contributed to scientific papers that utilize Hubble data.[2]

On January 10, 2021, as Eris made her annual direct station, the Space Telescope Science Institute in Baltimore announced the successful deployment of the primary mirror of the James Webb Space Telescope.

Since its launch, the James Webb Space Telescope has made groundbreaking discoveries about Kuiper Belt trans-Neptunian objects, expanding our understanding of the cosmos into previously uncharted territories. Its images reveal structures that appear almost magical, if not numinous, providing a glimpse into the unknown depths of space.

"The most significant discoveries of the James Webb Space Telescope include finding extremely distant galaxies from the early universe, detecting complex organic molecules on far-off planets, observing supermassive black holes in young galaxies, capturing detailed images of star formation regions, identifying the first exoplanets with the potential for life, and providing unprecedented views of the atmospheres of planets in our solar system, such as Jupiter and Uranus."[3]

This scientific breakthrough advances the ongoing effort to expand human consciousness on Earth. Our vision has also broadened as the repercussions of human frailties and spiritual imbalances, revealed and clarified over centuries and millennia, come to light.

---

2   https://science.nasa.gov/mission/hubble/overview/hubble-by-the-numbers/
3   https://science.nasa.gov/blogs/webb/

Eris introduces a shift in perception, recalibrating our moral compass. What we experience is a wake-up call. When we feel anger, we express it, releasing its energy. When we feel shame, we confront the discomfort it brings to process it. These emotions do not define us; instead, they serve as signals that guide us toward healthier relationships with ourselves and the world around us.

The Astronomy of Eris

Planetary Characteristics

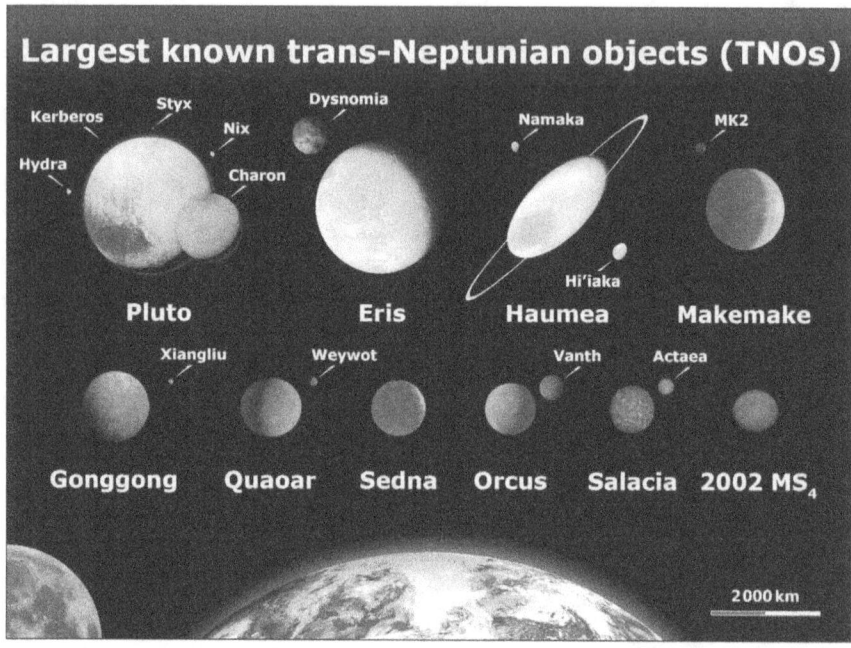

Eris is the second largest and the heaviest dwarf planet in the solar system and the eighth-heaviest object directly orbiting the Sun.[4]

In 2010, astronomers at the La Silla Observatory in Chile measured the diameter of the distant dwarf planet Eris for the first time when it passed in front of a faint star during an event known as an occultation.

The observations indicate that Eris is nearly a perfect twin of Pluto in terms of size. Its mass is approximately 0.27% that of Earth and about 27% greater than that of the dwarf planet Pluto, although Pluto is slightly larger in volume.

---

4   https://science.nasa.gov/dwarf-planets/eris//

Eris is likely a large, rocky body covered by a thin layer of ice. Its surface is highly reflective, bouncing back 96% of the light that strikes it. This reflectivity exceeds that of fresh snow on Earth, making Eris one of the brightest objects in the solar system.[5]

Due to her highly elliptical orbit, Eris spends roughly 20% of her 557 year orbit in the sign of Aries, which is currently her transit sign.

Eris is approximately three times farther from the Sun than Pluto. She has one known moon, Dysnomia, which symbolizes one of her mythical offspring and means "lawlessness."

Eris is a dwarf planet situated in the Kuiper Belt, recognized for its similarities to Pluto.

Here are its key astronomical characteristics:[6]

Orbit:

- Semi-major axis: ~67.7 AU (astronomical units)
- Eccentricity: 0.44 (highly elliptical orbit)
- Orbital period: ~557 Earth years
- Inclination: 44° to the ecliptic (highly tilted)

Physical Characteristics:

- Diameter: ~2,326 km
- Mass: ~0.27% of Earth's mass
- Density: ~2.52 g/cm^3 (suggesting a mix of rock and ice)
- Surface temperature: ~30–55 K (-243 to -218°C)

Surface and Composition:

- Covered in a layer of frozen methane and possibly nitrogen ice.
- Bright and highly reflective (albedo ~0.96), meaning it reflects most sunlight.
- Moons: One known moon is Dysnomia.
- Rotation: Estimated to be around 25.9 hours, but still uncertain.

---

5 Op. cit
6 ibid

The Mythology of Eris

"I am chaos. I am the substance from which your artists and scientists build rhythms. I am the spirit with which your children and clowns laugh in happy anarchy. I am chaos. I am alive, and I tell you that you are free."

—Principia Discordia[7]

In Homer's Iliad, Eris is described as the "sister and comrade" of Ares, though according to Geoffrey Kirk she is "not fully personified" here, and this genealogy is a "purely *ad hoc* description."[8]

Homer was known to be somewhat "creative" with his storylines. I prefer the myth that Eris emerged from the vast void, a daughter of Nyx (Night) herself. Without a father, lineage, or guiding hand to shape her, she is molded solely by the cold expanse of the cosmos and the weight of her own wild nature. She is born not from order but from the deepest abyss, where chaos and potential swirl together. Unlike her siblings she is neither constrained by the inevitability of fate nor the balance of cosmic justice. Instead, she is a force that disrupts, provokes, and shatters illusions. While others fear discord, she wields it like a weapon, slicing through stagnation and revealing hidden truths.

The Siblings of Eris

Also born of Nyx, they embody various forces of inevitability, suffering, and balance in the cosmos:

---

7   https://www.cs.cmu.edu/~tilt/principia/body.html
8   Kirk, Geoffrey Stephen, *The Iliad: A Commentary*. Volume I: Books 1–4, Cambridge, Cambridge University Press, 1985. ISBN 9780511620263. doi

- **Moros (Doom/Fate):** The daimon representing an unavoidable destiny, Moros embodies the inescapable end that looms over all beings, including the gods.
- **Thanatos (Death):** The daimon of peaceful, nonviolent death, Thanatos moves through the shadows, guiding souls to the afterlife without conflict. Unlike Eris, he does not revel in strife, but merely fulfills his duty.
- **Hypnos (Sleep):** As the twin of Thanatos, Hypnos brings rest and unconsciousness, countering Eris' disruptive nature by providing relief from turmoil.
- **Oizys (Misery/Distress):** The daimon of suffering and wretchedness, Oizys embodies the anguish and despair that often arise in the aftermath of Eris' conflicts.
- **Apate (Deception):** A daimon of falsehood and trickery, Apate flourishes in the chaos unleashed by Eris, illustrating how discord can cultivate illusions and manipulation.
- **Nemesis (Retribution):** As a force of divine justice and vengeance, Nemesis punishes excess and hubris—often as a direct consequence of the discord highlighted by Eris.
- **The Keres (Spirits of Violent Death):** These fearsome daimones haunt battlefields similarly to Eris, delighting in carnage and claiming the souls of the slain.

Together, these siblings create a pantheon of shadowy forces, each reflecting an aspect of fate, destruction, and cosmic balance—mirroring the role of Eris in the grand design of myth.

The Offspring of Eris

Eris' children, unlike their mother, are not distinct gods with unique personalities; instead, they are forces of nature—inevitable manifestations of discord and its consequences. They embody the fallout of conflict, whether in battle, within society, or deep in the human psyche:

- **Ponos (Toil/Labor):** The daimon of relentless hardship, Ponos symbolizes the struggles and exhaustion that come from conflict.

- **Limos (Famine):** The daimon of starvation, Limos represents the agony that emerges from war and societal collapse.
- **Algae (Pains/Sorrows):** A collective of spirits embodying both physical and emotional suffering—direct consequences of Eris' influence.
- **Hysminai (Battles):** The spirits of fierce combat, ever present among warriors, just like their mother.
- **Machai (Wars):** Daimones of large-scale conflict that embody war itself, rather than individual skirmishes.
- **Phonoi (Murders/Slaughter):** Spirits of bloodshed outside the battlefield, representing all forms of violent death.
- **Androktasiai (Manslaughters):** Associated with the Phonoi, these daimones represent personal killings and feuds fueled by discord.
- **Neikea (Quarrels/Feuds):** The spirits of unresolved grudges and disputes that divide relationships and communities.
- **Pseudea (Lies):** Falsehoods and deception arise naturally from discord and distrust.
- **Logoi (Disputes):** Personifications of argumentative and contentious discourse that extend Eris' influence into language and philosophy.
- **Amphillogiai (Confusion/Disagreement):** Associated with the Logoi, these daimones represent misunderstanding, indecision, and ambiguity in conflict.
- **Dysnomia (Lawlessness):** The daimon symbolizing societal collapse and the breakdown of order stemming from unchecked discord.
- **Ate (Ruin/Folly):** The power of reckless destruction and self-sabotage, compelling both mortals and gods to make disastrous choices.

Eris' offspring reveal the full extent of her power—not just as a bringer of chaos but as the source of the suffering, deception, and destruction that inevitably follow discord. Yet among them, figures like Ponos (toil) indicate that struggle and hardship are intrinsic to life itself, not merely products of strife.

Moreover, her children exemplify the escalating nature of conflict: a simple quarrel (Neikea) can lead to deception (Pseudea), disorder (Dysnomia), and ultimately cause destruction (Ate).

A minor disagreement (Neikea – quarrels) escalates into open hostility (Logoi – disputes). Hostility leads to deception (Pseudea – lies) or lawlessness (Dysnomia – disorder).

The breakdown of order invites violence (Hysminai – battles, Machai – wars). War and bloodshed (Phonoi – murders, Androktasiai – man-slaughters) lead to suffering (Algea – pains, Limos – famine).

Ultimately, unchecked discord results in ruin (Ate – folly).

This pattern suggests that Eris is not just a force of external chaos but also a psychological and societal influence, driving individuals and civilizations toward their breaking points.

Beyond mythology, Eris' children hold deeper symbolic and astrological significance. They embody her disruptive yet transformative influence, revealing the inescapable cycles of turmoil and renewal that shape both personal and collective evolution.

Eris' children do not emerge as distinct characters in myths; instead, they manifest as forces unleashed when strife prevails. Their presence illustrates the ripple effect of discord: once Eris sets conflict in motion, it spreads through hardship, deception, and destruction.

Eris as Conflict and Catalyst

While Eris and her offspring symbolize hardship, their role is not only destructive. They highlight what is broken, corrupt, or unsustainable, enabling transformation to occur. In myth and astrology, Eris reminds us that struggle is an essential part of growth, and even discord has its purpose.

The ancients neither revered her nor worshipped at her altar. Invoking Eris means inviting trouble and beckoning disaster. Yet, despite her fearsome reputation, she remains essential. She is the voice of the unheard, the breaker of false peace, and the midwife of transformation. Without her, illusions persist, corruption festers, and vital evolution is delayed. She compels us to confront what we refuse to acknowledge.

Eris does not bring chaos for its own sake; she highlights the fractures that already exist and the unsustainable structures on the verge of collapse.

She embodies a journey through shadows and the confrontation with our most challenging truths. Her presence is most palpable where injustice reigns, where power suppresses, and where voices are silenced. She fights for those who cannot fight for themselves: the marginalized, the wounded, and the forgotten. Women, children, plants, animals, and Mother Earth—she is their champion and untamed protector.

Engaging with Eris means confronting the discord within ourselves. She does not allow avoidance or complacency. The discord she incites reveals our shadow—the parts we suppress, the wounds we refuse to heal—so we can face them and strive for deep, authentic balance. Unlike the comforting whispers of harmony, she urges us to awaken our inner activists, compelling us to rise with sacred rage when injustice prevails.

Her sacred rage is not a reckless destruction but a divine force of reckoning. The fire fuels revolution, a raw power that dismantles what is false and restores what is true. Eris does not rush the process; her influence moves slowly, unraveling us when we need it, not necessarily when we are ready. We do not summon her—we awaken to her, often in times of great upheaval, when the soul or the world stands at the brink of transformation.

Historically and astrologically, Eris emerges when the collective reaches a breaking point. She does not initiate discord but instead reveals the fractures that have long existed beneath the surface. From civil rights movements to environmental revolutions, and from the voices rising against oppression to the dismantling of outdated power structures, her energy pulses through moments of necessary reckoning. She calls forth the rebel, the truth-seeker, and the warrior of justice within us all.

Understanding Eris in an astrological chart requires recognizing where we are called to disrupt, challenge, and resist compliance with falsehoods. Her placement reveals the area of life where we must confront uncomfortable truths, face distortions, and ignite transformation—not only for ourselves but also for the collective.

There is no nonsense or tiptoeing around with Goddess Eris. She is the wild force that moves through us when we declare, "No more." She is the voice that defies silence, the warrior who rises from within, and the force that ensures evolution never ceases. To walk with Eris is to walk through fire—but it is a fire that purifies, forges us anew, and demands we become nothing less than our most authentic, awakened selves.

Eris in Greek Classics

Much of our understanding of the mythology of Eris comes from classical literature, particularly the works of the Greek poets Homer and Hesiod.

The Greeks of the Classical period regarded Homer and Hesiod as their earliest authors. Therefore, these figures symbolize the initial phase of Greek literature, not just for modern readers. Moreover, it is a historical fact that the ancient Greeks ultimately credited Homer and Hesiod with establishing the foundation of Greek literature.

In both Hesiod's and Homer's works, Eris functions less as a traditional goddess and more as a daimon — a force that acts without personal motives, emerging whenever conflict occurs. She is both unavoidable and essential, exposing hidden unrest and guiding events to their natural outcomes.

The Iliad portrays a world where the gods actively shape the events of the Trojan War, taking sides and influencing mortal affairs. Eris, the goddess of discord and strife, plays a crucial role in escalating the conflict, aligning herself with the war-driven deities Ares and Athena.

Our primary source for this fact is none other than the so-called Father of History himself, Herodotus, who notes in his *Histories* that Homer and Hesiod, through their verses, have provided the Greeks with their first definitive expression regarding the gods. In a traditional society like that of the ancient Greeks, where defining the gods is akin to defining society itself, Herodotus's observation suggests that the works of Homer and Hesiod establish the groundwork for Greek cultural civilization.

Richard Alpert, known as Ram Dass, once said, "We are all walking each other home." Along the way, we encounter challenges and dangers in the world around us, as well as the threats that lurk within each of us. Upon returning home, like Odysseus, we must heal the ancestral wounds that have festered.

Homer

The Iliad recounts the epic battles that took place during the Trojan War. While *The Iliad* is often remembered for its grand battles, it is also a deeply tragic tale about the consequences of war. The poetic narrative recounts a father's sorrow as King Priam mourns the loss of his son Hector at the hands of Achilles, in contrast with the chaotic and often petty interventions of the gods. As a figure who thrives on strife, Eris reminds us that war involves not only valor and heroism but also suffering and irreversible loss.

The Iliad recounts the active involvement of Greek gods and goddesses, led by Ares, the god of war; Athena, the goddess of wisdom and strategy; and Eris, the goddess of chaos and discord, all under Zeus's guidance. According to Homer, these deities influenced both warring armies throughout the conflict.

Homer portrays Eris as an unstoppable force on the battlefield, gaining strength as the war escalates. In The Iliad, Eris plays a crucial role in escalating war and destruction. She is not merely a passive observer of the conflict; she actively engages, intensifying tensions and ensuring that once the gods and mortals embark on their paths, the consequences of their actions cannot be avoided. This aligns with her depiction in Greek mythology, where Eris embodies the essence of conflict—an inevitable, powerful influence that propels events forward.

In Book 4 of The Iliad, she is depicted as stalking the battlefield, reveling in the chaos and destruction. She is shown as a presence that fuels aggression, ensuring that strife remains relentless. Unlike Ares, who symbolizes the physical act of war, or Athena, who embodies strategic warfare, Eris represents the inevitability and escalation of conflict.[9]

In Book 11, Homer describes how Eris, *"only a little when she first arises,"* swells until *"her head reaches the heavens,"* illustrating how discord starts small but grows until it consumes everything. This reflects her role as a daimon—not a deity with personal motives but a force that ensures that once war begins, it cannot be easily controlled. She is described as "insatiable in war," walking among men and growing from small to enormous as the conflict escalates. In this sense, she acts as an amplifier of discord—her presence guarantees that once conflict starts, it only intensifies.[10]

Homer writes,

> *"The pressure held their heads on a line, and they whirled and fought like wolves, and Eris, the Lady of Sorrow, was gladdened to watch them. She alone of all the immortals attended this action. Ares drove these the Trojans on, and the Akhaians grey-eyed Athene and Phobos*

---

9 https://www.theoi.com/Text/HomerIliad4.htm
10 Homer, The Iliad 11

(Terror) drove them, and Deimos (Fear)...and Eris (Hate) whose wrath is relentless. She is the sister and companion of murderous Ares, she who is only a little thing at the first but thereafter grows until she strides on the earth with her head striking heaven. She then hurled down bitterness equally between both sides as she walked through the onslaught, making men's pain heavier."[11]

and,

"Zeus sent forth Strife unto the swift ships of the Achaeans, dread Strife, bearing in her hands a portent of war. And she took her hand by Odysseus' black ship, huge of hull, that was in the midst so that a shout could reach to either end, both to the huts of Aias, son of Telamon and to those of Achilles; for these had drawn up their shapely ships at the furthermost ends, trusting in their valor and the strength of their hands. There stood the goddess and uttered a great and terrible shout, a shrill cry of war, and in the heart of each man of the Achaeans, she put great strength to war and to fight unceasingly. And to them forthwith war became sweeter than to return in their hollow ships to their dear native land."[12]

Hesiod

Hesiod was one of the great Greek epic poets. His poem, *Theogony*, is a cosmological work that describes the origins and genealogy of the gods. His *Works and Days* discusses farming, morality, and rural life. Theogony translates to "genealogy" in Greek.

In *Theogony*, Hesiod writes *"Nyx (Night) bore hard-hearted Eris."*[13] He describes Eris as the "immortal offspring of Chaos." She is the daughter of Nyx, the female personification of night, and a significant cosmogonic figure integral to the origins of the Universe. Nyx is the offspring of Aether (Air) and Erebus (Darkness), primordial beings that emerged from 'The

---

11 Homer, *The Iliad*, trans. Richmond Lattimore (Chicago: University of Chicago Press, 1951), Book 4.441-444 and Book 5.738-742.
12 Homer, *The Iliad*, trans. A.T. Murray (Cambridge, MA: Harvard University Press, 1924), Book 11.3-12.
13 Hesiod, *Theogony* 211-225, trans. Hugh G. Evelyn-White (Loeb Classical Library).

Beginning Which Cannot Be Spoken." It is not created; it did not come to be; it has always existed.[14]

In *Works and Days,* Hesiod writes,

> "[Eris] is hateful . . . [she is the one] who builds up evil, war, and slaughter. She is harsh; no man loves her, but under compulsion and by the will of the immortals, men promote this rough Eris (Strife)."[15]

Hesiod also presents a different perspective of Eris,

> "It was never true that there was only one Eris (Strife). There have always been two on earth. There is one you could like when you understand her. The other is hateful. The two Erites have separate natures. There is one Eris who builds up evil war and slaughter. She is harsh; no man loves her, but out of compulsion and by the will of the immortals, men promote this rough Eris (Strife). But the other was born the elder daughter of black Nyx (Night). The son of Kronos, who sits on high and dwells in the bright air, set her among the roots of the earth and among men; she is far kinder. She pushes the shiftless man to work for all his laziness. A man looks at his neighbor, who is rich; then he too wants work, for the rich man presses on with his plowing, planting, and ordering of his estate. So, the neighbor envies the neighbor who presses on toward wealth. Such Eris (Strife) is a good friend to mortals."[16]

Virgil

Virgil was a Roman poet during the reign of Emperor Augustus in the 1st century BCE. His work includes *The Aeneid*, a twelve-book epic that describes the founding of Rome by the Trojan hero Aeneas, which is an integral part of this story.

In *The Aeneid*, Virgil writes,

> "Mars rages in the centre of the contest, engraved in steel, and the grim Furies in the sky, and Discord (Eris) in a torn robe strides joyously...

---

14 Op. cit
15 ibid
16 https://www.theoi.com/Daimon/Eris.html

maddening Discordia, her snaky locks entwined with bloody ribbons...Here [in battle], Eris strides, exulting in her torn mantle."[17]

Virgil presents her guarding the gates of Hell, *"Upon the porch and entrance to Hades." Here dwells . . . lunatic Discordia (Strife-Eris) whose viperine hair is caught up with a headband soaked in blood."*[18]

Aeschylus

Aeschylus was a 5th century BCE Greek tragedian from Athens. He famously wrote, *"Eris is the last of the gods to close an argument."*[19]

Aeschylus is also known for *"Prometheus Bound"*, which is based on the myth of Prometheus, a Titan who defies Zeus to protect mankind by giving them fire. For this act, he incurs Zeus's wrath and faces punishment. Richard Tarnas derived his work, *Prometheus the Awakener,* from this mythology, articulating the archetype of Uranus.

Eris was the *"daimon of the strife of war, haunting the battlefield and delighting in human bloodshed." Daimon* refers to a supernatural force, and in Homeric works the term is used almost interchangeably with *theos* to denote a god. The distinction lies in emphasis: while *theos* highlights the god's personality, *daimon* emphasizes its action. Thus, *daimon* often pertains to sudden or unexpected supernatural interventions that are not attributed to any specific deity.

In Greek thought a *daimon*[20] was not merely a lesser deity but a fundamental force—an active, often impersonal presence shaping human affairs. Unlike the Olympian gods, who had distinct personalities and motives, *daimones* embodied raw, elemental powers that emerged in moments of necessity. As the *daimon* of strife, Eris was not simply the goddess of discord; she was discord itself—an inevitable and inescapable force that surfaced wherever imbalance, tension, or injustice lay hidden.

In later Greek philosophy, *daimones* were sometimes reinterpreted as internal forces—guiding spirits, primal instincts, or uncontrollable impulses that shape human behavior. In this sense, Eris is not only a

---

17 Virgil, Aeneid 6. 268 ff (trans. Fairclough) (Roman epic C1st 24 B.C.)
18 Op. cit.
19 Aeschylus, Seven Against Thebes, line 1055, trans. Herbert Weir Smyth (Cambridge, MA: Harvard University Press, 1926).
20 https://www.theoi.com/Daimon/Eris.html

cosmic force but also a psychological one. She embodies the unrest within us, the voice that refuses to allow hidden tensions to remain buried. She arises when we are called to confront discomfort, injustice, or personal transformation, unraveling us not when we are ready but when we must awaken. Eris as a *daimon* is more than a mythological figure; she is a force of revelation, the necessary discord that brings truth to the surface. No illusion remains intact in her presence, and no shadow stays hidden.[21]

The Judgment of Paris and the Apple of Discord

The most famous story of Eris centers on the golden apple. These apples grew on the Tree of Life in the Garden of the Hesperides, a sacred orchard tended by the Hesperides—goddess-nymphs associated with the evening and the golden light of sunsets. Depending on the source, the Hesperides were regarded either as the daughters of Nyx (Night) or the heaven-bearing Titan Atlas.

The golden apple tree was a wedding gift from Gaia to Hera, symbolizing divine blessing and immortality. The Hesperides, who were responsible for its care, guarded the sacred fruit with Drakon, a formidable hundred-headed dragon, ensuring that no unworthy hands could claim its power.

The Hesperides and their radiant golden apples were seen as the source of the sunset's luminous light, a phenomenon that commemorated the marriage of Zeus and Hera, the king and queen of the heavens.

---

21 The daimon is a term from ancient Greek thought referring to a guiding spirit, an intermediary between the divine and human realms, often perceived as a personal inner force that shapes one's destiny, calling or genius. Unlike the modern connotation of "demon," the original daimon could be benevolent or ambivalent, and was regarded by philosophers like Socrates as a source of inner moral guidance or divine intuition. See James Hillman, The Soul's Code: In Search of Character and Calling (New York: Random House, 1996), 9–12. Hillman revitalizes the ancient notion of the daimon as the "acorn theory" of the soul, proposing that each person is born with an innate image or destiny that the daimon helps to unfold.

The Ubiquity of Apples in Culture and Mythology

Apples frequently appear in mythology, history, and culture, often symbolizing knowledge, fate, and transformation. In the Garden of Eden, the apple was viewed as the forbidden fruit, representing temptation and humanity's fall. An apple famously contributed to Isaac Newton's discovery of gravity, forever altering our understanding of the natural world. In fairy tales, Snow White falls into a deep sleep after biting into a poisoned apple, reinforcing the fruit's association with both danger and destiny.

Beyond myth and science, apples have influenced folklore and legend. Johnny Appleseed, the American frontiersman, became renowned for spreading apple trees throughout the early United States, blending horticulture with frontier expansion. Apple Inc. transformed the technological landscape with the goal of placing a computer on every desk and eventually in every hand.

This humble fruit is also deeply embedded in language, shaping idioms and expressions that reflect wisdom, caution, and identity:

- *The apple of my eye – a person cherished above all others.*
- *As American as apple pie, symbolizes national identity.*
- *An apple a day keeps the doctor away, linking apples to health and longevity.*
- *Comparing apples to oranges highlights the differences between things that cannot be compared.*
- *Don't upset the apple cart – a warning against disrupting order.*
- *The apple doesn't fall far from the tree, emphasizing inherited traits.*
- *The Big Apple, a nickname for New York City, embodies both opportunity and ambition.*
- *One rotten apple spoils the entire bunch – a reminder of the corrupting influence of a single bad element.*

From ancient myths to modern technology, and from folklore to everyday language, the apple remains a powerful and enduring symbol, intricately woven into the fabric of human experience.

The story of Eris and the Golden Apple begins with the wedding of Thetis and Peleus, the future parents of Achilles. Zeus hosted the wedding party and asked Chiron to send out the invitations. Knowing that Eris often caused disruption and that uninvited chaos followed her, Chiron left her off the guest list.

Nonetheless, Eris, embodying the necessity of disruption, arrived, bringing with her a golden apple from the Tree of Life. With a single act, she shattered the carefully curated harmony of the gathering by tossing the golden apple into the crowd and declaring, *"To the fairest"*.

In that moment, Eris fulfilled her archetypal role as the catalyst for transformation. The question ignited a rivalry among the Olympian goddesses Pallas Athena, Hera, and Aphrodite, each vying for the prize. Their contest unveiled the underlying dynamics of power, wisdom, and desire—forces that shape both human and divine narratives. To avoid entanglement in the dispute, Zeus appointed Paris, the son of Priam, King of Troy, as the judge. Hermes guided the three goddesses to the sacred spring on Mount Ida, where they bathed before Paris, enhancing the illusion of purity and beauty before offering their bribes.

Hera, queen of the gods, promised Paris dominion over both Europe and Asia. Athena, goddess of wisdom and strategy, offered him unparalleled intelligence and skill in battle. Athena also promised him exceptional intelligence and prowess in combat. Aphrodite, accompanied by the Goddesses of the Seasons, the Horai, adorned with flowers and song, pledged to grant him the most beautiful woman in the world—Helen of Sparta, who was already married to the Greek king Menelaus.

Paris, embodying youthful desires and shortsighted choices, awarded the golden apple to Aphrodite, sealing his fate and that of his city. By taking Helen to Troy, he unwittingly set in motion the forces of war, shifting the balance of power throughout the ancient world. What began as a competition of vanity escalated into a conflict that consumed the lives of heroes and altered the course of history.

Paris took Helen to Troy, provoking the Greeks, particularly the city-state of Sparta. The Greeks pursued Paris and Helen, which led to the Trojan War. By the end of that bitter conflict, all the legendary heroes of the Trojan War had descended to the Underworld, where Odysseus visited them during his ten year journey back to Ithaca. The Greek Classical Age had come to a close.

Helen of Troy

Euripides wrote that Helen never went to Troy. He narrated the story of how Hermes, following Zeus's instructions, stole Helen and took her to Egypt, where King Proteus kept her safe.

When Helen was rescued from Egypt by Menelaus, she told him,

"To Troy I went not: that ... a phantom was."[22]

and,

"Never to alien princes' bed, wafted by the wings of the oars I fled."[23]

By the end of the war, the iconic figures of the Trojan War—Achilles, Hector, Agamemnon, and Paris—had all perished. The Greek Classical Age began its transformation, heralding new cycles of civilization. Eris, whose presence had been shunned, unveiled hidden truths. Discord reveals what lies beneath the surface, forcing an evolution that might not happen otherwise. Her apple was not merely a source of conflict but a symbol of awakening, reminding us that chaos, though feared, is an essential force in the unfolding of destiny.

Helen was regarded as the most beautiful woman in the world. Due to the bloodshed she caused at Troy, she is also known as the Woman of Sorrow.

Eris is traditionally blamed for the bloodlust associated with the Trojan War. However, there is another version of the story about Eris and Helen that presents a much different narrative.

Mythology depicts Helen of Troy as the passive prize for which men fight, while Eris, the goddess of strife, incites conflict by tossing the golden

---

[22] *Euripides, Helen,* 582
[23] ibid, 668

apple marked "To the Fairest." But what if Helen herself represents the Erisian force, actively instigating the Trojan War? What if she were neither a victim nor a pawn, but rather a conscious disruptor- a force of chaos revealing the fragile foundations of power?

In his play *Helen* the Greek tragedian Euripides suggests that Helen of Troy, known as *"the face that launched a thousand ships"*, was responsible for the slaughter at Ilium. Helen was the wife of Menelaus, King of Sparta. At their wedding, all present signed a pact called the Oath of Tyndareus, stating that if anyone interfered with the marriage, war would ensue.[24]

Tyndareus was Helen's earthly father. Her true father by birth was Zeus, who seduced Leda by appearing to her as a swan. That very night, both Zeus and Tyndareus had relations with Leda. As a result, four children were born—hatched from a single egg—from the same mother but with different fathers: Castor and Polydeuces, known as the Dioscuri (meaning children of Zeus), and Clytemnestra and Helen. Among these four, Helen and Polydeuces were immortal, while Castor and Clytemnestra, being the children of Tyndareus, were mortal.[25]

Helen and Eris: Mirrors of Chaos and Revelation

Helen does not merely fall under Aphrodite's spell and leave with Paris out of love or duress. Instead, she sees through the hollow nature of patriarchal control—the way kings use women as bargaining chips and how war is justified under the pretense of honor. By willingly departing for Troy, she does not just provoke war; she prompts an unavoidable reckoning. She is not taken; she claims herself.[26]

Helen's departure serves as the Erisian moment that brings latent tensions to the surface. The Greeks, seeking any excuse for expansion, use her as justification for an already brewing conflict. The ensuing war is not merely about reclaiming Helen; it concerns deeper fault lines in Greek society—power struggles, greed, and a crumbling heroic ideal. She does

---

24 Op. cit.
25 Gantz, Timothy. *Early Greek Myth: A Guide to Literary and Artistic Sources*. Vol. 1 (Baltimore: Johns Hopkins University Press, 1993), 313–316.
26 ibid.

not create the conflict; she reveals it. Like Eris, she does not wield a sword, yet she is the most dangerous figure on the battlefield.

Helen, embodying the Erisian archetype, symbolizes the agent of discord that propels transformation. The resulting war destroys one era and ushers in another. This aligns with Eris' astrological role: the great unmasker, the force that dismantles illusions by making them impossible to overlook.

Helen: The Reflection of a Greater Illusion

Helen's abduction became the justification for war. Yet, as Euripides suggests in his play, the Helen who went to Troy may not have been real at all—merely a phantom, a divine illusion, while the true Helen remained in Egypt. This myth points to a deeper truth: Helen was never the cause of war but rather a symbol onto which men projected their desires, ambitions, and justifications for violence.

Euripides' *Helen* reshapes the traditional narrative. In his version, Hermes, following Zeus's instructions, steals Helen and takes her to Egypt, where King Proteus keeps her safe. Meanwhile, the Greeks and Trojans fight over a mere illusion—a phantom Helen. This revelation, delivered when Menelaus finally reunites with the real Helen, exposes the entire war as a misguided conflict based on deception and projection. As Helen herself states,

"To Troy I went not: that ... a phantom was my name alone."[24]

Through this lens, Helen embodies an archetype of Eris—she is not the active cause of destruction but rather the figure through which deeper conflicts manifest. Her beauty serves as a vessel for the ambitions of gods and men, just as Eris' golden apple merely brought divine tensions to a head.

Eris and Helen in Evolutionary Astrology

Herodotus offers an alternative version. In his account, Paris was shipwrecked off the coast of Egypt after eloping with Helen and a large amount of treasure. Betrayed by his own servants, he was brought before King Proteus, who condemned him upon learning of his misdeeds. Proteus kept Helen and the stolen riches as an act of moral restitution while sending Paris back to Troy in disgrace. In this version, Paris returned not with the real Helen but with a mere phantom—an ethereal likeness fashioned from clouds created by the gods.[27]

Other traditions further complicate the narrative by asserting that Paris and Helen were welcomed in Egypt, where they lived peacefully while the Achaeans and Trojans fought one another. This interpretation not only reframes Helen's role in the war but also emphasizes the fluid nature of myth, shaped by the perspectives and biases of various storytellers. Herodotus, known for his efforts to blend historical inquiry with mythology, may have been influenced by Egyptian traditions or sought to challenge the dominant Homeric account by presenting an alternative based on moral consequence rather than divine fate.

Ultimately, these variations enrich Helen's legend, transforming her from a passive object of desire into a figure of mystery—one whose very presence, or absence, reshapes the motivations and outcomes of one of history's most enduring tales of war.

After the fateful contest between Hera, Aphrodite, and Athena, Helen did not simply fall victim to fate—she embraced it. she willingly left her husband fully aware of the storm it would unleash, compelled by the irresistible force of the goddess's promise.

Was her choice truly her own, or had Aphrodite's divine influence rendered her powerless to resist? The line between free will and divine compulsion is blurred, leaving her legacy open to endless debate. Was she a betrayer, a pawn, or merely a woman ensnared by forces beyond her control?

Regardless, her departure shattered the delicate balance between kingdoms, igniting a war that would engulf men and the gods in its wrath. By choosing desire, whether of her own volition or another's, Helen set into

---

27 Herodotus, *Histories*, trans. A.D. Godley (Cambridge, MA: Harvard University Press, 1920), 2.112–120.

motion the defining tragedy of the age—one that would resonate through myth for centuries to come.

> *"Didn't Helen, who far surpassed all in beauty, desert the best of men, her husband and king, and sail off to Troy, forgetting her daughter and dear parents? Mere love's gaze made her bend and led her from her path."*—Sappho[28]

Helen as Disrupter

In *The Odyssey*, Homer recounts how Helen nearly unraveled the Greeks' clever plan after the Trojan Horse was brought inside the city walls. As she walked around the towering wooden structure, she called out to the warriors hidden inside, mimicking the voices of their wives with uncanny precision. Her taunts and illusions tested their resolve, tempting them to betray themselves by responding.[29]

This moment adds a layer of intrigue to Helen's character—was she trying to expose the Greeks out of loyalty to Troy, or was she simply playing a dangerous game, caught between both sides of the war? Her actions highlight the ambiguity that surrounds her throughout the myth: a figure of allure and deception, intelligence and unpredictability.

Aeneas and The Founding of Rome

In *The Aeneid*, Virgil recounts how, after the fall of Troy, Aeneas, a prince of the Trojan royal family, fled the burning city and embarked on a perilous journey to Italy. The son of the Trojan prince Anchises and the Greek goddess Aphrodite, Aeneas was destined for greatness. The epic chronicles his trials and tribulations as he faces divine wrath, battles formidable foes, and navigates the will of the gods, all of which lead to his ultimate fate as the progenitor of Rome.

---

28 Sappho, *Fragment 16*, in *Greek Lyric: Sappho and Alcaeus*, trans. David A. Campbell (Cambridge, MA: Harvard University Press, 1982), 51.
29 Homer, *The Odyssey*, trans. Robert Fagles (New York: Penguin Books, 1996), 4.271-289.

> "*Aeneas... shall build a city and establish laws, and from him will spring the race of Romans, the rulers of the world.*"[30]
> "*To these, I set no bounds, either in space or time:*
> *Empire without end have I granted them.*
> *Even harsh Juno shall come to better counsels ...*
> *Then will come the age of iron, and Romulus shall receive the people...*"
>
> — Virgil, Aeneid 1.257–260[31]

Eris reveals her power as a force capable of overturning or obliterating anything that has resisted previous attempts at peaceful resolution. Her reputation in myth has long tied her to the relentless bloodlust of the Trojan War, where discord led to destruction. Yet, at her core, Eris embodies a deeper archetypal potential—one that seeks to rectify unresolved conflicts, compelling transformation when all other means have failed.

Eris' mythology and history suggest a more complex and even hopeful outcome. Although often associated with chaos and strife, she is also credited with initiating events that led to the founding of the Roman Empire, a civilization that endured for over a thousand years. The legacy of ancient Rome continues to influence the liturgy, ideology, and mysticism of the Roman Catholic Church. Even after nearly twenty eight centuries, Rome's foundations remain deeply rooted in the ashes of Troy, which stands as a testament to Eris' role in cycles of destruction and renewal.

---

30 Virgil, *Aeneid*.
31 Op. cit.

The Astrology of Eris

Outer Planet Transits to Eris

Due to its highly elliptical orbit, the periodic aspects of the outer planets in relation to Eris vary significantly, creating irregular cycles of influence. The chart below shows the average number of years Eris spends in each zodiac sign during a single orbit. This correlation reflects the evolutionary pacing of Eris, revealing extended periods of development in certain signs and shorter transitions through others.

Eris spends most of its transit in the signs of Aries, Taurus, Gemini, Aquarius and Pisces—especially in Aries and Aquarius where it spends over 100 years in each sign. It moves more swiftly through Leo, Virgo, Libra, Scorpio, Sagittarius and Capricorn—spending less than 20 years in Cancer, Leo, and Virgo, due to the shape of its orbit. This uneven

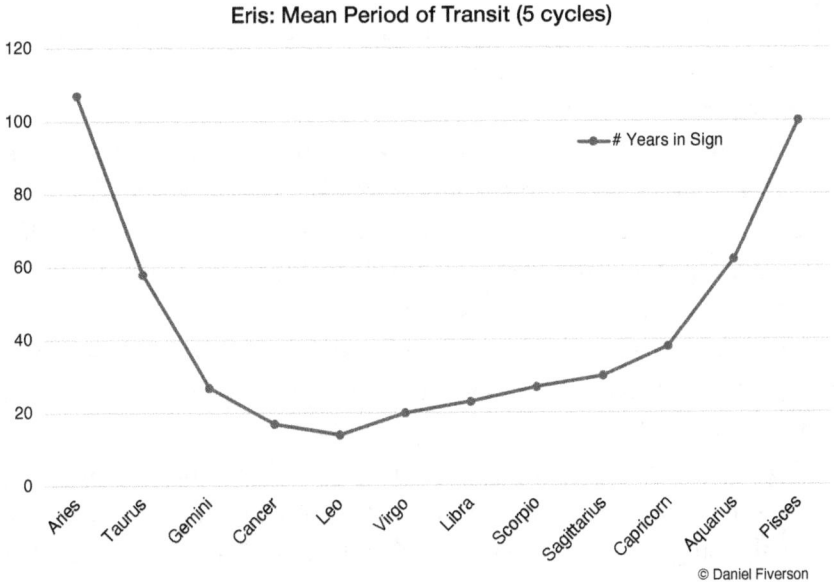

© Daniel Fiverson

distribution means that planetary aspects to Eris, particularly from Neptune and Pluto, occur at irregular intervals, shaping the course of history in concentrated bursts of evolutionary intensity. These long-term cycles define epochs of transformation as Eris disrupts existing paradigms, exposes hidden truths, and challenges power structures.

The Recent Last Quarter Square Between Pluto in Capricorn and Eris in Aries

The tremendous social and political pressures of our times reflect Eris' influence on the global landscape and the long-term changes initiated by her rare last quarter square to Pluto in Capricorn. This waning square, which occurred between 2017 and 2024 and perfected five times between 2020 and 2021, will not happen again until 2459 to 2519, making it one of the most significant astrological events of the early 21st century.

The last quarter square, signifies a crisis of reorientation, marking the breaking point of outdated power structures, economic systems, and societal frameworks. In Evolutionary Astrology, squares symbolize crises and evolutionary necessity. The Pluto–Eris last quarter square represents a phase that Dane Rudhyar called a "crisis in consciousness"—a moment when the old evolutionary paradigm is no longer sustainable, yet a new one has not fully emerged. This period entails profound reckoning, deconstruction, and reorientation.

Pluto in Capricorn relates to consensus reality—established power structures, governments, corporate control, and the old guard—elements that serve to maintain power hierarchies. This indicates entrenched authority, systemic regulation, and the ruling elite. Eris in Aries represents rebellion against exclusion, the awakening of suppressed identities, and the chaos necessary for new evolutionary breakthroughs. Eris reveals those marginalized by existing power structures, sparking discord, uprisings, and a call for justice.

This last quarter square represents the final crisis before the upcoming Pluto–Eris conjunction in Taurus in 2115. It suggests that everything currently being deconstructed is preparing the way for a new paradigm that won't fully materialize for another 90 years. The evolutionary purpose of this closing square is to raise awareness of unsustainable power dynamics and the need to reconfigure how societies distribute power, resources, and agency.

The five exact Pluto–Eris squares from 2020 to 2021 heightened global tensions and ignited evolutionary turning points that will reshape human consciousness.

The first Pluto–Eris square on January 26, 2020, planted the seeds of collapse as the world became aware of COVID-19, which rapidly developed into a global pandemic that transformed the world forever.

In 2019 Donald Trump became the fourth U.S. president in history to be impeached. On April 15 much of the world watched in horror as fire raged at Notre Dame de Paris in France, destroying the spire and much of the roof of the beloved 850 year old cathedral. The brutal arrest and death of George Floyd occurred in 2020, launching the Black Lives Matter movement. Brush fires devastated Australia and burned millions of acres across the American West.

The Pluto–Eris square exposed vulnerabilities in healthcare, economics, and leadership, illustrating how fragile human-made power structures can be. Pluto demands transformation through destruction, while Eris, the disruptor ensures that no illusions remain intact. What many had taken for granted—economic stability, access to healthcare, and political trust—began to unravel, compelling the collective into an evolutionary crisis of survival and adaptation.

The second square on June 14, 2020, coincided with the eruption of mass uprisings following the murder of George Floyd. The social justice movement against racial violence and systemic inequality ignited worldwide, fueled by the core Eris theme of marginalized groups demanding justice. With Pluto in Capricorn undermining systems of control and Eris in Aries insisting on raw truth, institutions faced significant resistance from the collective. The militarized response to protest movements characterized this transit, along with the spread of misinformation and the struggle to redefine justice. The tension between power and rebellion intensified, revealing that the world was approaching a breaking point.

By December 10, 2020, when Pluto and Eris squared for the third time, the world entered what could be called the "dark night of the soul." This period was marked by exhaustion, grief, and rising psychological distress. The second wave of the pandemic struck, and societies came to understand that an immediate return to "normal" was unlikely. Governments struggled to manage the economic and social fallout as increasing division within nations deepened. It was a time when Pluto urged surrender while Eris fueled resistance, leading to deep psychological and spiritual turmoil at a collective level. The traditional structures that once provided a sense of order could no longer ensure stability, yet a new paradigm had not yet emerged. This third square compelled humanity to confront uncertainty and reevaluate who truly holds power. On January 6, 2021, supporters of Donald Trump stormed and ransacked the U.S. Capitol.

On the day of the fourth square on August 27, 2021, a devastating suicide bombing occurred outside the Kabul airport, killing 13 U.S. troops and dozens of Afghan civilians. The fourth Pluto–Eris square also initiated a retroactive reckoning. Many wounds from 2020 resurfaced as new protests erupted against vaccine mandates, lockdowns, and government overreach. People felt the full impact of the loss and trauma experienced over the past year, yet many institutions attempted to return to pre-pandemic norms. The tension between these forces—one clinging to control and the other demanding freedom—intensified.

At the same time, digital surveillance, technological governance, and the expansion of cryptocurrency accelerated, fundamentally reshaping the distribution of power for the decades to come. The failure of outdated economic and political systems to adapt to the evolving needs of the population became increasingly evident, illustrating that the past could not be sustained and that resistance to change was futile. The conflict between Pluto's demand for systemic control and Eris' pursuit of autonomy continued to intensify, creating a noticeable divide between those who wished to maintain the status quo and those advocating for radical change.

The final Pluto–Eris square on October 9, 2021, marked the beginning of a rebuild. Although the global crisis was far from over, this last exact square indicated that the peak moment of confrontation had passed, and new solutions—albeit chaotic—were starting to emerge, advocating for decentralization, technological sovereignty, and collective governance. Cryptocurrencies, digital communities, and alternative economic models assumed a more significant role, reflecting a shift away from the rigid Capricornian model of top-down authority. The final Pluto–Eris square marked the moment when it became evident that there was no turning back to the old world. Transformation was now inevitable, and the power structures would either need to adapt or collapse entirely.

The previous Aries ingress occurred more than 600 years ago. During the late 15th and early 16th centuries, the world witnessed the Italian Renaissance, the fall of Constantinople, and Gutenberg's invention of the printing press.

During those same years, there were significant events:

- Columbus' voyage to the Americas, resulting in the conquest and genocide of indigenous peoples
- Magellan's circumnavigation of the Earth
- Joan of Arc
- Martin Luther
- Leonardo da Vinci
- Michelangelo
- Lorenzo de' Medici
- Hernán Cortés
- the establishment of the Inca Empire
- the birth of Guru Nanak Dev
- and the start of the transatlantic slave trade

These events bore unmistakable Erisian signatures—upheaval, revelation, and irreversible change. It was an age of intense collisions: old worlds collapsing, new ones emerging, and individuals confronting truth at great personal and collective costs. Beneath the ventures and conquests, the art and reform, a deeper current flowed—one that shattered familiar meanings and rewrote the structures of power. The Earth was circled, new continents claimed, inherited faiths challenged, and human brilliance unleashed. But vision didn't come without violence. For every frontier that opened, another was crushed. These lives—and the systems they broke or built—bear the mark of Eris: a force that shatters what no longer serves, exposes what has been hidden, and demands transformation. In the 15th and 16th centuries, she didn't whisper change—she forced it through tremors that shook land, soul, and memory. These events exemplify strong Erisian themes of upheaval, revelation, and forced transformation.

Eris again entered Aries in 1927, conjunct retrograde Uranus—two disruptive forces moving backward through the fire sign of identity, initiative, and will. Their encounter didn't whisper; it roared. Retrograde Jupiter in late Pisces formed a balsamic conjunction to both, signaling a karmic ending to a collective dreamscape that had run its course. The belief systems and ideologies holding the world together were beginning to fray. Saturn, stationed in Sagittarius, cast a trine to the conjunction—offering the illusion of stability, but from a position rooted in dogma and institutional authority that could no longer hold the center.

This wasn't just another outer-planet alignment. Eris, the archetype of discord, arrived in Aries not to destroy for destruction's sake, but to expose what had been excluded, denied, or forcibly silenced. Uranus lit the fuse. Saturn tried to hold the line. But something fundamental had already begun to unravel.

By 1929, the myth cracked. The stock market collapse didn't just trigger a global depression—it marked the breakdown of a collective delusion: the belief in infinite growth, in markets that could self-correct, in the supremacy of reason to master fate. A deeper crisis emerged—a loss of meaning. Psychologically, it was a rupture in the modern psyche itself: the end of the Promethean bargain that promised progress without consequence.

Eris in Aries refused compliance. Provoked by Uranus and constrained by Saturn, she forced a confrontation—not just with failing systems, but with the psychic architecture behind them. Her disruption was not random. It asked: What have we refused to see? What lies beneath the stories we tell about progress, order, and control?

What surfaced was not just economic collapse, but the shadow side of modernity. Authoritarianism took root. Fascism rose—not as an aberration, but as a reflection of the very structures that had collapsed. Eris had pulled back the veil. What had been buried came into view: the cost of exclusion, the violence masked as civility, and the brittleness of a world built on denial.

As we move forward, Saturn, Uranus, and Neptune will keep influencing each cycle of Eris in Aries, driving conflict, revelation, and a redefinition of power. The themes established by the Pluto-Eris squares of

2020–2021 will continue to unfold, preparing humanity for the upcoming phase of radical transformation. The evolutionary impulse of these transits is undeniable—what is breaking down now is simply the precursor to what will be reconstructed in the decades ahead. The disruptions of this era act as catalysts for the transformations that will define the next century.

Pluto–Eris and Neptune–Eris Cycles

Catalysts of Transformation and Ideological Reckoning

The table below presents the cycles of the outer planets, including Neptune, Pluto, and Eris, along with their durations and characteristics. This chart illustrates how Eris integrates into long-term evolutionary themes—introducing discord into power structures, emphasizing exclusion, and driving the world toward radical transformation. Eris appears in conjunctions or aspects with Neptune and Pluto, both of which are associated with profound, gradual shifts in consciousness, power, and societal structures.

Perfections of Eris by Aspect and Sign

In the chart opposite:

- Aries embodies raw initiation, rebellion, and individual will, reinforcing Eris' archetype of disruption and self-assertion. This conjunction perfects 15 times.
- Pisces carries significant weight (perfects 15 times) symbolizing spirituality, collective dissolution, and endings, indicating that many of these cycles align with periods of transition and ideological transformation.
- Capricorn (perfects 3 times) is linked with established power structures, indicating moments when rigid systems are challenged.

Pluto–Eris and Neptune–Eris Cycles

Outer Planet Cycles			# Years Cycle	Number of Perfections			
				By Aspect		By Sign	
765	BCE	Neptune-Eris	258	Pisces	3	Aries	15
578	BCE	Uranus-Neptune-Pluto	494	Taurus	1	Taurus	13
466	BCE	Pluto-Eris	355	Scorpio	1	Gemini	10
507	BCE	Neptune-Eris	229	Libra	1	Cancer	0
278	BCE	Neptune-Eris	186	Pisces	3	Leo	0
111	BCE	Pluto-Eris	471	Aries	3	Virgo	0
92	BCE	Neptune-Eris	299	Aries	1	Libra	1
84	BCE	Neptune-Pluto	495	Taurus	1	Scorpio	1
207	AD	Neptune-Eris	186	Aquarius	3	Sagittarius	0
360	AD	Pluto-Eris	477	Aries	5	Capricorn	3
393	AD	Neptune-Eris	286	Aries	5	Aquarius	3
411	AD	Neptune-Pluto	494	Taurus	3	Pisces	15
679	AD	Neptune-Eris	201	Capricorn	3		
837	AD	Pluto-Eris	472	Pisces	3		
880	AD	Neptune-Eris	196	Aries	3		
905	AD	Neptune-Pluto	494	Taurus	1		
1076	AD	Neptune-Eris	290	Gemini	3		
1309	AD	Pluto-Eris	447	Pisces	3		
1366	AD	Neptune-Eris	185	Pisces	3		
1398	AD	Neptune-Pluto	493	Gemini	3		
1551	AD	Neptune-Eris	297	Taurus	3		
1756	AD	Pluto-Eris	447	Sagittarius	1		
1848	AD	Neptune-Eris	189	Pisces	3		
1891	AD	Neptune-Pluto	493	Gemini	3		
2037	AD	Neptune-Eris		Aries	3	© Daniel Fiverson	

Pluto and Eris: Cycles of Power and Upheaval

Throughout history, the pas-de-deux between Pluto and Eris has marked eras of profound transformation. In the language of Evolutionary Astrology, Pluto is the force of death, rebirth, and karmic necessity—an archetype that exposes and dissolves structures that no longer serve the soul's evolution. Eris, the cosmic disruptor, reveals what has been cast aside. She tears the veil from what's been hidden or denied and insists that truth, however unwelcome, be included in the story.

When Pluto and Eris engage in hard aspects—especially conjunctions, squares, and oppositions—the result is never quiet. What has been solidified over generations begins to crack. Pluto holds the archetypal weight of entrenched power, and Eris meets it with defiance. She does not dismantle for the sake of destruction, but to bring forward what has been silenced. Their tension, both astronomical and archetypal, reshapes the collective terrain. Pluto uncovers the deep roots of soul and structure; Eris fractures the illusions that sustain exclusion.

Though rare, these meetings are pivotal. They illuminate suppressed rage, systemic imbalance, and the compulsion for both individual and collective reckoning. Their alignments force the question: what is power built on, and who has been left out of the narrative?

Historically, Pluto and Eris have conjoined roughly every 445 years. The most recent cycle began in 1756 in Sagittarius, a sign associated with empire, ideology, and expansion. That cycle opened just as empires rose and revolutions stirred. It seeded democratic ideals and individual freedoms, while also cementing capitalist hierarchies and colonial violence. The Enlightenment offered liberty but also justified domination. It gave birth to human rights alongside human exploitation.

Earlier Pluto–Eris conjunctions reflect similar patterns. In 466 BCE, near the time of the Peloponnesian War, Athens and Sparta clashed in a brutal struggle for dominance. In 111 BCE, Rome's imperial ambitions expanded as older Hellenistic empires began to fade. In 360 CE, the Western Roman Empire began its slow collapse. In 837 CE their alignment mirrored the Viking expansion and the fracturing of centralized authority in Europe. In 1309, their meeting coincided with the Avignon Papacy and the breakdown of medieval religious power structures. Each cycle reflects a breakdown of old orders and the emergence of new power dynamics.

Fast forward to the present: Pluto entered Aquarius in 2024, maybe reaching the most radical turning point yet in the current cycle. The systems forged under the last conjunction are faltering. Technology, governance, and identity are being rewritten. Pluto in Aquarius excavates collective structures and demands their transformation. With Eris still in Aries—where she has been since 1927—the pressure is eruptive.

The Pluto–Eris squares of 2020 and 2021 were accelerants. The first exact square occurred on January 26, 2020, just as the COVID-19 outbreak was declared a global health emergency. The second, on June 14, followed the death of George Floyd and mass protests for racial justice. The final square, on December 10, 2021, landed amid rising political division and institutional collapse. These were no ordinary transits—they cracked open systems already under strain. Pluto exposed the rot. Eris made sure we saw it. The myth of linear progress gave way to volatility and reckoning.

These upheavals weren't isolated. They marked the unraveling of systems birthed under the 1756 cycle. If the old world was built on hierarchy, the new must be built on mutuality. If the past centered domination, the future must root itself in accountability. The evolutionary arc that began over two centuries ago is now reaching a threshold, calling for a rebirth of collective power rooted in truth.

Neptune and Eris: Cycles of Myth and Revelation

While Pluto and Eris confront power and structure, Neptune and Eris operate on the level of belief, myth, and collective imagination. Neptune dissolves boundaries. It governs dreams, illusions, and spiritual yearning. When it meets Eris, the myths we live by come under pressure. What we worship, what we believe in, what we use to frame meaning—it all becomes subject to rupture.

Neptune and Eris meet approximately every 494 years, though this varies due to Eris' eccentric orbit. Their conjunctions signal periods of ideological upheaval and spiritual transformation. They are not about material revolution, but about the rewriting of collective meaning.

The last Neptune–Eris cycle began in 1848, when the two conjoined at 1° Pisces. That year, revolutions erupted across Europe. Monarchies trembled. New ideals surged—socialism, nationalism, spiritual reform. As Neptune turned retrograde and re-met Eris on August 30, the dream turned murky. Revolutions faltered or reversed. Disillusionment followed. Yet the myth had already seeded itself. Concepts like equality, worker's rights, and spiritual self-determination began to circulate widely.

By the final conjunction on January 4, 1849, the uprising had dimmed, but its aftershocks endured. The mythic currents of that time persisted through later movements: abolition, feminism, spiritual revival, and the eventual collapse of monarchic dominance in Europe.

This cycle progressed through key moments of crisis and reflection. By the 1890s, Neptune squared Eris, and the world saw Plessy v. Ferguson enshrine racial segregation in the U.S.—an ideological betrayal cloaked in legality. Eris exposed the hypocrisy. Neptune blurred the ethical lines.

In the 1940s, during their opposition, the world was again engulfed in rupture. World War II, the Holocaust, decolonization, and the formation of the United Nations all unfolded within this arc. Neptune promised redemption. Eris revealed the cost.

Now, that cycle is nearing its close. In 2037, Neptune and Eris will conjoin once again—this time in Aries. Neptune will conjoin Eris at 28° Aries on June 6. This marks a decisive shift from Piscean surrender to Arian ignition. No longer are we dreaming of justice; we are being asked to enact it.

This Aries conjunction falls just before the summer solstice and comes with other significant alignments: Eris square the lunar nodes, opposing the U.S. natal Saturn–Moon conjunction in Libra. The archetypal message is unmistakable—myths must now be embodied or dismantled. Beliefs must meet action. Ideals must prove themselves in lived experience.

Neptune and Eris in Aries will not be soft. They demand courage, confrontation, and clarity. What began in the dream of 1848 now seeks expression in fire. The myths that carried us—religious, nationalist, capitalist—are either burning out or being reborn.

These outer planet cycles do not offer comfort. They reveal. They rupture. But they also open the path toward truth—not the truth we inherit, but the truth we are willing to live.

The Rise of Authoritarianism and Social Disruptions (2016–Present)

Since 2016, the accelerating surge of authoritarianism, mass violence, and social unrest has mirrored the intensifying presence of Eris—now in the last decan of Aries, a sign associated with raw instinct, identity, and individual assertion. Her archetypal role as cosmic revealer, challenger of false order, and catalyst for evolutionary truth has unfolded on the global stage with increasing urgency.

The 2016 U.S. presidential election, marked by foreign interference and the manipulation of disinformation, occurred during Uranus's conjunction with Eris in Aries. Uranus, the planet of disruption, innovation, and social shock, combined with Eris, whose mythic apple reveals the fractures beneath the façade, created a volatile environment where long-simmering tensions erupted. This was not just about who won—it was about what was revealed. The illusion of democratic resilience crumbled, exposing a landscape rife with data manipulation, racialized fear, and technological surveillance.

Shortly after, in October 2017, the Las Vegas mass shooting—the deadliest in modern U.S. history—shocked a nation already destabilized. By then, Eris remained within the orb of Uranus, with Pluto in Capricorn dismantling outdated hierarchies. This violence, random and unexplainable, echoed a deeper chaos—one not created by Eris, but exposed by her. The social contract was unraveling, and Eris served as the midwife to the reckoning.

In 2020, as the pandemic exposed structural inequality on a global scale, George Floyd's murder became a flashpoint for collective grief and rage. That summer, Mars in Aries joined Eris, forming multiple conjunctions and igniting mass uprisings worldwide. Simultaneously, Jupiter, Saturn, and Pluto were tightly conjunct in Capricorn, dismantling the skeletal framework of authority, capitalism, and control. This alignment created a volatile crucible in which ancestral pain could no longer be concealed. Eris, energized by Mars, demanded that suppressed voices emerge. The chaos was not merely destruction—it was the birth pain of evolution.

The Capitol riot on January 6, 2021, represented the culmination of these forces: conspiracy-fueled insurrection, the rejection of truth, and the attempted overthrow of institutional order. On that day, Mars, in the final anaretic degree of Aries, was conjunct Eris, forming a square with Saturn in Aquarius and getting ready to conjoin Uranus. This tense square between Mars, Uranus, Saturn, and Eris indicated an explosive confrontation between personal will, entrenched power structures, and destabilized social contracts. The insurrection wasn't merely political theater—it was the visible expression of a psychic civil war, long brewing beneath the surface, now ignited by Erisian discontent.

Throughout this period, Eris in Aries squared Pluto in Capricorn within a widening orb. Eris is to have an unprecedented nine squares to U.S. Pluto between 2026 and 2030. The evolutionary groundwork for these initiations has already been laid. The cycle that began with the Eris–Uranus conjunctions is unfolding toward its next crescendo, not only the collapse of political norms or democratic institutions, but the *unmasking* of a collective identity crisis, as evolutionary pressure forces confrontation with the soul-level consequences of exclusion, suppression, and denial.

Eris does not *cause* the upheaval; she reveals what is already in motion. She names the lie, exposes the imbalance, and holds up the mirror. The evolutionary demand is not obedience but awakening. These transits are not a detour; they are the curriculum.

Eris and Climate Change – Earth's Reckoning

Eris, embodying the fierce feminine force of nature, speaks through ecological catastrophes. She does not merely disrupt human systems—Eris speaks on behalf of Earth itself. In the planetary orchestra of evolution, she is the voice that howls through wildfire smoke, churns through hurricane winds, and bleeds through oil-slicked oceans. She is not a destroyer but the revealer of imbalance, an emissary of natural law who calls humanity to account for centuries of domination, extraction, and denial. When the ecological body suffers, Eris rises.

In April 2010, the Deepwater Horizon oil spill ruptured in the Gulf of Mexico—an industrial wound that poured over 200 million gallons of oil into the sea. At that time, Pluto in Capricorn—ruthlessly dismantling systems of hierarchical power—was inching into a long square with Eris in Aries. Though not yet exact, the tension was growing. Pluto, representing the drive for control and resource exploitation, faced off against Eris, who responded with ecological vengeance. The spill was not just a disaster—it was a revelation. It exposed the blind arrogance of corporate power, the illusion of human mastery over nature, and the cost of violating the elemental feminine.

Then came 2017, a year when Eris and Uranus conjoined precisely in Aries. Against this backdrop, a triad of devastating hurricanes—Harvey, Irma, and Maria—pummeled the Caribbean, Gulf Coast, and Puerto Rico in rapid succession. Each storm shattered records, displaced millions, and revealed the political and racial inequities that determined who received aid—and who did not. The evolutionary symbolism was unmistakable. Eris, fused with Uranus, stripped away the thin veneer of climate denial. These weren't isolated meteorological events. They were global wake-up calls, infused with soul-level urgency.

The wildfires of 2020, which scorched vast stretches of California, Australia, and the Amazon, brought the fury of Eris into sharper focus. During this time, Mars in Aries repeatedly activated Eris through conjunction, igniting flames both literal and figurative. Simultaneously, Jupiter, Saturn, and Pluto in Capricorn formed a long-standing square to Mars and Eris—a cardinal T-square pressurizing collapse, confrontation, and reckoning. The Earth itself seemed to scream for recognition, not in metaphor but in fire. From a karmic perspective, these fires revealed more than ecological mismanagement; they exposed the soul wound of humanity's severance from nature.

What is happening is not merely a climate crisis—it is an evolutionary emergency. And Eris, as the fierce feminine guardian of natural law, is not interested in our comfort or convenience. She demands integrity. She holds up the mirror and says: "This is the cost of forgetting that the Earth is alive." Eris is not here to punish. She is here to awaken. And in the face of fire, flood, and storm, her message remains unyielding: reconnect, or perish.[32]

---

32 ibid

Earth-Based Spiritual Traditions – Reweaving the Sacred Web

In the face of a mounting ecological crisis, many are returning to Earth-based spiritual traditions that honor the planet not merely as a resource, but as a living, conscious being. Long before modern institutions severed spirit from matter, ancient peoples recognized the Earth as Mother, Kin, Ancestor, and Teacher. These traditions—from the Orphic and Eleusinian rites of Greece to Indigenous cosmologies across the Americas, Africa, and Australia—carried the embodied wisdom that all life is interwoven, cyclical, and reciprocal.

Eris, as the embodiment of untamed feminine power, aligns with these ancient streams of reverence. She does not exist within the sanitized temples of patriarchy. She thrives in the wild spaces, the dark moonlit forests, the volcanic fault lines, the margins. Her current transits demand not only systemic change but also a re-enchantment of the world—a restoration of our spiritual relationship with Earth. Her disruptions are not random acts of violence but sacred alarms urging us to remember what we have forgotten: the holiness of water, the dignity of soil, the breath of trees, the consciousness of the elements.

To heed Eris is to listen once more—to the rustle of leaves, the tremor of the ground, the grief of whales singing to a dying ocean. Her evolutionary function is not only destruction; it is remembrance. Through chaos, she restores the soul's connection to the sacred web of life.

A Nation at the Crossroads of Power and Discord

From 2026 to 2030 we approach another critical crossroads as Eris in Aries forms nine exact squares with the United States' natal Pluto at 25°44' Capricorn, based on the chart cast for July 6, 1775, at 11:06 am in Philadelphia, PA.[33]

These alignments are not merely astrological events; they act as ritual gates, each symbolizing an intensification in the long evolutionary journey of a nation standing at a precipice. These moments are not isolated in time but rather pulses—pressure points in the body of a country compelled to confront its deepest contradictions.

The echoes of the US Pluto return in 2021 still reverberate. That transit exposed the fault lines long buried beneath American exceptionalism, the belief that a specific nation, culture, or society is unique and different from others, often implying superiority, revealing cracks surrounding race, power, economy, and truth. Eris arrives not to quietly observe but to shout from the margins. If Pluto represents the soul's evolutionary imperative, Eris is the uninvited truth-teller, revealing what others refuse to see. She is the voice of the excluded, the whistleblower, and the rebel goddess with a blade. A collective confrontation becomes inevitable as she clashes with Pluto, the gatekeeper of power and shadow. This is not just a political reckoning; it is a spiritual one.

Each square that Eris forms with Pluto represents another moment when Eris presses her finger against the festering wounds of empire. Each square raises the question: will the United States evolve, or will it resist?

---

33 On this date the 2nd Continental Congress passed an act to "bear arms" against Great Britain. The next day they passed an act to raise a standing army and named George Washington to be Commander-in-Chief.

58   Eris

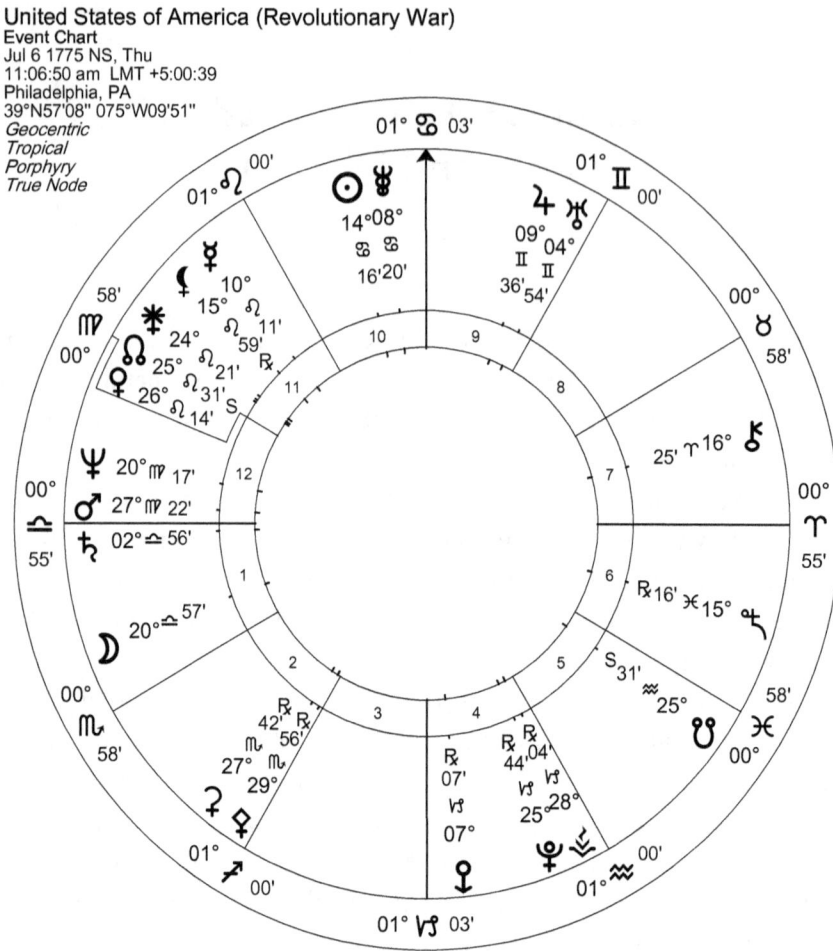

These alignments are not coincidental in number. In myth and mysticism, nine signifies initiation, culmination, and rebirth. A human child gestates for nine months before entering life. Odin, in Norse myth, hung on the World Tree for nine nights in search of wisdom. In Greek tradition, the Nine Muses embody the full spectrum of divine creativity. Nine represents the end before a new beginning, the final contraction before birth.

These transits will not be gentle. They will tear at the seams of denial, corresponding to moments of intensifying polarization, institutional crisis, environmental upheaval, and grassroots uprising. Whistleblowers will emerge, much like the mythic Eris who disrupted the banquet of the gods by revealing the hypocrisy beneath the surface. Climate disasters may rage with divine fury, demanding accountability from systems that have treated the Earth as a commodity. Economies will shake under the weight of accumulated imbalance, just as they did in other years influenced by Eris: the stock market crash in 1929; the Black Monday crash in 1987; the Global Financial Crisis of 2008; and the pandemic in 2020. Globally, American hegemony will face tests—militarily, ideologically, and spiritually.

Yet, beneath the collapse lies opportunity. A new generation—those born with Pluto in Sagittarius and Capricorn—will rise to claim a future not yet written. Their voices will not emanate from the centers of power but from its periphery, demanding not only justice but a complete restructuring of meaning itself. At the heart of this confrontation is the essential question: who holds power, and at what cost?

Pluto in Capricorn, where it resides in the US chart, symbolizes empire—top-down authority, institutional control, and the legacy of hierarchical systems.

Eris in Aries blazes, wild, and unwilling to be tamed. She is not satisfied with representation or token reform. She refuses to seek permission. In Aries, she embraces the role of the warrior. She arrives not as an academic critique but as raw, uncompromising truth. Her transit activates cosmic energies that narrate their own myth: the man with too many gifts to hold, the lost opportunity reclaimed through imagination, and the disappointed audience yearning for substance over spectacle. Her movement is slow and relentless, with each retrograde cycle peeling back more layers of illusion.

The squares unfold in three distinct but overlapping phases. The first phase, from mid 2026 through mid-2027, ignites the initial rupture. Transiting Pluto in Aquarius is retrograde during the first exact square, indicating that power structures are being destabilized from within. Like a match struck in a dry forest, the confrontation begins with whistleblowers and decentralized dissent. The soul of the nation stirs. Forgotten voices find their breath. Technologies emerge that challenge traditional hierarchies. Local communities start forming networks of mutual aid. Official narratives can no longer suppress the truth. This is the spark that ignites the fire.

As 2027 transitions into 2028, the second phase of the project begins with the second square. The fire intensifies. The pressure between transiting Eris and the US Pluto grinds like tectonic plates. The mask slips further, and the emperor stands exposed. Trust in government, media, and major institutions starts to erode. Scandals erupt. Protests mount. Surveillance tightens its grip. Attempts to silence dissent only amplify the call for justice. The divisions grow louder: generational, cultural, and economic. The old power structures, reluctant to yield, intensify repression.

Yet beneath the surface, alternative systems quietly take root—cooperative economies, decentralized governance, and cultural healing practices. The nation teeters on the edge of chaos, and yet, within the storm, something more resilient begins to grow.

By 2029 and into 2030, the final phase arrives: the Phoenix Gate.[34] While Pluto transits through Aquarius and paves the way for the new paradigm, Eris delivers her ninth and final square to the US Pluto. This is a threshold. Whatever has been suppressed can no longer remain hidden. Illusions die. Denial crumbles. Systems must either evolve or fall. Constitutional reform becomes a possibility. Economic restructuring looms. Cultural tipping points may emerge—mass boycotts, collective spiritual awakenings, or ecological shocks that force a new reckoning with nature. The old myths of supremacy no longer hold. A new story strains to be born.

This is the moment everything hinges upon. Will the nation cling to its imperial inheritance or dare to become something radically different? Will it retreat into censorship and control, or step forward with courage, truth, and humility?

There are three likely paths. At its lowest expression, the US could intensify authoritarianism, leveraging technology to suppress dissent, discrediting Erisian figures who speak inconvenient truths, and strengthening Pluto's fortress of control.

In a middle expression, there may be endless cycles of protest and repression, exposure and burnout, and change that lacks coherence.

However, at its highest expression, the nation could choose to evolve. Truth could become sacred. Institutions could gracefully fade, allowing something new and aligned with the soul to emerge. Power could be

---

34 A Phoenix Gate might symbolize a portal of transformation, where something must die or be destroyed in order to be reborn anew—a threshold moment akin to passing through fire. It evokes Pluto, Eris, or even Chiron energy in astrology—catalytic destruction leading to rebirth. It is an alchemical or evolutionary astrology concepts: a gate of purification, ego death, or soul initiation.

distributed, transparent, and accountable. The revolutionary impulse of 1775 could finally fulfill its promise—not in words, but through embodied action.

Even after 2030, the work remains unfinished.

- The Eris–Pluto dynamic will remain in the collective of the US until its final ingress into Taurus in 2048. A deeper metamorphosis will unfold over the decades.
- From 2044 to 2048, Eris will dance at Taurus' doorstep, finally ingressing and shifting the focus to land, the body, and value systems.
- By then, Pluto will have reached the final degrees of Aquarius and transitioned into Pisces, fundamentally transforming technology, communities, and the overall power structure.
- In 2037–38, Neptune's conjunction with Eris could signal a moment of spiritual reckoning or revelation.

The nine squares between Eris and the US Pluto symbolize the flames of initiation. What follows is the ongoing care of the fire. This work is mythic. It demands the restoration of truth as a sacred value, the reimagining of power as relational rather than coercive, and the healing of the ancient rift between insiders and outsiders.

This is not the end of the story; it is the turning point. The nine squares represent the descent. The gate stands open, and Eris waits with sword in hand while Pluto watches in silence. Do we dare to walk through? Do we let the fire strip us of illusion so that only essence remains?

If we respond to this call with courage, vision, and soul, then perhaps a different kind of empire may emerge—not one built on dominion, but one founded on truth, justice, and awakened collective power.

As the United States completed its Pluto return in late 2021, Eris emerged as a key figure in the nation's reckoning with its shadow. The repeated squares of Eris to the US Pluto from 2026 to 2030 reflect not only collective upheaval but also a mythic confrontation between the forces of truthful rebellion and the entrenched structures of power, control, and secrecy.

We are witnessing the unraveling of the American democratic experiment—a 250-year-old social contract, albeit an experiment—under the pressures of authoritarianism, disinformation, and widespread wealth inequality. In many ways, this is not the fall of democracy but rather its trial by fire. The shadow of empire, long obscured by mythic narratives of freedom and justice, now stands revealed.

Donald Trump's return to power—and his wielding of it with autocratic flair—can be viewed as the final gasp of Pluto in Capricorn, a dying breath of patriarchal authority trying to crown itself king over the ashes of the Republic. He embodies a distorted archetype of the "strongman", a Pluto figure unhinged from ethical restraint, aligning himself with the desires of plutocrats and oligarchs who seek to rule rather than govern.

Eris, squaring the US Pluto during this time, plays a different role. She is not aligned with institutional power; rather, she stands outside it as the voice of the excluded, the enraged, and the revelatory. In mythology, she exposes the hypocrisy of false order. In the present moment, she symbolizes the chaos that arises when justice is perverted and truth is suppressed. She brings disruption not for its own sake but as a crucible through which deeper truths must be confronted.

What we are witnessing is a test of collective consciousness. Will America evolve or sink into deeper regression? Will Eris' voice resonate as a call to restore integrity, accountability, and truth—or be drowned out by the chaos of scapegoating, violence, and lies?

The Billionaire Class and Plutocracy's Last Stand

As billionaires manipulate the media, exploit legal loopholes, and fund extremist candidates, we are witnessing the climax of the Pluto in Capricorn era. The wealth gap has grown into a chasm. This is no longer capitalism; it is oligarchy, and Eris knows it. Her square to Pluto raises the question: who has been excluded from the social contract? Who has been cast into the wilderness while a privileged few hoard the spoils?

Eris stands with those who rise not in polished protest but in raw fury—those who recognize that the system has failed them. However, she also urges us not to allow our rage to lead to self-destruction. There is a fine line between revolution and reaction, between truth and vengeance. It is this crucible that will define the nation's next chapter.

What Comes After the Empire?

We are at a moment of mythic proportions: a dying empire encounters the trickster goddess at the gate. The outcome is not predetermined. The Eris squares to the US Pluto, along with Neptune's ingress into Aries and Pluto's entry into Aquarius, suggest that a new era is possible—but only if we undertake the necessary spiritual, ethical, and imaginative renewal.

Evolutionary Astrology reminds us that outer events are not merely symptoms but reflections. The chaos in the external world signals the need for inner evolution—both personally and collectively. If the United States is to survive as a democracy, it must undergo not just reform but transformation. This represents the higher octave of Pluto and the initiatory gift of Eris: to birth a new order from an honest reckoning with the shadow.

Soul Navigation Through the Storm: Aligning with Eris as Sacred Disruptor

To navigate this era, we must see clearly and anchor ourselves in deeper ground. Eris encourages us to respond with awareness rather than react blindly.

This storm cannot be avoided, but it can be transformative. The square between Eris and the US Pluto is not just a battleground—it is a rite of passage. We are being asked:

- What truth have we hesitated to confront?
- What illusions of order or safety do we still cling to?
- What inner authority can we regain as external structures fall apart?

Eris invites us to:

- Speak the truth without apology—even when it challenges consensus.
- Refuse to be complicit in systems of harm, even when they offer false comfort.
- Honor the voices of outsiders, rebels, and the uninvited, both within and outside.
- Embrace chaos not as destruction but as the foundation for reinvention.

Practices for Alignment

- Discernment: In an age of disinformation, cultivate inner clarity. Not every scream signifies truth, and not every silence reflects wisdom.
- Sacred Rage: Allow anger to be your sacred fuel, not a destructive fire. Transform it into action grounded in love and collective liberation.
- Community: Discover your soul allies. While Eris may stand alone in myth, her voice resonates most powerfully when joined with others who share a commitment to truth.
- Mythic Vision: Remember, this is not merely politics; it is a myth that unfolds throughout history. We are the midwives of a new collective narrative.

This is not the end. It is the beginning of the next cycle.

Eris in Our Charts: Working with Eris

Like Pluto, Eris is a rogue—an outsider by nature, orbiting on her own terms. She does not circle the Sun like a dutiful servant of order, but carves her path through the cosmos with a wild and ancient will. Where Pluto stirs the undercurrents and sends tremors before the quake, Eris arrives without warning—her presence unmistakable, her timing irrevocable. Pluto may whisper that change is coming; Eris arrives like a rupture. By the time you recognize her, the negotiation is over. The mirror is shattered, and you are staring at your own reflection in a thousand sharp pieces.

For those born since 1928, Eris resides in Aries, where she will remain until 2048—a fiery, extended journey that signifies a collective initiation. In the natal chart, this indicates that her house placement—not her sign—is the primary key to her evolutionary function. It is in this area of life that the soul grapples with the deeper meanings of identity, authenticity, disruption, and truth.

And yet, like all planetary forces, Eris rarely acts alone. Her touch is subtle, complex, and seldom confined to a single bold aspect. A conjunction may shout, a square may strain—but her influence runs deeper than any one angle. To seek a dominant theme is to overlook her method. Like Pluto, Eris expresses according to karmic necessity. Her role is not to reward or punish, but to reveal what has been hidden, cast out, or long denied.

What must we confront? What must we release? What, in this lifetime, cannot be resolved—and must simply be endured or transformed? These are the riddles she presents. There is no final answer, no moral hierarchy. Only movement.

For we are all evolving—each of us walking the spiral path from the instinctual to the conscious, from fragmentation to wholeness. From the animal soul to the human spirit, and onward still. No one is ahead, and no one is behind. We are simply standing at different bends in the same long road—called not to compete, but to awaken.

And Eris, fierce and loyal, stands as the gatekeeper at one of its wildest turns.

Eris and Your Natal Planets

The presence of Eris in aspect to the personal planets—**Sun, Moon, Mercury, Venus, and Mars**—infuses an individual's core identity, emotional body, communication style, values, and drive with Eris' disruptive, revelatory, and fiercely independent qualities. When **Eris** aspects the **Sun**, the individual's sense of self is shaped by themes of exile, defiance, and the necessity of carving a unique path outside conventional norms. This can manifest as a lifelong challenge to societal structures, potentially evolving into a beacon of empowerment for others who feel displaced or unseen. A distorted expression may involve deep struggles with rejection, leading to an excessive need to prove one's worth through conflict or rebellion. The enlightened path emerges through self-acceptance, enabling the individual to wield their disruptive power constructively.

When Eris influences the **Moon**, the emotional body becomes immersed in themes of survival, alienation, and deep instinctual responses to feelings of exclusion or betrayal. This aspect may suggest early life experiences marked by emotional turmoil, a sense of being cast aside within the family dynamic, or a strong desire for autonomy in emotional connections. The shadow side can result in defensive isolation or emotional volatility, while conscious integration enhances the ability to nurture oneself and others who have been marginalized, transforming personal pain into a source of wisdom and healing.

With **Mercury**, Eris disrupts traditional ways of thinking, communicating, and perceiving reality. The individual may possess an uncompromising mindset, seeking hidden truths and challenging accepted narratives. They might incline toward radical thought, activism, or the ability to dismantle conditioned mental structures. Distortion can manifest as a disruptive or confrontational communication style, yet at its highest expression, this placement sharpens intellect into a tool for revelation, awakening, and the deconstruction of illusions.

When Eris meets **Venus**, relationships, values, and aesthetic expressions take on an unconventional, even rebellious quality. Individuals may challenge societal expectations of love, attraction, and material value, often gravitating toward connections that defy norms or serve as catalysts for personal transformation. There can be an inherent struggle with self-worth stemming from past experiences of exclusion in love or friendships, yet this ultimately paves the way for a more liberated, self-defined approach to connection.

Eris in aspect to **Mars** fuels a warrior spirit that thrives on breaking through limitations and resisting oppression. The drive and desires carry a disruptive edge, and the individual may encounter themes of power struggles, anger, and the assertion of will in environments that seek to suppress them. A distorted expression may manifest as impulsive destruction or rebellion for its own sake, while conscious engagement allows this energy to be directed toward liberating oneself and others from restrictive or unjust circumstances.

When Eris interacts with the outer planets—**Jupiter, Saturn, Uranus, Neptune, and Pluto**—its revolutionary impact extends beyond personal identity, influencing collective consciousness, cultural structures, and the profound evolutionary currents of society.

With **Jupiter**, there is a strong urge to challenge philosophical, moral, and ideological systems. Individuals may be drawn to radical belief systems or a quest for truth that dismantles outdated traditions of wisdom. At its best, this alignment fosters a fearless visionary; at its worst, it can manifest as dogmatic or extreme views.

When Eris encounters **Saturn**, the struggle against control, hierarchy, and limitation becomes clearer. Individuals may face systemic oppression or feel burdened by rigid structures that aim to stifle their authenticity. A constant tension can exist between following the rules and breaking them, with the evolutionary lesson centered on redefining authority on one's own terms.

Eris' connection with **Uranus** enhances the disruptive, rebellious, and innovative qualities of both planets, leading to an individual who embodies radical change. There may be sudden, unforeseen breaks from tradition, an electrifying genius that flourishes through unconventional methods, and a refusal to be constrained by outdated paradigms.

With **Neptune**, Eris faces illusions, dismantling spiritual, religious, and artistic ideals that obscure deeper truths. People may encounter disillusionment with false transcendence, seeking a genuine form of spirituality that acknowledges chaos, raw truth, and the need for confrontation instead of escape.

The meeting of Eris and **Pluto** is one of profound evolutionary intensity, bringing an uncompromising force of transformation. The themes of death, rebirth, power, and the exposure of the hidden are magnified, often manifesting as an individual who uncovers deep, buried truths within themselves and society. There may be an inherent connection to the collective undercurrents of destruction and renewal, with the potential to serve as a guide through the shadows of human experience.

The relationship between Eris and the **lunar nodes** reveals the evolutionary path of the soul's journey through chaos, disruption, and liberation.

When Eris is conjunct, square, or in opposition to the **South Node**, the past-life imprint carries themes of exile, marginalization, and the necessity of fighting for survival. The individual may hold deep memories of being cast aside or compelled to rebel, with unresolved patterns of defensiveness, rage, or a tendency to instigate discord as a way of asserting their existence. The evolutionary imperative is to recognize these imprints, integrate the wisdom gained from past disruptions, and transcend reactionary cycles.

When Eris aligns with the **North Node**, the soul's path involves courageous individuation, embracing the role of an initiator of change. There is a call to engage with the world as a catalyst, whether by breaking barriers, revealing hidden truths, or guiding others through necessary upheaval. The challenge lies in learning to harness this energy in ways that promote collective evolution rather than perpetuating alienation or destruction for its own sake.

Eris, whether related to the personal planets, the outer planets, or the lunar nodes, emphasizes the need to confront disorder as a means of awakening. She demands authenticity, courage, and a willingness to explore the edges of existence, where the structures of false security crumble, revealing only the raw, unfiltered truth of one's evolutionary journey.

Eris' influence in the natal chart acts as both a catalyst and a crucible. She compels individuals to confront uncomfortable truths, dismantle entrenched structures, and reclaim their power. Through personal transformation, artistic expression, or activism, her role is to ignite the necessary chaos for new paradigms to emerge. Understanding her placement in relation to personal planets offers profound insight into where an individual is called to challenge, disrupt, and ultimately reshape their world.

Eris does not offer an easy path, but she ensures that what was hidden can no longer remain in the shadows. She is the voice that must be heard, the spark that ignites revolution, and the force that propels us toward genuine evolutionary growth.

Eris Through The Houses

"The zodiac correlates to the total structure of consciousness in human form. The archetypes within the zodiac correlate to bringing that consciousness to life, and thus setting in motion consciousness itself."

—Jeffrey Wolf Green

The natural zodiac is a twelve-letter, multidimensional alphabet. The sequence from Aries to Pisces reveals the pathway and cycle of Eternal Return. We enter Time and Space, time after time, lifetime after lifetime. The Soul, Higher Self, Guardian Angel, Source of All That Is, Overlord, or however one perceives that which is greater than ourselves, projects into 3D "reality". The Earth serves as a school for the soul. Each of us is an agent sent by our Soul on an evolutionary path of self-knowledge to learn about Itself. We are each waves of a Great Ocean. The wave that rises from the ocean first senses an exhilarating feeling of freedom and independence. It feels individual and unique. It feels separate. Yet, it is anything but separate.

Ultimately, the wave's outward momentum fades. It has experienced all the joys and wonders of the earth and sky. The wave senses its new gravitation back to the vast expanse from which it originated. It is returning to the great Void from which it emerged. Lifetime after lifetime, cycle after cycle in nonlinear, five-dimensional time and space, we navigate 3D reality. Our life story follows the zodiacal circle as it unfolds through the house, their corresponding signs, and planetary rulers that shape the journey.

In numerical order, each house symbolizes the archetypal frequency associated with the natural zodiac. In other words, the 1st house represents the frequency of Mars and Aries; the 2nd house represents the frequency of Venus and Taurus; the 3rd house represents the frequency of Mercury and Gemini, and so on.

A planet in a house reflects the archetype of the sign in the natural zodiac that governs that house, along with its inherent frequency. For instance, the Moon in the 2nd house will wear a Taurus "face." The hour of our birth serves as a third element, positioning our planets within the houses and contributing to the essential archetypal pattern.

All archetypes are expressed in both light and shadow. Sometimes, a single sign filled with an abundance of planets reveals its polarity. For example, I have encountered instances where someone with multiple Libra planets is antisocial, demonstrating the Aries polarity.

Each archetype has a wide range of expressions from enlightenment to distortion. The way an archetype expresses itself is a reflection of the stage of evolution the individual has reached. At its least evolved level the archetype will seek to conform to societal standards and norms. The more individuated self will rebel against the consensus and foster their own unique self expression. At the most spiritual level, life is led in accordance with natural law.

Each individual's level of evolution will influence the balance of light and shadow in their lives, affecting the opportunities, challenges and crises they come face to face with. Our consciousness expands over many lifetimes. We are all on the same journey, each at different mile markers.

Each astrological house signifies an awakening. The energetic frequency of every house alternates between yin, which symbolizes energy moving inward toward the center, and yang, which represents energy moving outward from the center. This reflects the Hermetic Principle of Polarity, a fundamental rhythm of the cosmos. We observe it in the Moon's monthly cycle of emergence and retreat, as well as in the Sun's rising and setting. It manifests as light and shadow, black and white, dark and light, male and female, and day and night. It captures the journey of the Soul, known as Eternal Return; the separation from and the reconnection to the Source of All That Is.

We are like a wave that has separated from the ocean. The wave perceives itself as a free-flowing, distinct entity. However, this is merely an illusion of water. After many "sea-sons," the wave comes to realize that it is not "all there is." The awareness of being part of something much greater than itself begins to emerge. Our nonlinear journey through the houses and archetypes reflects this experience.

There is some controversy about who exactly said, "We are not human beings having a spiritual experience; we are spiritual beings having a human experience." However, the fact remains that this statement holds truth. Throughout our various incarnations, each lifetime serves as an extension of our soul, much like the network of roots of an ancient oak tree. Consider that time is an illusion. The soul lives all its terrestrial lifetimes simultaneously, though we only perceive one iteration. The soul seeks security through self discovery lifetime after lifetime.

In each lifetime, we are "equipped" with a specific set of instinctual desires that draw us to the people and situations necessary for our growth. Over time, through its many incarnations, the soul experiences every aspect of human life. These desires encompass the entire spectrum of human experience. Every variation of gender, religion, culture, social status, rejection, material abundance, or scarcity will be "experienced" by the soul.

We travel through time on the same family bus as part of an ensemble cast. Each family role is experienced: the loving mother, the absent father, the empowered sister, the violent brother, the incestuous uncle, the nurturing grandmother, and all the various manifestations of each.

This karmic framework accompanies us. In rotation, the astrological houses initiate us and assemble the "parts" of ourselves. The angles of the chart—Ascendant, Imum Coeli (the Nadir of the Sky), Descendant, and Medium Coeli (the Midheaven)—correlate with our four identities: instinctual expression, self-image, personality, and public image.

The Eastern Hemisphere of the birth chart, which includes the 3rd through the 10th house, is related to personal aspects and the self. The Western Hemisphere, covering the 4th to the 9th house, pertains to others. The Southern Hemisphere, spanning the 1st to the 6th house, connects to our inner world, including self-esteem, self-image, sense of self, and feelings of inadequacy. The Northern Hemisphere, extending from the 7th to the 12th house, pertains to our outer world and the social sphere.

Each house holds significance and applies to both natal and mundane astrology. The interpretations of an individual's chart may also relate to mundane charts.

Because Eris has a 577-year orbit, everyone on the planet today was born with Eris in Aries. I have selected contemporary individuals as examples of this planetary placement. Bearing that in mind, let's explore some examples of Eris across the houses.

> Author's note: Each chart included in this work includes of a short biography of the individual. Evolutionary Astrology is not a "one-size-fits-all" paradigm. No two individuals are alike. Two babies born side by side, just minutes apart, express highly individualized life patterns. The details of an individual's life are critical for understanding the functioning of their natal charts.
>
> In my consulting work and forecasting, I use a broader range of planets and asteroids. However, for simplicity and ease of understanding for all readers, I am limiting the charts to 10 planetary objects, Chiron, and the lunar nodes, and only the significant aspects—conjunction, opposition, trine, and square—unless otherwise indicative of an essential Erisian dynamic.

1st House ~ How We Meet The World

The Ascendant, serving as the gateway to this house, marks the exact moment of birth, the transition from spirit to matter. It signifies the emergence of the individual, a moment of involution where consciousness meets form. The 1st house correlates to Aries, the outward, initiating force of the fire triad, embodying the purest expression of yang energy. It represents the instinctual drive into existence, the initial spark of self-awareness that launches one into the world.

This house is linked to Mars, giving the sign on its cusp a dynamic, initiatory quality. As a species, we enter the world headfirst, eyes wide open, uncertain of what lies ahead and instinctively driven to exist. While someone is typically present to offer both physical and emotional security, the emotional support may not always be dependable.

The 1st house describes our engagement with the world, not through intentional projection but through instinctive response. It represents the unfiltered immediacy of our presence, reflecting how our energy interacts with the external environment before our thoughts intervene. There is no pretense, no calculation—only raw engagement with experience. Each person's approach is shaped by the sign on the cusp, its planetary ruler, and any celestial bodies within the house. This is the space where the world meets us as we are, and where we, in turn, encounter the world in a continual process of becoming. We step forward into life with an evolving sense of self, experimenting through direct experience.

The essence of the 1st house is encapsulated in the phrase "I am," yet this sense of identity remains fluid and is still in its early stages of development. There is no fixed understanding of what "I" signifies; instead, it is something to be uncovered through experience. The nature of this house is inherently experimental, functioning through trial and error. Choices are made, some yielding positive outcomes while others lead to dead ends, all contributing to the individual's evolving self-concept. In many spiritual traditions, particularly Hindu philosophy, this process is likened to "neti neti"—"not this, not this." The self is shaped not only by what it embraces but also by what it discards, distilling experiences to resonate with the soul's deeper truth.

The 1st house, along with the sign on its cusp, the planetary ruler of that sign, and any celestial bodies present within, reflects the *desires* that drive the soul's evolutionary journey. These desires exist on a broad spectrum, and each must be explored, embodied, and ultimately exhausted before the soul can advance beyond them. This process resembles water seeking to fill every space it encounters—no aspect of desire can be bypassed until its purpose is fulfilled.

The impulse of the 1st house is relentless in its pursuit of self-exploration; however, this journey is not without tension. Aries, the natural ruler of this house, forms a square with both Cancer and Capricorn, introducing necessary friction between the instinct for self-determination and the desire for security and responsibility. The need for personal autonomy is balanced by recognition of emotional bonds and societal obligations. Additionally, Aries opposes Libra, highlighting the challenge of balancing self-interest with relational awareness, requiring ongoing negotiation between independence and partnership.

For those with Eris in the 1st house, existence manifests as an act of defiance. These individuals navigate the world with a rebellious spirit, inherently self-motivated and largely indifferent to external validation. Their journey is one of disruption, breaking away from convention to forge an identity unbound by societal norms or expectations. They traverse life in a creatively unconventional manner, often challenging the status quo merely by being themselves. Their presence alone can evoke discomfort in those who cling to tradition, yet they do not seek conflict for its own sake. Instead, their existence demands authenticity, and they refuse to conform at the expense of their truth. This relentless assertion of selfhood shapes the trajectory of their lives, influencing how they engage with the world and those around them. Every choice, every act of defiance, and every refusal to yield serves as a declaration of their right to exist.

Allen Ginsberg

Allen Ginsberg was a pioneering poet of the Beat Generation, and his radical voice helped shape American counterculture. Best known for his groundbreaking 1956 poem *Howl*, he challenged societal repression, sexual taboos, and cultural conformity—sparking a landmark obscenity trial that advanced literary freedom.

Openly gay and deeply spiritual, Ginsberg infused his work with personal experiences and Buddhist philosophy. He lived simply in New York's East Village while remaining politically active for decades, protesting war, capitalism, and censorship. His legacy endures at the intersection of poetry, activism, and spiritual inquiry.[35]

Eris at 1° Aries in the 1st house, rising just behind the Ascendant, ignites Allen Ginsberg's chart like a primal scream breaking through generations of silence. She does not whisper or negotiate. In Aries, she bursts forth with the unfiltered urgency of becoming. In the 1st house, she resides in the body, the presence, the physical voice—she *is* the self that refuses to be made small. For Ginsberg, this placement not only defined his evolutionary path but also shaped the manner of his very existence. His life was an act of confrontation, not for rebellion's sake, but because truth had to be spoken, lived, and made flesh. The trine to Saturn in Scorpio retrograde in his 8th house authorized him to plumb the depths of his psyche for what had been hidden away and resurrect it as his spiritual pathway.

Conjunct Uranus at 29° Pisces, also in the 1st house, Eris is accompanied by a companion of electrified vision and cosmic rupture. Uranus in Pisces doesn't just disrupt society—it rips open the veil between the visible and invisible, shocking the dream awake. With Uranus at the

---

35 Paraphrased from https://en.wikipedia.org/wiki/Allen Ginsberg

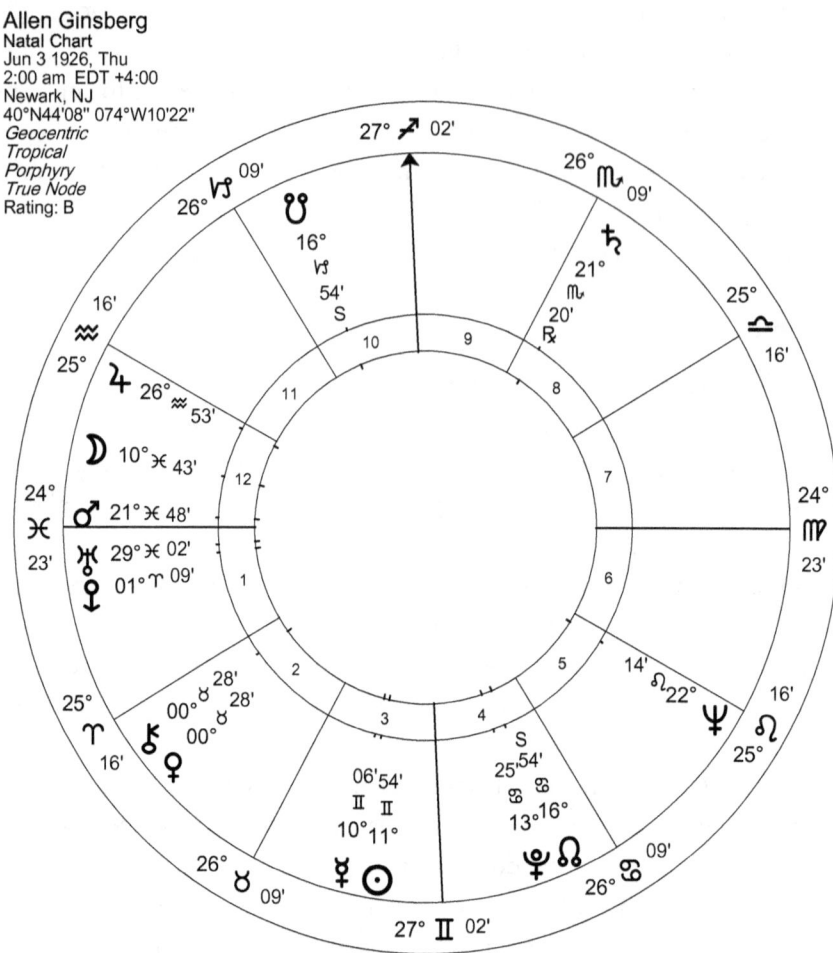

anaretic degree, their conjunction marked Ginsberg as a lightning rod for revelation, a channel for truths that had long been repressed in culture, family, sexuality, and spirit. The fusion of Eris and Uranus created a presence that could not conform, would not hide, and burned too brightly to be ignored.

That flame needed a voice, and it found it in the Sun at 11° Gemini and Mercury at 10° Gemini, both in the 3rd house—the realm of speech, rhythm, and meaning. These placements charged Ginsberg's identity with a powerful urge to communicate, but this wasn't just ordinary conversation. Eris, blazing from the 1st house, transformed that voice into a howl—a shout, a cry, a declaration. His words emerged raw, syncopated, breathless, like ecstatic confessions channeled straight from the underworld. *Howl*, his most famous poem, is the living embodiment of this astrology: unedited, unleashed, sacred, and obscene. Its opening line—*"I saw the best minds of my generation destroyed by madness…"*—roars with Eris' outrage and Uranus's shock, while the poem's structure—a sprawling litany of pain, desire, and revelation—mirrors Mercury's quicksilver rhythm pushed to its evolutionary edge.

Then there is *Kaddish*, his poetic elegy to his mother. In it, the Moon in Pisces in the 12th house mourns and remembers, while Pluto in Cancer in the 4th exhumes the emotionally dead. This was not a sanitized tribute. It was a psychic exorcism of ancestral grief, generational madness, and the unspoken wounds of the tribe. Ginsberg did not write from a distance—he wrote with his entire being, and Eris in the 1st house ensured that the pain would not be edited out for respectability. He gave voice to the places most people bury, sanctifying the unspeakable.

His sexuality was never peripheral; it was central to the defiance of his soul. Chiron and Venus conjunct at 0° Taurus in the 2nd house reveal a wound surrounding self-worth, sensuality, and the yearning for safety and love. Chiron aches from the rejection of the embodied self, while Venus seeks beauty through that very embodiment. There is no gentle trine to Eris here, no ease—only tension and the courage to name the ache. Ginsberg did not conceal his desires. He wrote them down, read them aloud, and made love a revolutionary act. His poetry—explicit, erotic, and devotional—was not obscenity for its own sake; it was truth-telling. It was sacred transgression. The queer body, the desiring self, and the vulnerable ache of longing all became scripture in his hands.

In the 12th house, Mars at 21° Pisces conjunct his Ascendant, and the Moon at 10° Pisces deepen the mystical, erotic undertow of the chart. Mars here doesn't act with force; it flows through surrender, dreams, and yearning. The Moon, saturated in the waters of the collective unconscious, makes him a vessel for emotions too vast for a single voice to hold. And yet…Eris in the 1st house compels him to contain them anyway, if only for a moment, long enough to inscribe them into poems that pierce the collective skin. Without Eris, he might have drowned in these waters. With her, he transforms into a witness, a mystic, and a prophet of vulnerability.

Also residing in the 12th house is Jupiter at 26° Aquarius, enhancing his inner vision and belief in collective transformation. In Aquarius, Jupiter envisions liberation—not just personal, but global. In the 12th, this vision flows through silence, meditation, and spiritual experience. It whispers dreams of a renewed world. However, Eris, relentless and embodied, demands that those dreams manifest in action and word. Ginsberg didn't keep his ideals private—he embodied them. He protested, marched, and wrote until the truth could no longer be ignored.

Neptune at 22° Leo in the 5th house reveals the sacred performer—the poet as priest, the artist as ecstatic. Neptune here spiritualizes creativity, and in Leo, that creativity is personal, radiant, and dramatic. The 5th house transforms his work into play, his devotion, and his erotic offering. However, Neptune can blur and escape. Eris would not allow that; she cut through fantasy to reveal something real. When Ginsberg stood on stage, reading *Howl* to stunned audiences, often weeping or naked in voice or flesh, it was Neptune's dream channeled through Eris' fire.

The ancestral and emotional foundation of his soul's evolution lies in Pluto at 13° Cancer in the 4th house, conjunct the North Node at 16° Cancer. He came to reclaim the emotional truths buried in the family line—especially grief, madness, love, and the fractured essence of belonging. The South Node in Capricorn in the 10th house indicates past lifetimes characterized by public control, rigid performance, and emotional repression. In this life, he was called home—to intimacy, to memory, to the vulnerability of love and loss. Eris aided him in shedding the mask, dismantling what no longer served the soul's becoming.

Saturn at 21° Scorpio in the 8th house, retrograde, serves as a furnace for psychological transformation. Scorpio governs death, sex, and the underworld, while Saturn demands mastery and responsibility. When in retrograde, its lessons become internal and profound. Ginsberg was well acquainted with darkness—his poetry does not shy away from it. However, Eris gave that darkness a voice. She compelled him to express the unspoken, explore the forbidden, and transform taboo into revelation. This was not just poetry—it was alchemy.

All of this resides within a chart illuminated by Eris, forged in fire, softened by water, and given voice by air. She is the root from which all other planets emerge. She is the refusal to be silenced. She is the scream, the kiss, the chant, the prayer. She is *Howl*. She is *Kaddish*. She embodies the radical tenderness of a man who loved too deeply, spoke too freely, and lived, always, on the edge where spirit and body converge.

In Allen Ginsberg's chart, Eris in Aries in the 1st house does not merely represent an aspect of him; she embodies him—his rage and radiance, his wound and his witness, his body and his word. Through her, he shattered boundaries, redefined poetry, reclaimed sexuality, and blazed a trail for others to follow.

Through Eris, he didn't just find his voice; he became the voice.

Joan Baez

Joan Baez is an American singer, songwriter, and activist whose folk music has long served as a powerful vehicle for protest and social justice. Throughout her 60-year career, she has released over 30 albums, leaving a lasting impact on both music and activism.

Though rooted in the counterculture of the 1960s, Baez's style has evolved over time, drawing on a variety of influences. Raised in a Quaker household, she has remained committed to pacifism and advocacy, reflecting her lifelong dedication to nonviolence and human rights.[36]

Eris at 3° Aries in the 1st house, closely aligned with the South Node at 5° Aries, signifies Joan Baez's incarnation as one shaped by the karma of visibility, independence, and confrontation. In Aries, Eris is not patient; she does not wait for permission. She asserts and exposes. In the 1st house, she embodies the visible force of the soul's mission—unmistakable, instinctual, and present. Baez entered public consciousness not merely as a voice but as a presence: principled, piercing, and unafraid to stand alone. The conjunction with the South Node reveals a soul with past-life experience in fighting for personal truth and justice, perhaps with a tendency toward isolation or carrying the shadow of being misunderstood. In this life, the North Node at 5° Libra in the 7th house calls her toward relatedness, peace, and co-creation. Yet Eris, fused with the South Node, insists that she should not abandon her independence to achieve that. The task is to carry the warrior's fire into relationships—to become a partner in peace without forfeiting her capacity to disrupt.

The square from Eris to Venus at 24° Sagittarius in the 9th house, within a 9° orb, introduces a central tension between love and liberation, as well as between personal values and collective ideology. Venus in Sagittarius seeks love through truth, freedom, and philosophical alignment. However,

---

36 Paraphrased from https://www.britannica.com/biography/Joan-Baez

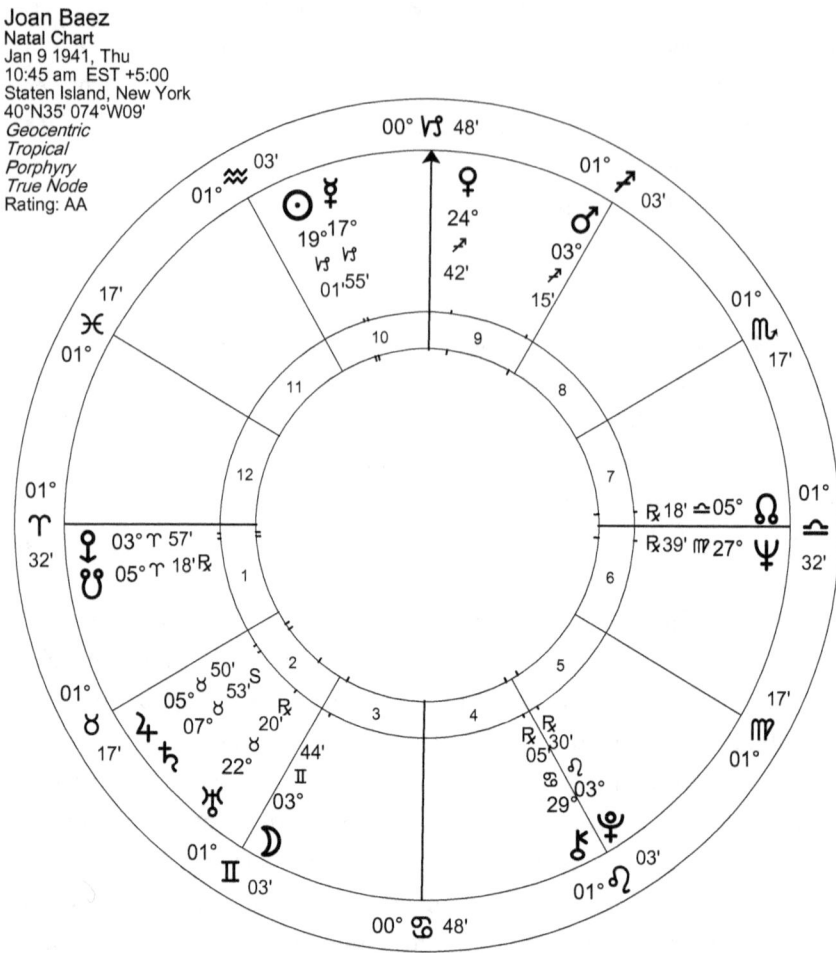

the square to Eris reveals friction: her unapologetic selfhood may clash with romantic expectations, social niceties, or cultural norms of feminine behavior. This dynamic challenges Baez's ability to reconcile her need for intimacy with her calling to remain politically and spiritually untamed. Yet, it also fuels the power of her message—her voice carries not just melody, but also confrontation, longing, defiance, and vision.

This vision receives fiery support from the trine between Eris and Mars at 3° Sagittarius in the 9th house, exact in orb. Mars in Sagittarius embodies the crusader—the one who acts on truth, takes risks to defend ideals, and seeks justice on a global scale. In the 9th house, his actions are influenced by principle, belief, and worldview. The trine to Eris creates a natural alliance between instinctual courage and philosophical purpose.

This represents the fearless activist who sings truth to power, driven not only by rage but also by a deeply embedded moral code. Baez's protests and her performances for civil rights and peace were never separate from her identity—they were an extension of it.

Another strong current arises from Pluto at 3° Leo in the 5th house, forming a close trine to the Eris–South Node conjunction. Pluto in Leo emanates transformational power through self-expression, and in the 5th house, that expression becomes creative, courageous, and heart-centered. This trine indicates that her soul's authority manifests through performance, but not for egoic attention—rather, as a force of regeneration. Baez's artistry was never separate from her integrity. She utilized her voice not only to create beauty but also to channel the deeper emotional and spiritual realities of her time. The Pluto trine strengthened Eris' demand for truth with presence, charisma, and a fierce creative heart.

Eris' opposition to Neptune at 27° Virgo in the 6th house introduces a polarity that shapes her journey through service and disillusionment. Neptune in Virgo spiritualizes labor, healing, and sacrifice, envisioning a world purified through devotion to higher ideals. However, Eris resists the tendency to lose herself in service or fall into savior fantasies. She emphasizes discernment: When is service empowerment, and when is it erasure? Baez often walked that line—serving movements, causes, and collective needs, but always returning to her own fierce moral compass. The opposition clarifies: she was not here to dissolve in others; she was here to serve by *standing fully in herself.*

The Moon at 3° Gemini in the 3rd house brings emotional fluency and a communicative instinct that supports Eris' need for directness. The Moon in Gemini processes feelings through speech, curiosity, and connection. In the 3rd house, it fosters a lifelong emotional relationship with voice, message, and language. Saturn at 7° Taurus, which is Venus's house and sign, enhances her ability to translate feelings into language—an essential gift for someone whose life has called her to speak not only personally but also politically and poetically.

Saturn and Jupiter, positioned at 7° and 5° Taurus respectively, occupy the 2nd house, grounding her values in endurance and substance. Saturn in Taurus offers persistence, stability, and a willingness to navigate challenges slowly and patiently. Jupiter in Taurus enhances this quality through sensuality, ethical self-reliance, and a commitment to what is lasting. These placements strengthen her ability to give her ideals structure—creating a life and body of work rooted not only in momentary conviction but also in enduring principles.

Uranus at 22° Taurus, retrograde in the 2nd house, introduces a sense of inner rebellion regarding security and value. It resonates with her theme: challenging the status quo, rejecting material expectations, and crafting personal definitions of worth. This placement showcases her artistic integrity—prioritizing ethics over fame and truth over convenience.

Chiron at 29° Cancer in the 4th house reveals a profound wound in the areas of home, belonging, and emotional grounding. It establishes the foundational tone for this incarnation. Eris rising in the 1st may have developed, in part, as a defense mechanism and a compensation for that wound: if safety could not be assured, then truth would be her essence. She discovered home in the fierce clarity of her values.

At the top of the chart, Mercury at 17° Capricorn and the Sun at 19° Capricorn in the 10th house shape her public identity. Mercury in Capricorn thinks with maturity, precision, and ethical responsibility. The Sun highlights qualities of leadership, respect, and endurance. These placements lend structure and credibility to Eris' fire—they allow her message to resonate, not as an outburst, but as wisdom. Baez did not merely disrupt; she *led*. And she did so not by claiming authority, but by *embodying it*.

Eris in the 1st house of Joan Baez's chart serves as the axis around which everything else revolves. She defines the evolutionary edge, and her conjunction with the South Node anchors this life in the memory of solitary courage. Trined by Mars and Pluto, opposed by Neptune, and squared by Venus, she is not only active—she is challenged, tested, and empowered. Her placement reveals why Baez could never simply perform love songs or retreat into comfort. Her soul demanded presence, action, and fire. She was not just a voice of peace—she was its spear. Through Eris, she became the embodied conscience of a generation, wielding melody as a mirror and truth as a blade.

John Coltrane

John Coltrane was an American jazz saxophonist, bandleader, and composer, widely regarded as one of the most influential figures in jazz and 20th-century music. Emerging from the bebop and cool jazz traditions, he led over fifty recording sessions and collaborated with legends such as Miles Davis and Thelonious Monk. As his career evolved, Coltrane's music took on a deeply spiritual dimension, culminating in his landmark album *A Love Supreme*. His legacy endures through numerous posthumous honors, including a Pulitzer Prize and recognition from the African Orthodox Church. His second wife, Alice Coltrane, continued his musical and spiritual path.[37]

Eris at 0° Aries in the 1st house rises at the threshold of the zodiac with explosive clarity in John Coltrane's chart. As the first degree of the first sign in the 1st house, this Eris serves as a primordial force of becoming, marking Coltrane's incarnation as one of profound initiatory intensity. Here, Eris appears as the warrior of consciousness, fully embodied and determined to break the silence through sound—not for attention, but for truth. His identity—his very presence—was disruptive in a sacred sense, not as rebellion for its own sake, but as an urgent demand to express what could not be repressed. This Eris doesn't wait; she is the call, the spark, the ignition. Coltrane's relentless innovation, his elevation of music into a spiritual offering, and his refusal to remain confined by form or genre all reflect this placement. His very being acted as a rupture in the collective sonic field, beginning with Eris on the horizon at 0° Aries, announcing that the world would not be the same after this.

Eris is accompanied in the 1st house by Uranus at 27° Pisces, retrograde and conjunct within 3°. Uranus, the planet of awakening, electrifies Eris' fire with visionary frequencies from the dream realms of Pisces. While Eris demands incarnation, Uranus pierces through illusion, bringing sudden downloads of truth from beyond the veil. Their conjunction charges the self with a revolutionary force. For Coltrane, this fusion gave rise to a form of soul-jazz mysticism—a sonic language that was not merely innovative but revelatory. He wasn't just changing music; he was channeling divinity through disruption, allowing Uranus to flood Eris' fiery emergence with transcendent insight.

---

37 https://www.britannica.com/biography/John-Coltrane

Eris

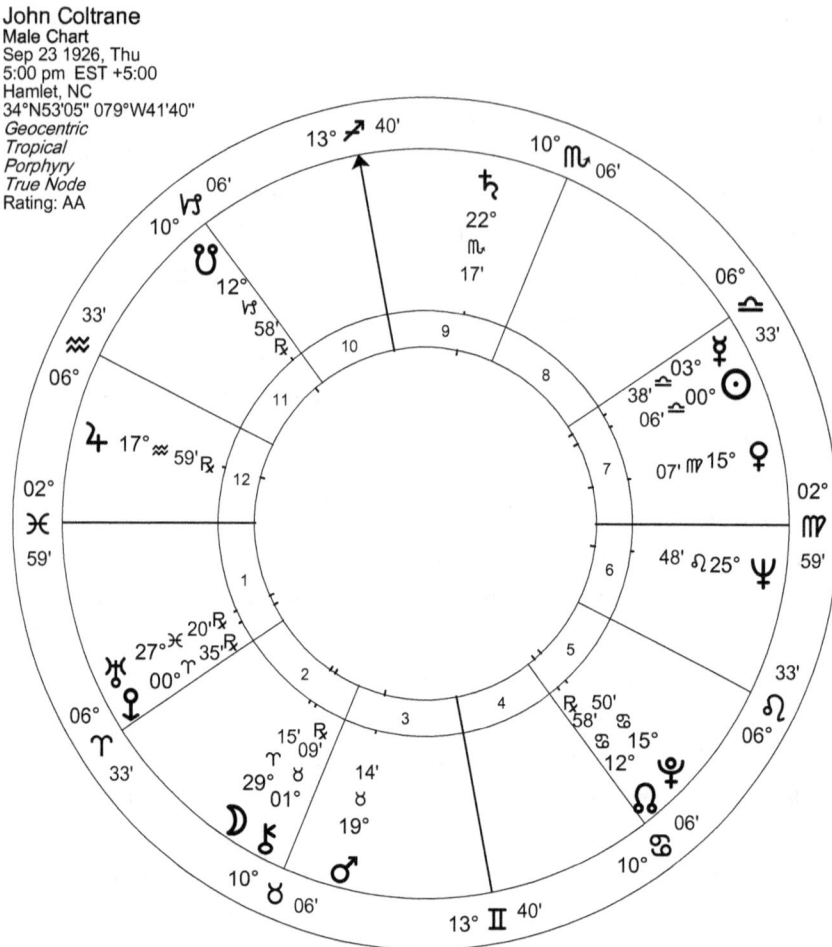

Eris is in direct opposition to the Sun at 0° Libra in the 7th house, another critical threshold degree. The Sun at 0° Libra seeks identity through harmony and the reflection of the Other. In the 7th house, it emphasizes relational balance, shared purpose, and aesthetic refinement. However, Eris at 0° Aries stands in absolute opposition, insisting that the self takes precedence—not in an egotistical sense, but fundamentally. This dynamic creates tension between asserting individual truth and accommodating external expectations or roles. Coltrane's music often explored this polarity—soulful, relational, deeply collaborative, yet unmistakably rooted in his unique voice. The Eris–Sun opposition illustrates a man caught between partnership and presence, unity and individuation, constantly recalibrating the sacred tension between them.

Mercury at 3° Libra, also located in the 7th house, conjoins the Sun while forming a close opposition to Eris. In this placement, Mercury conveys beauty, grace, and diplomacy—but Eris demands unfiltered, raw, and real truth. This aspect indicates that Coltrane's intellectual and communicative style carried an inherent friction. His thoughts and expressions, though refined, could not conform. The opposition of Eris to Mercury compels one to articulate what others avoid, using language—or in Coltrane's case, sound—as a liberating act of confrontation. Every note in his later works—particularly *Ascension* and *Interstellar Space*—embodies the tension between Eris and Mercury: language pushed beyond its polite limits into revelation.

In the 2nd house, the Moon at 29° Aries and Chiron at 1° Taurus retrograde are closely conjunct, positioned just behind the Eris-Uranus pair. The Moon at 29° is at the anaretic degree—a karmic completion point—suggesting a culmination of instinct, identity, and emotional drive concerning Aries themes. The emotional body has already faced tests regarding courage, autonomy, and desire. Chiron at 1° Taurus, just over the threshold, signifies a wound related to worth, embodiment, and the ability to feel grounded or secure in the material realm. These two—Moon and Chiron—create an emotional field of profound vulnerability wrapped in fire. Coltrane may have carried immense inner sensitivity, masked by strength. The conjunction reflects emotional wounds transmuted through voice, touch, and sound. Located in the 2nd house of values and resources, they also symbolize his unique emotional imprint as a form of spiritual currency. These placements immediately follow Eris, reinforcing the notion that after emergence comes pain—and the healing power to transform it.

In the 6th house, Neptune at 25° Leo adds a devotional element to daily work and practice. Neptune here spiritualizes routine—Coltrane's tireless practice, musical discipline, and sacred view of sound all arise from this placement. Neptune's opposition to Jupiter at 17° Aquarius retrograde in the 12th house creates a powerful polarity between visionary idealism and mystical faith. Jupiter in Aquarius, hidden in the 12th, speaks to a private but unwavering faith in collective awakening and evolutionary truth, that guided Coltrane to channel music not for personal meaning, but in service to the future of human consciousness. These two placements suggest a soul devoted to universal uplift, even at personal cost. Neptune also squares Saturn at 22° Scorpio in the 9th house, indicating a crisis between faith and control, between spiritual desire and the need for depth and authority. This dynamic tension required deep soul work.

Saturn also forms a close opposition to Mars, creating a crucible of pressure, will, and mastery that demanded profound internal discipline to navigate. Eris in the 1st house acts not as an escape from these tensions but as the *catalyst through which they can be expressed and integrated.*

The Sun at 0° Libra and Eris at 0° Aries, both positioned on critical degrees, form the central axis of this chart. These degrees serve as gateways, inherently initiatory. They reveal the story of a soul embarking on something radical—not just musically, but evolutionarily. Eris ignites the soul with its fire, pain, and voice, while the Sun provides the aspiration for peace and balance. However, Eris insists that this peace must not be false. In John Coltrane's chart, Eris compels transformation of the self through sound, structure, and struggle.

The fixed grand cross formed by Saturn in Scorpio, Mars in Taurus, Neptune in Leo, and Jupiter in Aquarius creates an intense, unyielding matrix of pressure, internal conflict, and eventual mastery. Each planet in this configuration occupies a fixed sign, revealing a soul shaped by deep resistance to change yet paradoxically driven by the evolutionary necessity to break through stasis. In Coltrane's chart, this cross holds the elemental forces of will, discipline, faith, and vision—and Eris, rising in Aries in the 1st house, stands outside this cross as both witness and ignition point.

Eris interacts with this configuration not through a direct aspect, but as the *catalyst that sets the entire structure in motion*. The grand cross inherently tends toward containment—tension locked within a closed system. However, Eris at 0° Aries exists precisely to crack open such systems. She embodies the evolutionary force that refuses to let this fixed structure harden into paralysis. She challenges each corner of the cross to express itself more fully:

She challenges Saturn in Scorpio to conquer fear and control in favor of emotional honesty and spiritual authority.

And she activates Jupiter in Aquarius to bring its quiet, visionary idealism into a tangible expression—not someday, but right *now*.

If the fixed grand cross holds the inner crucible, Eris is the spark that ignites its potential. She ensures that the struggle is not in vain. The immense tension of the cross becomes not a prison, but a pressure chamber for alchemical transformation—reflected in Coltrane's later musical explorations, which pushed structure to its breaking point in search of the divine.

The Earth grand trine formed by Mars in Taurus, Venus in Virgo, and the South Node in Capricorn establishes a grounded channel of karmic mastery—rooted in form, discipline, and an instinctive ability to navigate and refine structure. This configuration reflects a soul already deeply practiced in the realms of embodiment, skill, and pragmatic creation. Mars in Taurus brings steady, deliberate will; Venus in Virgo adds precision, discernment, and devotion to craft; and the South Node in Capricorn carries the imprint of past-life experience in responsibility, endurance, and mastery of material or social systems.

However, the evolutionary call in this chart emphasizes transformation rather than repetition. Pluto, conjunct the North Node in Cancer, indicates a soul journey away from rigid frameworks of duty and external achievement, shifting toward a deeper reclamation of emotional truth, vulnerability, and soulful belonging. Eris in Aries in the 1st house amplifies this movement. She challenges the comfort and control of the earth trine, urging that the tools of the past be used not to reinforce old paradigms but to spark new ways of being. Through her fire, the stability of the trine transforms into a crucible for inner revolution—fueling Coltrane's ability to turn technical mastery into spiritual, emotional, and artistic rebirth.

The fixed grand cross and the earth grand trine together form the structural and expressive core of Coltrane's chart. Eris, though not geometrically enmeshed in either, acts as the evolutionary agent that pierces the grid and propels the soul forward. She is the wild flame that breaks open the closed circuit and asserts: *you are not here to master form—you are here to transmute it into freedom.*

He responded with nothing short of a revolution of the spirit.

Through Eris in the 1st house, Coltrane emerged as a vessel of divine fire—not merely to innovate but to *initiate*. Every dissonance he played and every phrase that transcended the known carried the essence of Eris: the raw, unyielding insistence to become more fully, more truly, and more eternally real.

2nd House ~ What do I need to Survive?

The 2nd house serves as the astrological foundation of our survival instinct, embodying an innate drive to secure resources, sustain life, and establish stability in a material world. It is where the biological imperative to survive is most profoundly felt, rooted in the physical body's need for food, shelter, and safety. While the 1st house initiates life itself—the emergence of identity and the will to exist—the 2nd house ensures that existence continues through tangible means. It represents the bridge between survival and self-sufficiency, shaping our relationships with security, resources, and self-worth.

At its most basic level, the 2nd house reflects our responses to the fundamental reality that, as physical beings, we need sustenance and protection to survive. This house corresponds to Taurus, a fixed earth sign, which echoes our instinctual need to ground ourselves in a stable environment. Just as animals claim territory, seek nourishment, and defend their resources, the 2nd house in a natal chart reveals how we instinctively secure our well-being. This drive extends beyond mere survival to encompass how we create continuity and comfort—how we build a life that enables us to persist and thrive.

The survival instinct of the 2nd house operates on both material and psychological levels. Materially, it impacts how we secure and manage resources, such as money, food, possessions, and any external support that provides a sense of stability. This instinct reflects our attitude toward work, our ability to create financial security, and whether we accumulate or struggle to retain what we need. The planetary rulers and aspects associated with the 2nd house indicate whether this instinct manifests as self-sufficiency, financial prudence, or challenges like scarcity, fear of lack, or compulsive accumulation. For example, a strong, well-supported 2nd house may suggest an individual who instinctively knows how to generate stability, while challenging aspects could imply difficulties with financial insecurity or an excessive attachment to material possessions as a means of feeling safe.

On a psychological level, the 2nd house governs our sense of self-worth and how this internal valuation influences our ability to attract and maintain resources. In Evolutionary Astrology, survival is not merely about acquiring possessions; it relates to the vibrational frequency we emit regarding what we believe we deserve. If a person feels worthy of abundance and security, they are more likely to make choices that foster stability. However, if they internalize a sense of lack—whether due to conditioning, trauma, or past-life karma—they may unknowingly create patterns of financial struggle, dependency, or difficulties in sustaining what they achieve.

Venus, the ruler of the 2nd house, governs attraction and magnetism, illustrating how our inner sense of worth determines what we draw into our lives. This also relates to survival instincts, as our ability to attract resources, opportunities, and even supportive relationships is directly connected to the frequency we emit. When we feel secure internally, we naturally gravitate toward situations that reinforce stability. Conversely, if insecurity exists, we may struggle to attract what we need or even repel it through self-sabotage.

The evolutionary lesson of the 2nd house is to learn to trust in one's ability to provide for oneself—not only materially but also emotionally and energetically. It raises important questions: What do I need to survive, and how do I secure it? Do I believe I am worthy of having enough? Do I trust in life's abundance, or do I fear scarcity? These questions guide the soul's journey through this house, shaping how we cultivate a sustainable foundation for our existence.

The aspects of the 2nd house reveal how our survival instincts are either supported or challenged. The Sun on the 2nd house cusp may indicate someone who identifies strongly with their ability to sustain themselves, perhaps measuring their self-worth through financial or material achievements. A challenging square from Pluto to the 2nd house planets or the ruler of the 2nd house might introduce profound fears of loss, power struggles over resources, or an intense drive to secure wealth as a means of control. Saturn may signify lessons about self-sufficiency, teaching patience and endurance in the pursuit of security, while Neptune might lead to a tendency to idealize, escape, or experience uncertainty in material matters.

The opposition between the 2nd and 8th houses is particularly significant regarding survival instincts. The 2nd house represents what we can personally control—what we earn, possess, and claim as our own—while the 8th house governs what is beyond our control, such as shared resources, inheritances, and the transformative forces of life and death.

This polarity highlights the tension between self-reliance and trust, the need for stability, and the inevitable changes that compel us to evolve. At its highest expression, the 2nd house teaches us that survival is not only about acquiring and clinging to possessions but also about cultivating a deep, intrinsic security that external circumstances cannot undermine.

Through the lens of Evolutionary Astrology, the 2nd house symbolizes the soul's journey toward understanding how to sustain itself in a way that aligns with its values and purpose. Here, we develop self-sufficiency, foster trust in our ability to navigate the material world, and ultimately cultivate an unshakable sense of worth that transcends the physical. When we master the lessons of this house, we move beyond mere survival into authentic stability—an inner state of security that enables us to face life with confidence, knowing we possess both the inner and outer resources to sustain ourselves through any challenge.

Barack Obama

Barack Hussein Obama II served as the 44th president of the United States from 2009 to 2017, becoming the first African American to hold the office. His presidency centered on healthcare reform, climate change, diplomacy, and social justice, with landmark achievements such as the Affordable Care Act, the Paris Agreement, and the operation that led to the killing of Osama bin Laden.

Born in Honolulu in 1961, Obama's multicultural upbringing—both in Hawaii and Indonesia—shaped his global perspective. He earned a political science degree from Columbia University and graduated magna cum laude from Harvard Law School, where he became the first African American president of the *Harvard Law Review.*

Before entering national politics, Obama served as a community organizer, civil rights attorney, and constitutional law lecturer in Chicago. He was elected to the Illinois State Senate in 1997 and the U.S. Senate in 2004, gaining national prominence after delivering his keynote speech at the 2004 Democratic National Convention.

Elected president in 2008 and re-elected in 2012, Obama led efforts to recover from the Global Financial Crisis, expand healthcare, and restore global alliances. He appointed Supreme Court Justices Sonia Sotomayor

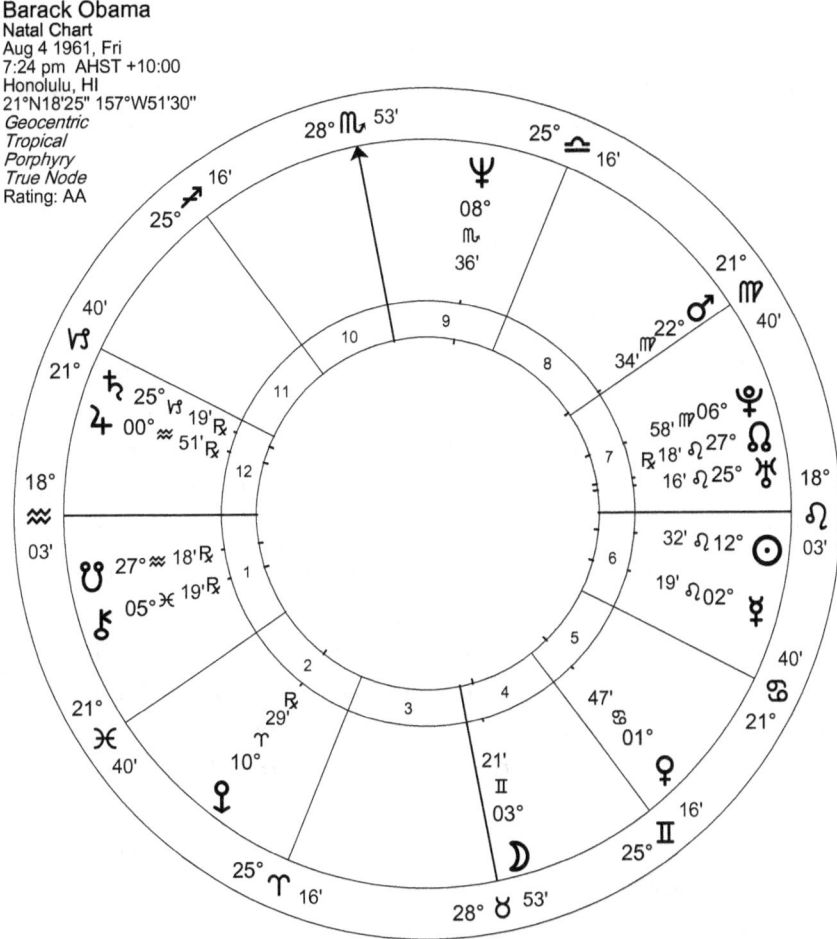

and Elena Kagan, and he won the 2009 Nobel Peace Prize for advancing international diplomacy.

Since leaving office, Obama has stayed active through the Obama Foundation, concentrating on leadership, climate action, and youth empowerment. His legacy continues to influence national and global discussions on progress and justice.[38]

With Eris retrograde at 10° Aries in the 2nd house, Barack Obama's evolutionary journey carries a significant subtheme of reclaiming individual agency, self-worth, and survival strength through a process of radical self-definition. In Evolutionary Astrology, the 2nd house relates to

---

38 Paraphrased from https://en.wikipedia.org/wiki/Barack Obama

the development of inner resources—the foundational values and internal security that sustain the soul. With Eris in Aries, the soul confronts layers of collective and ancestral conditioning that have obstructed or distorted the natural instinct to assert identity, value, and will. This placement suggests an evolutionary history in which personal value has faced challenges or devaluation, particularly in contexts of cultural conflict, ideological conformity, or survival pressure. Retrograde, Eris emphasizes an internalized, karmic reclamation—one that cannot depend on external approval and must be forged from within.

The trine between Eris and the Sun at 12° Leo in the 6th house provides an empowering thread in this process. The Leo Sun in the 6th house learns to express its will and identity through humble service, daily discipline, and commitment to craft. This trine indicates that Obama's core vitality is supported by his efforts to embrace authentic values. His ability to lead with strength and calm authority is nourished by the energy of Eris—by that deep, often hidden warrior who has fought to reclaim worth from fragmentation or rejection. This harmonious flow allows the disruptive and independent qualities of Eris to enhance the clarity and dignity of the Sun's purpose. He can shine without seeking the spotlight for its own sake because Eris has taught him the importance of grounding in true, tested value.

Eris also trines Mercury at 2° Leo, strengthening the voice of this warrior. Mercury in Leo in the 6th house speaks with precision, warmth, and authority, and this trine suggests that Obama's ability to advocate for the marginalized or unspoken carries an intuitive charge of justice and clarity. The integration of Eris with Mercury and the Sun enables him to bring truth to light with grace—his words contain a quiet heat, a strategic edge, but they rarely provoke overtly. Eris enhances the strength of his message's content, even if its delivery is measured and refined.

The South Node in Aquarius in the 1st house reflects a past-life identification with causes, ideologies, or group affiliations—often to the detriment of emotional presence or individual self-expression. The North Node in Leo in the 7th emphasizes a shift toward personal authenticity, relational warmth, and creative leadership. Although not in aspect, Eris' focus on inner worth and individual instinct supports this transition, particularly as Obama's journey involves moving away from intellectual detachment or collective roles (Aquarius) and embracing a more visible, heart-centered presence (Leo) in service to others.

The conjunction of Uranus and the North Node in Leo, located in the 7th house, alongside Pluto at 6° Virgo, forms a powerful configuration that enhances this trajectory. Together, Uranus and Pluto symbolize soul-level evolution through relational transformation. Within the 7th house, they underscore a karmic necessity to liberate oneself and others from outdated relational contracts and power dynamics. Pluto in Virgo demands discernment and integrity, whereas Uranus in Leo calls for bold, creative innovation. These energies amplify the importance of conscious relationships, not only with others but also with oneself.

In this context, Eris in Aries in the 2nd house supports the evolutionary process by requiring that Obama never lose his center—never allow relational roles, cultural demands, or social expectations to dictate his intrinsic values. It may not be loud, but it's unshakable: a private fire that insists on self-definition as the foundation for all outer engagement.

Mars at 22° Virgo in the 8th house provides a complementary thread. Although not aspecting Eris, Mars in this placement shows a profound concern for purification, integrity, and power dynamics. This is a strategic, surgical Mars—relentless in the pursuit of reform, especially beneath the surface. His drive to transform broken systems aligns with Eris' impulse to challenge what is unjust or exclusionary, even when that impulse is often hidden behind diplomacy and reason.

Chiron at 5° Pisces retrograde in the 1st house signifies a wound surrounding personal identity—especially regarding feelings of being unseen, misrepresented, or spiritually fragmented. This profound wound, although it does not aspect Eris, amplifies the significance of her placement in Aries: both represent the struggle to reassert selfhood after its erasure or distortion. Together, they illustrate a soul healing its way back to embodiment, presence, and self-trust.

The conjunction of Saturn at 25° Capricorn and Jupiter at 0° Aquarius in the 12th house adds a layer of collective karma and spiritual responsibility. Saturn here carries ancestral weight, the burden of institutions, and the task of navigating invisible structures. With Jupiter newly in Aquarius, there is a focus on visionary reform and spiritual expansion. Although these planets don't directly aspect Eris, their placements in the hidden house and signs of governance and reform further emphasize the quiet gravity of Obama's path—one where disruption and transformation are internalized, intentional, and deeply rooted in a sense of karmic obligation.

A water grand trine involving 9th house Neptune in Scorpio, 5th house Venus in Cancer, and 1st house Chiron retrograde in Pisces endow him with profound emotional intelligence and visionary leadership. Neptune in the 9th house represents a higher calling and an intuitive understanding of global and philosophical dynamics. Venus in Cancer in the 5th house gives him a heartfelt connection to others and a desire to inspire those around him. Chiron retrograde in Pisces in the 1st house signifies a karmic wound related to identity and belonging, but it also conveys a significant gift: the ability to rise above personal pain and provide healing to others through his presence and actions.

Ultimately, Eris in the 2nd house serves as a quiet yet foundational force in Barack Obama's chart. She symbolizes the slow, hard-won reclamation of personal value from the remnants of social fragmentation. Her fire warms the solar purpose and refines the voice. She does not engage in surface-level conflict; rather, she shapes the core of character. In this chart, she does not represent aggression; instead, she signifies a refusal to compromise one's essence—an evolutionary strength that empowers Obama to lead from a place of profound, internal authority, forged by fire yet expressed with grace.

> *"Obama's resolute solitude—his isolation and alienation from the other players and power centers of Washington, be they rivals or friends—emerged as the defining trait of his time in office: a community organizer who works alone."*
> —Vanity Fair, 2013

Jane Fonda

Jane Fonda, the daughter of actor Henry Fonda, was born into privilege but also faced personal tragedy—losing her mother to suicide during her childhood and growing up in the shadow of her father's fame. She rose to prominence as an acclaimed actress, winning two Academy Awards in the 1970s, yet her influence has extended far beyond Hollywood.

From the 1970s onward, Fonda emerged as a bold voice in left-wing activism, particularly in her opposition to the Vietnam War. Her controversial 1972 visit to North Vietnam and a photo of her seated at an

Eris Through The Houses 95

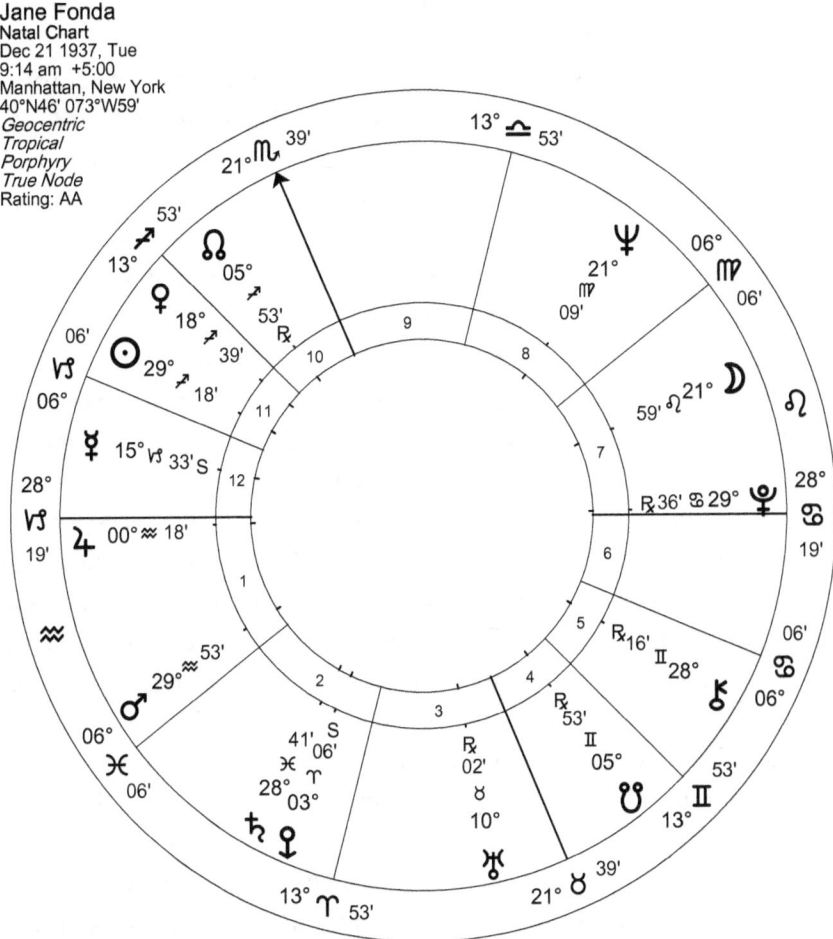

anti-aircraft gun drew fierce criticism and earned her the nickname "Hanoi Jane." Although she later expressed regret for the photo, she maintained her anti-war convictions and continued her lifelong commitment to social justice.

In the 1980s, she transformed into a fitness icon with a bestselling workout series that helped finance the Campaign for Economic Democracy, which she co-led with her then-husband Tom Hayden. A passionate advocate for women's rights, she co-founded the Women's Media Center in 2005 to promote gender equity in media.

In recent years, Fonda has concentrated on climate activism, engaging in high-profile protests and acts of civil disobedience to draw attention to the climate crisis. Since returning to acting in 2005, she has balanced her creative endeavors with relentless activism, solidifying her legacy as both a cultural icon and a catalyst for change.[39]

With her 2nd house Eris retrograde in Aries and conjunct Saturn in the final degrees of Pisces, Jane Fonda stood in her self-reliant authority, inspired by her father's success in Hollywood, and discovered her authenticity through acting and activism. The 2nd house, which governs personal values, self-worth, and material resources, provided her with the inner resilience necessary to navigate the shifting tides of Hollywood while maintaining a strong sense of her own priorities.

In Aries, Eris erupts with the need to assert "I am"—not merely in egoic terms but in existential terms. The soul here has faced lifetimes where its intrinsic worth was threatened, devalued, or forcibly subordinated to collective demands. This time, the soul returns to break the pattern and reclaim the fierce clarity of being, acting from personal necessity, and knowing its own value regardless of societal permission. Fonda's life reflects this clearly; her transition from objectified film icon to political activist and deeply reflective elder embodies Eris in Aries in the 2nd: the warrior who has fought to both own her voice and reshape her values on her own terms.

This Eris placement reinforced her ability to recognize what was truly essential in her life, compelling her to forge her own path instead of simply inheriting success. She cultivated self-sufficiency and remained unwavering in her commitment to her principles, ensuring that her work— whether in film, fitness, or activism—reflected her deeper values rather than external expectations. Born into a Hollywood family business, she navigated the arduous ascent up the success ladder as an actress. She also possessed a profound sensitivity to the world around her, using her many resources to seek ways to heal the societal ills she observed. Her Eris is ruled by 1st house Mars in Aquarius, which enhances her sense of individuality and creativity.

In Jane Fonda's chart, Eris in early Aries squares her Sagittarius Sun in the 11th house and her retrograde Chiron in Gemini in the 5th, forming a mutable T-square with the Sun opposing Chiron. This powerful configuration has catalyzed continuous transformation in her life— from award-winning actress to fitness icon to relentless activist and

---

39 Paraphrased from https://www.britannica.com/biography/Jane-Fonda

back again—driven by a fundamental tension between personal identity, wounded creativity, and a deeper evolutionary call to disrupt collective norms.

This transition has been supported by a grand trine from Eris to her retrograde Pluto in the 7th house, along with the karmic influence of her North Node in Sagittarius located in the 10th house. Pluto serves as the focal point of a yod formed by her Sun and Mars.

Eris is in a conjunction with Saturn at 28° Pisces, a placement that indicates a karmic burden related to themes of value and survival. Saturn in this position carries a legacy of sacrifice, guilt, or disempowerment, particularly regarding spiritual or ideological systems. In the 2nd house, it may reflect lifetimes marked by poverty, servitude, or internalized shame about material and personal value. The conjunction with Eris suggests that part of Jane Fonda's evolutionary work involves confronting inherited or unconscious guilt while reforging her personal authority. She is not meant to follow scripts dictated by society or patriarchy. Instead, she is destined to define, earn, and embody her value from the ground up, in ways that may challenge conventional norms but are true to her soul.

Eris squares Chiron at 28° Gemini in the 5th house, creating a core tension between the wounds of communication or expression and the need to assert self-worth. Chiron in Gemini in the 5th highlights the pain of not being heard and the struggle to express joy, sexuality, or creative truth. This may reflect past-life experiences where her voice, opinions, or artistry were mocked, silenced, or misunderstood. This square poses a soul dilemma: how to express oneself freely when the wounds of rejection still ache. However, it also presents a path to healing—by daring to speak even while trembling and by persevering through discomfort to do so publicly, Fonda has transformed this square. Her legacy of speaking out against war, patriarchy, and injustice, even when vilified, embodies this aspect.

A subtler but significant dynamic emerges with Eris forming a trine to Pluto at 29° Cancer in the 7th house. Pluto in Cancer in the 7th indicates a profound soul history of intense relational dynamics—possibly involving manipulation, emotional enmeshment, or familial roles that constrained her autonomy. The evolutionary intention is to transform how she engages in partnerships, breaking bonds of codependency or societal relational scripts. Eris in Aries in the 2nd, squaring this Pluto, demands that she cease giving away her power for the sake of emotional safety or social harmony.

The inner warrior must rise and declare: "I will not be defined through relationship. I define myself." This is particularly poignant considering Fonda's well-known personal evolution through multiple marriages and her eventual self-ownership as an independent figure.

Meanwhile, Mars at 29° Aquarius and Jupiter at 0° Aquarius in the 1st house add a bold surge of individualism. This pair brings immense courage and idealism, but also risk: these degrees are at the threshold of transformation, bridging the personal and the transpersonal. In the 1st house, this duo reflects a soul who leads with unapologetic authenticity and a fierce commitment to liberation. These placements energize the Erisian project—providing her not only with the will (Mars) but also the philosophical breadth (Jupiter) to act with conscience, strategy, and vision. The 3rd house Uranus in Taurus has endowed her with the self-confidence to become the star and prominent personality she is today.

Her 11th house Sun at 29° Sagittarius, the anaretic degree, near the Galactic Center, also carries the signature of a visionary: someone who can see and articulate the future. The Sun here is filled with purpose, idealism, and the need to radiate truths that transcend dogma. In square to Eris, the Sun offers opportunities for self-actualization—her capacity to lead movements, reimagine womanhood, and embody elder wisdom all reflect the creative fire of Sagittarius guided by Eris' uncompromising authenticity. Her inner values fuel her social vision. She was determined to live the individuality she embodied and to "go to war" for what she believed in.

The Sun is accompanied in the 11th house by Venus at 18° Sagittarius, enhancing the theme of social reform and collective purpose. Venus in this position links beauty and love with truth, freedom, and justice. Although not in direct aspect with Eris, it resonates with her Aries mission—fighting for what matters, even at the risk of public backlash.

Uranus at 10° Taurus retrograde in the 3rd house provides an evolutionary backdrop of mental rebellion—original thought, sudden insights, and a refusal to conform intellectually. Although not in direct aspect to Eris, it adds depth to the narrative: her voice is electrified, resistant, and defiant. She is not here to echo cultural norms but to disrupt and reform them.

Her 8th house Neptune in Virgo reflects the challenges of her childhood and the personal growth they necessitated. The Sagittarius

Sun's expansive nature trines her 7th house Moon in Leo, representing her multiple marriages as her awareness has expanded over the years.

Her 4th house South Node in Gemini, ruled by the 12th house Mercury stationed retrograde, seeded the deep compassion she expressed through her acting career and her dedication to protest movements. She is the living embodiment of the warrior goddess Athena.

The North Node at 5° Sagittarius in the 10th house reveals that her evolutionary aim is to engage in public truth-telling, bringing wisdom and ethical fire into her career while serving as a teacher and moral compass in society. Eris in the 2nd, conjunct Saturn and square to Chiron, supports this mission with unshakeable personal values—she cannot serve truth without first knowing and living her own.

In sum, Eris in the 2nd house in Aries in Jane Fonda's chart serves as the sovereign heartbeat of her evolution. She begins by confronting the internalized shame of patriarchal value systems, breaks the silence surrounding feminine rage and dissent, and forges an identity grounded in radical worth. The conjunction with Saturn signifies the karmic crucible where the soul must earn freedom through discipline and internal fortitude. The square to Chiron uncovers the wound but also provides the portal to healing through creative self-expression. The chart is rich with late and early degree power signatures that cluster around 29° and 0°, amplifying the stakes of evolution and indicating that this is a life of culmination and transition—where the soul comes to claim its authority, not as a crown bestowed, but as a flame fought for and won.

Jim Morrison

Jim Morrison, the charismatic and enigmatic frontman of The Doors, captivated audiences with his poetic lyrics, magnetic presence, and defiant spirit. As the lead singer and lyricist, he became a defining voice of 1960s counterculture, challenging societal norms with his provocative performances and rebellious ethos. His life burned brightly with artistic brilliance, excess, and self-destruction, culminating in his death in Paris at the age of 27.

A pivotal childhood event profoundly influenced Morrison's creative vision. At around five years old, he witnessed the aftermath of a fatal car accident involving Native American workers in the New Mexico desert—an

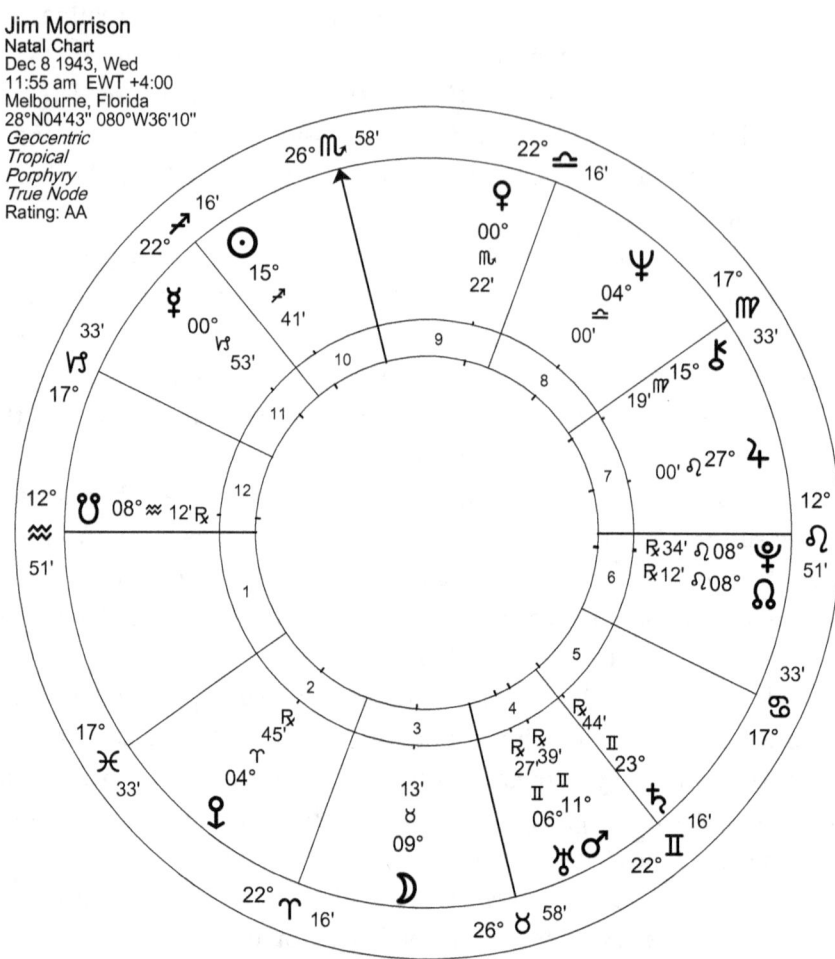

image he later described as haunting and transformative. This experience fueled his lifelong fascination with mysticism, death, and the supernatural, which became central to his poetry and his shamanic stage persona.

As a teenager, Morrison was a voracious reader and a philosophical nonconformist. He immersed himself in the works of Nietzsche, Blake, Ginsberg, and Kerouac, cultivating a literary identity and a disdain for authority. His passion for poetry deepened during his film studies at UCLA, but music became the ideal outlet for his vision. In 1965, he co-founded The Doors with Ray Manzarek, Robby Krieger, and John Densmore. Their fusion of blues, rock, and psychedelia—combined with Morrison's dark, introspective lyrics—quickly set them apart. The breakout success of *Light My Fire* in 1967 launched them to international fame.

At the height of his success, Morrison's behavior became increasingly erratic. His heavy drinking and drug use fueled an infamous stage persona that spiraled into chaos, culminating in controversial performances and legal troubles—most notably the 1969 Miami concert incident that resulted in charges of indecent exposure.

In 1971, seeking an escape from the pressures of fame and ongoing court battles, Morrison moved to Paris with his longtime partner, Pamela Courson. There, he immersed himself in poetry and reflection—but the respite was short-lived. On July 3, 1971, Morrison was found dead in his apartment. With no autopsy performed, speculation surrounded his passing. He was buried in Père Lachaise Cemetery, where his grave became a lasting site of pilgrimage.

Morrison's legacy endures as one of rock's most iconic and enigmatic figures. His voice, infused with intensity and existential longing, expressed a generation in rebellion. Through his surreal, defiant lyrics and mythic persona, the *Lizard King* remains a timeless emblem of rebellion, mysticism, and artistic transcendence.[40]

Jim Morrison's lifestyle was profoundly shaped by a cardinal T-square, with his 2nd house Eris retrograde in Aries opposing 8th house Neptune in Libra and squaring 11th house Mercury in Capricorn. This configuration reflects a self-image intricately molded by deep-seated struggles with depression, alcoholism, sexual dependency, and drug addiction. The 2nd house, governing self-worth, values, and resources, became an arena where Morrison wrestled with his identity and personal power. The presence of Eris retrograde in Aries in this house indicates a fractured sense of self that oscillated between rebellion and a desperate search for authenticity.

The opposition to 8th house Neptune in Libra enhances the theme of dissolving boundaries, particularly through intoxicants, sexuality, and a nearly mystical surrender to chaos.

His 11th house Mercury in Capricorn, squaring Eris and Neptune, channels conflicts into poetic expression, structuring his inner turmoil into lyrics and philosophical musings that both captivate and disturb his audience. This T-square not only contributes to his struggles but also serves as the source of his intense music and singing voice, as if his very breath carries the echoes of an existential battle.

---

40 https://www.biography.com/musicians/jim-morrison

The presence of 6th house Pluto in Leo retrograde, conjunct his North Node, further underscores the inescapable force of his evolutionary journey. Pluto trining Eris propelled him toward fame but simultaneously ensnared him in a crisis of addiction and self-destruction. The 6th house, associated with daily routines, health, and service, became a battleground where Morrison's compulsions and need for control played out, particularly in his excessive lifestyle. The Pluto-North Node conjunction suggests a karmic imperative to confront power, death, and transformation—themes deeply embedded in his poetry and music. Yet, his entanglement with fame and excess hints at his struggle to wield this power responsibly.

Pluto engages in a fixed grand cross involving the lunar nodes, the 3rd house Moon in Taurus, and the 9th house Venus at 0° Scorpio. This complex pattern emphasizes emotional crises that shaped his relationships and creative expression. His Taurus Moon in the 3rd house indicates a deeply sensual nature, yet one that conflicts with his need to intellectualize and communicate his feelings. Opposing his 9th house Venus in Scorpio, his emotional world teetered between material security and an insatiable desire for intensity, transformation, and destruction.

These tensions activated two distinct "skipped steps":[41] one through Venus and the other through the Moon, compelling him to reconcile his need for stability with his radical, boundary-shattering creative impulses. The fixed grand cross, a formation requiring resolution, consistently positioned Morrison at existential crossroads, urging him to confront issues of attachment, identity, and personal evolution.

His 10th house Sun in Sagittarius serves as a beacon for his public persona and existential quest, opposing his 4th house Mars conjunct Uranus in Gemini, while squaring Chiron in Virgo. This dynamic fueled his fame and defiant image, yet it was rooted in an internal struggle to discover his truth and self-reliance. Uranus-Mars in the 4th house, both in retrograde, indicates a chaotic and unstable foundation—perhaps linked to his upbringing—that spurred a revolutionary, rebellious approach to life. The square to Chiron in Virgo reveals a wound surrounding perfectionism, service, and health, manifesting as a profound internal crisis that

---

41 A skipped step is an Evolutionary Astrology condition where a planet squares the lunar nodes. The issues surrounding the node that was last transited by the squaring planet are now amplified to be resolved in the current lifetime.

Morrison attempted to drown in excess. The opposition between his Sun and Uranus-Mars created a relentless push-and-pull between public life and private turmoil, as his need for personal freedom clashed with an underlying sense of volatility and alienation.

His air grand trine, connecting his Uranus-Mars conjunction, Neptune, and the South Node, provided an innate fluidity of thought, imagination, and radical self-expression. However, this trine was "kited" at two axes by the Eris-Neptune opposition and the Pluto-South Node opposition, transforming it into a conduit for both creative genius and self-destruction. The opposition between Eris and Neptune infused his visionary abilities with elements of chaos, illusion, and existential struggle, while the Pluto-South Node opposition anchored him to past-life trauma, ensuring that crises—both internal and external—would serve as inescapable catalysts for his personal and artistic growth. His compassionate nature, deeply intertwined with his radicalized worldview, bore the weight of past-life wounds that continually generated obstacles. These very challenges, however, became the driving forces that accelerated his evolution, rendering his life both a cautionary tale and a testament to the transformative power of suffering expressed through art.

Howard Sasportas

Howard Sasportas was a profound and influential figure in contemporary astrology, recognized for his pioneering integration of astrology with psychological and spiritual insight. Born into a Sephardic Jewish family, he was raised in a traditional environment, yet his spiritual path ultimately embraced a diverse range of perspectives that continued to reflect his deep-rooted heritage.

His fascination with the human psyche led him to study at the Psychosynthesis and Education Trust and the Center for Transpersonal Psychology in London. This training enriched his astrological work, grounding it in a compassionate and transformative understanding of the self.

In 1983, he co-founded the Centre for Psychological Astrology with Liz Greene, shaping its curriculum and vision. Their collaboration resulted in four volumes of widely respected seminars and offered students an intuitive yet rigorous framework for psychological chart interpretation.

104   *Eris*

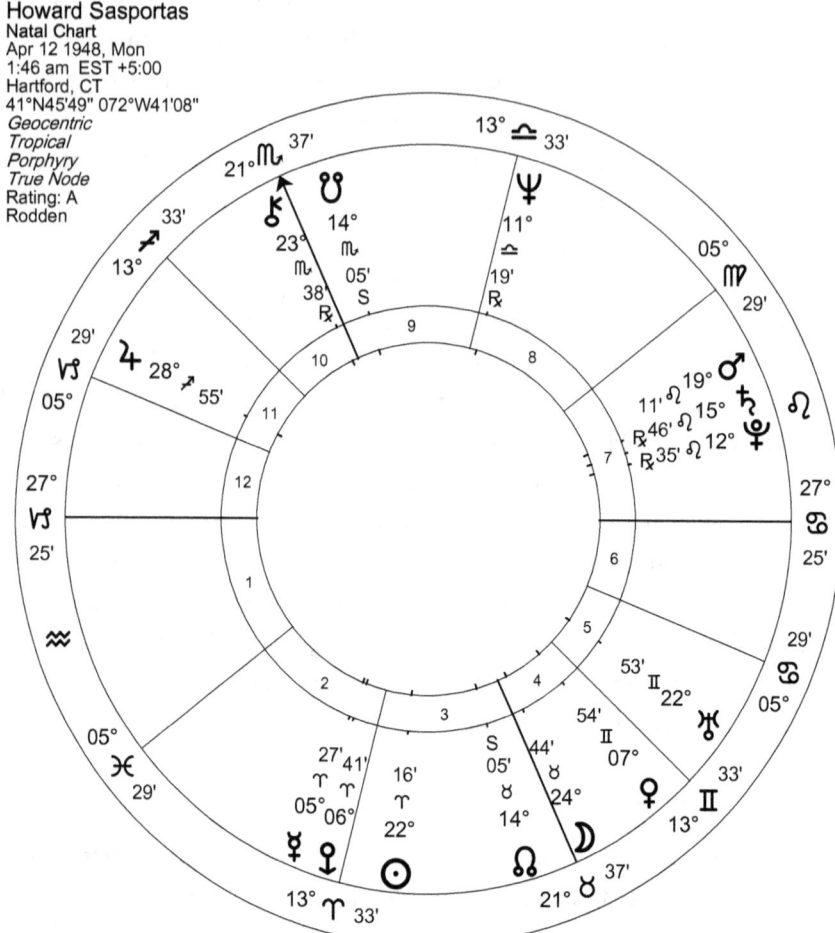

Howard's teaching was marked by warmth, clarity, and humor. He had a rare gift for making astrology accessible while honoring its depth, guiding countless students and readers to a more meaningful understanding of their life journeys.

In his later years, he faced significant health challenges, including spinal surgeries and a long battle with AIDS. Nevertheless, he remained active in teaching, writing, and advocacy, continuing to travel and support others with courage and generosity—even as his illness confined him to a wheelchair.

Howard Sasportas passed away in May 1992, leaving behind a body of work that continues to inspire astrologers worldwide. His legacy lives on through his writings, his students, and the lasting influence of his compassionate approach to astrology and the soul.

Howard Sasportas had a 2nd house Eris in Aries conjunct Mercury, a placement that fundamentally shaped his self-worth, values, and how he asserted himself in the world. The 2nd house, commonly associated with material and psychological resources, activated his chart by granting him an unyielding determination to carve out his own intellectual and professional path. His Eris-Mercury conjunction imbued his voice with an uncompromising directness, compelling him to challenge existing paradigms in astrology and psychology. His insights were not only innovative but also incisive, often piercing through illusions and societal conditioning to reveal deeper truths.

Eris' opposition to his 8th house Neptune retrograde in Libra further catalyzed this disruptive and revelatory energy, amplifying his ability to perceive the underlying psychological currents that influence human behavior. The 8th house governs transformation, shared resources, and the mysteries of the unconscious. With Neptune retrograde, Sasportas exhibited acute sensitivity to the unseen forces shaping both personal and collective experiences. His work often delved into the murky waters of the psyche, translating ethereal insights into grounded, practical knowledge. However, this aspect also posed the challenge of navigating the fine line between inspiration and disillusionment, requiring him to develop discernment and resilience amidst life's more nebulous complexities.

His 2nd house Eris also squared his 11th house Jupiter in Sagittarius, reinforcing his expansive intellectual pursuits and his role within a broad network of students and seekers. The 11th house, associated with vision, community, and collective ideals, amplified his ability to disseminate knowledge on a grand scale. Jupiter's Sagittarian influence infused him with a philosophical curiosity and a hunger for meaning, which found expression in his teaching and writing. This square required him to balance his independent, self-directed approach with the wisdom and perspectives gained through community engagement and higher learning.

Eris trined his 7th house Pluto, retrograde in Leo, which was conjunct retrograde Saturn, adding a layer of profound intensity and endurance to his personal evolution. The 7th house, governing relationships and partnerships, became a realm of transformation for Sasportas, where his interactions with others—whether students, colleagues, or close personal connections—served as catalysts for both his growth and theirs. Retrograde Pluto's presence in Leo indicated a deep need to reclaim personal authority through creative self-expression, while the conjunction with retrograde Saturn emphasized the necessity of discipline, structure, and mastering karmic lessons related to responsibility and self-definition. This trine provided him with a reservoir of inner strength, particularly in confronting the immense physical challenges that accompanied his illness.

The foundational structure of his teaching and writing arose from a formidable fixed T-square involving his Pluto-Saturn conjunction in Leo and his 10th house Chiron retrograde in Scorpio, along with his 3rd house-9th house nodes in Scorpio and Taurus. This configuration demanded both tenacity and unwavering commitment to his calling. The Moon in Taurus in the 4th house anchored him in the tangible, providing emotional stability and endurance, while the 10th house Chiron retrograde in Scorpio unveiled the wounds he carried in his public role, compelling him to transmute pain into wisdom. The Scorpio-Taurus nodal axis further emphasized his evolutionary path, requiring him to move beyond reliance on external validation (South Node in Taurus) and delve into the depths of psychological transformation and mastery.

His capacity for self-actualization was further enhanced by a fire grand trine involving his 3rd house Aries Sun, 11th house Jupiter in Sagittarius, and 7th house Mars in Leo. This dynamic synergy of fire signs fostered an unquenchable drive for personal growth, intellectual discovery, and leadership within his field. The Aries Sun in the 3rd house equipped him with sharp mental acuity and a pioneering spirit in communication, while Jupiter in Sagittarius in the 11th house ensured that his knowledge reached a global audience. Mars in Leo in the 7th house infused his relationships with assertiveness and charisma, further enhancing his ability to inspire and influence others.

This grand trine was "kited out" by his 5th house Uranus in Gemini, placing astrology and innovative thinking at the heart of his life's work. The 5th house, governing creativity and self-expression, became the arena where his Uranian brilliance flourished, allowing him to break new ground in the study of astrology and human psychology. His unconventional approach and ability to synthesize complex ideas made his teachings revolutionary, ensuring his legacy as a transformative force in the field.

The culmination of his purpose and mentorship role was highlighted by a yod—a "finger of fate"—created by his Aries Sun and Gemini Uranus, both directing towards his 10th house Chiron retrograde in Scorpio. This alignment positioned his Chironian wound and healing journey at the forefront of his public identity, reinforcing his role as a guide for others navigating their own transformations. His work was not just theoretical; it was profoundly personal, stemming from his own trials and suffering. Chiron in Scorpio in the 10th house indicates that his greatest contribution emerged through his capacity to hold space for others' deepest vulnerabilities while integrating his own.

By powerfully activating his 2nd house Eris, Howard Sasportas cultivated the resilience to challenge established norms, articulate profound psychological insights, and leave a lasting impact on the study of astrology. His legacy embodies courage, intellectual authenticity, and an unwavering commitment to helping others navigate the complexities of their inner worlds.

3rd House ~ Voice in the World

In the 3rd house, the mind awakens to the world, stirring the intellect into motion and shaping how we perceive and interact with our surroundings. Here, cognition takes shape, creating an essential bridge between the self and the external environment. The 3rd house represents the mutable yang expression of the Gemini archetype, embodying adaptability, curiosity, and an insatiable hunger for knowledge. Ruled by Mercury, this house oversees communication, language, thought processes, and how we gather, analyze, and disseminate information. It is where we first recognize our presence—we are "here"—fully engaged in a world that extends beyond the self, offering a continuous stream of stimuli for the mind to navigate.

Perception becomes a defining theme in this field because it is through perception that we understand the structure and fluidity of reality. Our immediate environment serves as the first classroom, shaping our early mental frameworks. Siblings, neighbors, and schoolmates emerge as the primary figures with whom we interact, and each engagement refines our ability to communicate, express, and interpret information. Early schooling, social interactions, and sibling relationships act as catalysts for intellectual development, shaping the voice that will carry us through life. This house signifies the moment when language begins to take shape, allowing thoughts to find articulation and enabling the mind to weave the fragments of experience into something meaningful.

As consciousness expands, the 3rd house begins the categorization process, distinguishing between various objects, concepts, and experiences to create a functional model of reality. In infancy, awareness is initially rooted in the self and immediate caregivers, as illustrated in the 1st and 2nd houses. However, awareness broadens as the 3rd house develops, encompassing an increasingly complex social and intellectual landscape. The world is no longer confined to the safety of parental care; it now includes siblings, peers, and members of the immediate community. This expansion requires developing communication skills to express personal needs, exchange ideas, and engage with the external world in a way that fosters understanding.

Mercury, like Venus, governs two signs. In Gemini, it presides over the rational, left-brain functions that define the lower mind. This realm involves active processing, where facts are collected, experiences are categorized, and patterns are recognized. The essence of Gemini energy lies in collection—the gathering of information, data, and perspectives, often without immediate concern for deeper synthesis. This phase is driven by curiosity, where the mind remains open and exploratory, accumulating the "bits and bobs" of life that will later form the foundation for broader intellectual growth. Words become tools, symbols gain meaning, and the ability to define and classify the world fosters a structured cognitive approach to reality.

The pursuit of security within the 3rd house involves constructing an intellectual framework that provides a sense of order amid the vast influx of information. The mind aims to clarify an otherwise chaotic world in this realm, often prioritizing empirical knowledge and firsthand experience over faith-based understanding. Gemini's curiosity fuels a continuous desire to uncover facts, explore new ideas, and engage with diverse subjects and perspectives.

However, this relentless pursuit of knowledge presents challenges. The inherent tension between Gemini and both Virgo and Pisces highlights potential distortions in this process. Without discernment, gathering facts may lead to mental clutter rather than clarity. The difficulty with Virgo energy stems from an overemphasis on critical analysis, which fragments knowledge into isolated details without holistic integration. In contrast, Pisces introduces the risk of an overly diffuse, ungrounded perspective, where information is absorbed but not always logically structured. The opposition to Sagittarius further reveals a polarity within the learning process—while the 3rd house collects information in a raw and immediate manner, Sagittarius seeks to synthesize and derive broader meaning. When this balance is disrupted, there is a risk of fragmented understanding, where knowledge remains a collection of scattered ideas rather than a cohesive worldview.

This house also demonstrates how one articulates their thoughts and engages with the world through verbal and written expression. Speech, writing, storytelling, and even singing are manifestations of this house, reflecting an individual's ability to communicate their inner landscape outward. The influence of siblings in this realm is particularly significant, as they often shape the ways in which communication patterns develop during early life. Whether through rivalry, camaraderie, or shared learning experiences, siblings play a critical role as some of the first individuals with whom one must negotiate thoughts and expressions, ultimately influencing intellectual development and shaping the nature of interpersonal exchanges.

At its core, the 3rd house embodies the perpetual student, a mind in motion, and the insatiable thirst for knowledge that drives one into the complexities of life. It is the realm of discovery, teaching us how to navigate an ever-expanding world through perception, intellect, and communication. Curiosity is the guiding force here, compelling the mind to ask questions, explore, gather, and process. This is where we first acquire the language of the world, not only in a literal sense but also in how we connect, interpret, and express the reality around us.

Malcolm X

Malcolm X, born Malcolm Little in 1925 in Omaha, Nebraska, was raised in a family grounded in black pride and Garveyite resistance. After his father's death under suspicious circumstances and his mother's institutionalization, Malcolm was placed in foster care, where he experienced the harsh realities of systemic racism. A teacher's dismissal of his ambition to become a lawyer left a lasting impression.

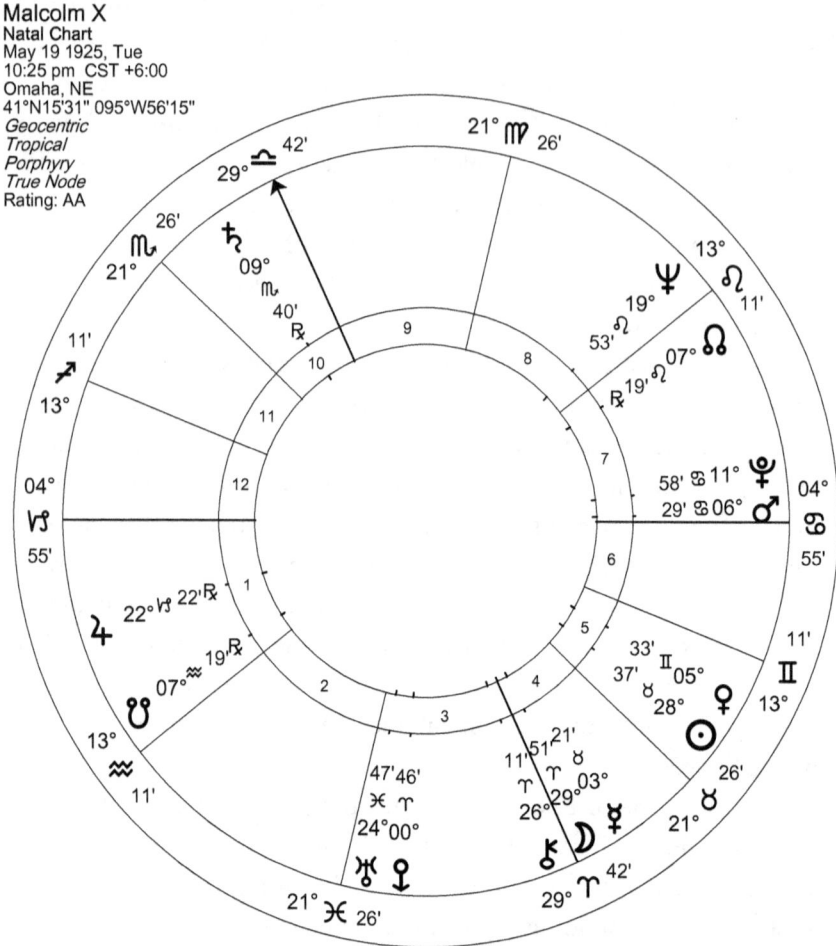

As a young man, Malcolm embraced street life in Boston and Harlem, later serving a prison sentence for burglary. While in prison, he underwent a profound transformation, immersing himself in study and joining the Nation of Islam. Upon his release in 1952, he adopted the name Malcolm X, rejecting his "slave name" and quickly rising as a powerful voice for black empowerment.

By the late 1950s, Malcolm had become a national figure—admired and feared for his militant stance and rejection of nonviolence. Although critical of Martin Luther King Jr., he acknowledged their shared goal of freedom. In 1964, disillusioned by Elijah Muhammad's misconduct and the Nation's rigid doctrines, Malcolm left the organization, marking a transformation in his thinking.

A pilgrimage to Mecca exposed him to Muslims of all races and transformed his views on race, prompting a more inclusive vision of global human rights. Back in the U.S., he called for unity among civil rights groups, even meeting privately with Coretta Scott King, saying his presence could strengthen King's cause by offering a radical alternative.

On February 21, 1965, Malcolm X was assassinated in Harlem. Although he and King never fully aligned, King mourned his death and acknowledged his evolving perspective. Malcolm's legacy endures as a symbol of unwavering resistance and revolutionary vision, inspiring generations in the ongoing fight for racial justice.[42]

Malcolm X's 3rd house Eris in Aries conjoined Uranus in Pisces, marking him as a revolutionary thinker whose words embodied the disruptive force of truth. His voice was not merely a tool for communication but a weapon against systemic oppression. The 3rd house, which governs perception, learning, and speech, became electrified by this conjunction, making his intellect unpredictable, piercing, and unwavering. Eris, embodying discord as a catalyst for transformation, found in Uranus a partner that demanded radical shifts in consciousness. His words, infused with the shocking revelations of Pisces, were meant to awaken, dismantle illusions, and expose hidden injustices. This relentless mental energy trined his 7th house North Node in Leo, emphasizing his destiny to form relationships as a leader and truth-bearer. He was not meant to work in isolation—his voice needed to resonate with the public, challenge, and inspire. The North Node in Leo indicated his role as a visionary, a beacon illuminating the path for his people.

However, his 3rd house Eris also squared his 7th house Mars in Cancer, revealing the tension between his uncompromising voice and the emotional rage that fueled his fight. Mars, the warrior, was deeply personal in Cancer, connecting to ancestral pain and the protective instinct of a man who viewed his entire race as family. This Mars, in turn, was ruled by and in mutual reception to his 4th house Moon in Aries, which conjoined Mercury in Taurus. His emotional body and intellect operated in unison, driven by the fire of Aries and the fixed, deliberate grounding of Taurus, shaping him into a speaker of immense weight and authority. His words were deliberate, steady, and uncompromising—rooted in survival and

---

42 Paraphrased from https://www.britannica.com/biography/Malcolm-X

the lived truth of his people. The Moon's placement in Aries reinforced his need for independence, action, and courage, while Mercury in Taurus ensured that his speech carried a tone of permanence and conviction, less about quick wit and more about building an unshakable argument. He did not simply debate; he declared, embodying the urgency of liberation with unwavering certainty.

His 5th house Sun in Taurus, conjunct Venus in Gemini, provided the emotional foundation necessary for him to act on his values and priorities. His Taurean Sun rooted him in an unshakable understanding of his worth, identity, and the enduring legacy of his people. This was not a man who wavered in the face of opposition; his sense of self was immovable, and with Venus in Gemini, his ability to articulate beauty, love, and justice was unparalleled. These placements endowed him with the necessary magnetism and charm to communicate his message with force and grace. He understood his role and purpose as a black man and lived that reality with unwavering determination and conviction.

His 1st house Jupiter retrograde in Capricorn, ruled by his 10th house Saturn retrograde in Scorpio, reflected the weight of ancestral history he carried and the discipline with which he wielded his influence. Jupiter, representing expansion and philosophy, was tempered in Capricorn, making him a man who did not waste words or energy. His growth came through struggle, through breaking chains rather than merely dreaming of freedom.

With his South Node in Aquarius, also in his 1st house, his soul bore the revolutionary imprint of past lives dedicated to collective progress. He possessed an innate understanding of rebellion, of challenging structures that sought to suppress the human spirit. However, in this life, his destiny was not to remain a detached observer; he was meant to embody the fire of Leo's North Node, to step onto the stage, command attention, and lead with an unyielding sense of purpose.

Malcolm X was the outspoken advocate for generations of African Americans whose voices had been silenced or denied for centuries. His 3rd house Eris, working in tandem with his 1st house Jupiter in Capricorn, made him a fierce orator, a radical thinker, and an unrelenting force for lack liberation. He did not seek comfort or compromise; he embraced the discord necessary for revolution. His presence was not merely personal but archetypal—a living testament to the evolutionary necessity of truth spoken without fear.

Oprah Winfrey

Oprah Winfrey is an American television personality, actress, entrepreneur, and philanthropist whose influence has transformed media, literature, and social activism. Her groundbreaking talk show, *The Oprah Winfrey Show*, redefined daytime television with its blend of entertainment, emotional honesty, and cultural dialogue. Over 25 years, it became the highest-rated talk show in the U.S., helping Oprah become one of the most powerful women in media.

Born into poverty in Mississippi in 1954, Oprah overcame a traumatic childhood characterized by abuse and instability. After moving between various homes, she ultimately found stability while living with her father in Nashville. She excelled in school, earning a scholarship to Tennessee State University and started her broadcasting career at age 19. After initial positions in local news, she discovered her voice on a Baltimore talk show, *People Are Talking*, and soon relocated to Chicago to host *AM Chicago*, which evolved into *The Oprah Winfrey Show* in 1986.

Her impact extended far beyond television. In 1985, she received an Oscar nomination for *The Color Purple and* then founded Harpo Productions, becoming the first black woman to own a major production company. She later launched Harpo Films, *O, The Oprah Magazine*, and *Oprah's Book Club*, which became a dominant force in publishing. In 2011, she established the Oprah Winfrey Network (OWN) and continued to lead powerful conversations through *Oprah's Next Chapter*.

Winfrey is also a committed philanthropist. She established Oprah's Angel Network and created the Oprah Winfrey Leadership Academy for Girls in South Africa. She has championed education, child welfare, and disaster relief, leveraging her platform to advocate for those in need.

Her numerous honors include the Presidential Medal of Freedom, the Jean Hersholt Humanitarian Award, and the Cecil B. DeMille Award at the Golden Globes, where her 2018 speech on justice and equality made headlines. She is also a bestselling author, delving into themes of trauma, healing, and personal growth.

114 *Eris*

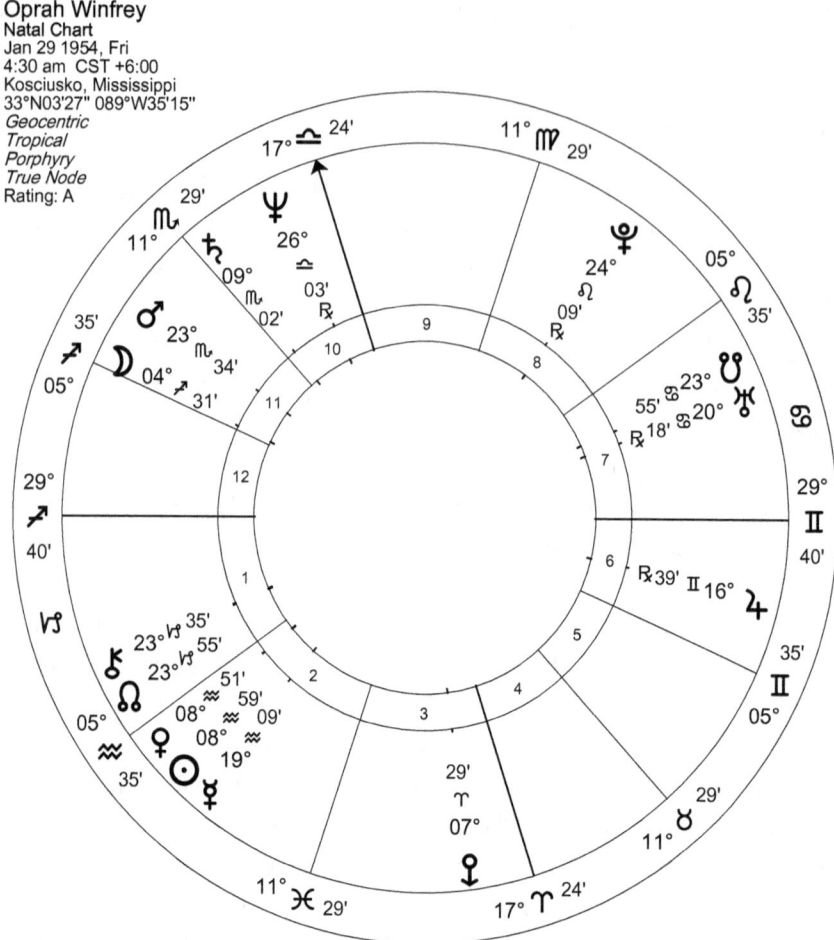

Oprah Winfrey's legacy is one of resilience, authenticity, and visionary impact—shaping culture, media, and humanitarian efforts for generations.[43]

Oprah Winfrey's Moon in Sagittarius, positioned in the 11th house, forms a flowing trine with her Eris in Aries, located in the 3rd house. This alignment emphasizes how her profound emotional intelligence and inherent compassion became an expansive and fearless voice against intolerance. Her message resonated globally, amplified by the natural rulership of the 3rd house of communication, broadcasting, and idea exchange. This placement endowed her with an unwavering drive to tell

---

43 Paraphrased from https://www.britannica.com/biography/Oprah-Winfrey

stories that challenged existing paradigms, empowering others to uncover their own truths. The energized 3rd house, fueled by Eris, enhanced her ability to disrupt conventional narratives, while the 11th house Moon broadened this reach, allowing her to cultivate a community of millions who saw her as a beacon of wisdom and inspiration.

Her 8th house Pluto retrograde in Leo, which governs deep psychological evolution, empowered her with unwavering determination to reshape societal perspectives through television, print media, and personal storytelling. She did not merely create content; she cultivated a space where truth could emerge, where vulnerability became strength, and where individual stories could resonate with universal struggles. This Plutonic influence ensured that her network possessed profound emotional and psychological depth, unafraid to confront trauma, healing, and transformation.

The 10th house symbolizes public reputation and professional mastery. Saturn's presence in Scorpio introduced a layer of emotional resilience and determination. This aspect necessitated ongoing recalibration between the significant responsibilities she carried and the deeply personal nature of her work. Her capacity to uphold authority and credibility in the public eye while navigating the intense emotional landscapes of those she uplifted represented a delicate balance that defined her career.

The conjunction of Venus and the Sun in Aquarius in the 2nd house served as a cornerstone for her ability to manifest wealth and resources aligned with her values. This conjunction provided her with self-assurance, charisma, and a visionary approach to financial matters, enabling her to build a philanthropic and lucrative empire. The 2nd house, which governs material security and personal priorities, became the foundation to enact her higher ideals. Oprah did not accumulate wealth solely for personal gain; her financial empire became a vehicle for global generosity, funding educational initiatives, humanitarian efforts, and cultural movements that reflected her Aquarian principles of collective upliftment and progressive change.

A deeply karmic dynamic emerges as her 7th house South Node conjoins Uranus retrograde in Cancer, forming a direct opposition to Chiron in Capricorn in the 1st house, which is conjunct her North Node. This opposition reveals a soul contract that challenges systemic limitations and forges a path of healing, not only for herself but also for those who resonate with her struggles. Her 1st house Chiron-North

Node in Capricorn signifies an imperative to transmute personal wounds into a guiding light for others, transforming past pain into a mission of empowerment.

The South Node-Uranus reflects the disruptive, revolutionary energy she has carried from past experiences—an inherited genius for change-making that, when activated, launches her into a role of global influence. This axis of growth and healing defines her voice of conscience, not only for her African heritage but for women and the oppressed, wherever they may be found.

The 3rd house Eris in Aries has served as the catalyst that set all these forces into motion. As the realm of intellect, communication, and media, the 3rd house provided the stage for her battle cry against injustice to be heard. Eris, the disruptor, ensured that her voice was never one of passive observation but rather of bold, necessary confrontation. Through television, books, and personal dialogue, she redefined what it meant to engage in meaningful discourse, utilizing her 3rd house activation to shatter silence, amplify marginalized voices, and instigate collective transformation.

Bob Dylan

Bob Dylan is a musical chameleon whose career has spanned over six decades, marked by bold reinvention and boundary-breaking artistry. Rising to prominence in the early 1960s as a folk troubadour in New York's Greenwich Village, Dylan's early acoustic work—deeply influenced by Woody Guthrie—captured the spirit of protest and social commentary.

In 1965, Dylan shocked fans and critics alike by going electric at the Newport Folk Festival, a pivotal moment that changed the landscape of popular music forever. Blending rock, blues, and surreal lyricism, albums like *Highway 61 Revisited* and *Blonde on Blonde* redefined the role of the singer-songwriter and expanded the possibilities of lyrical and sonic expression.

Over the decades, Dylan continued to evolve—experimenting with country (*Nashville Skyline*), gospel (*Slow Train Coming*), and roots rock (*Time Out of Mind*), often staying ahead of cultural trends. His ever-changing voice and aesthetic kept audiences guessing, while his relentless touring earned him the nickname *The Never Ending Tour*.

Eris Through The Houses   117

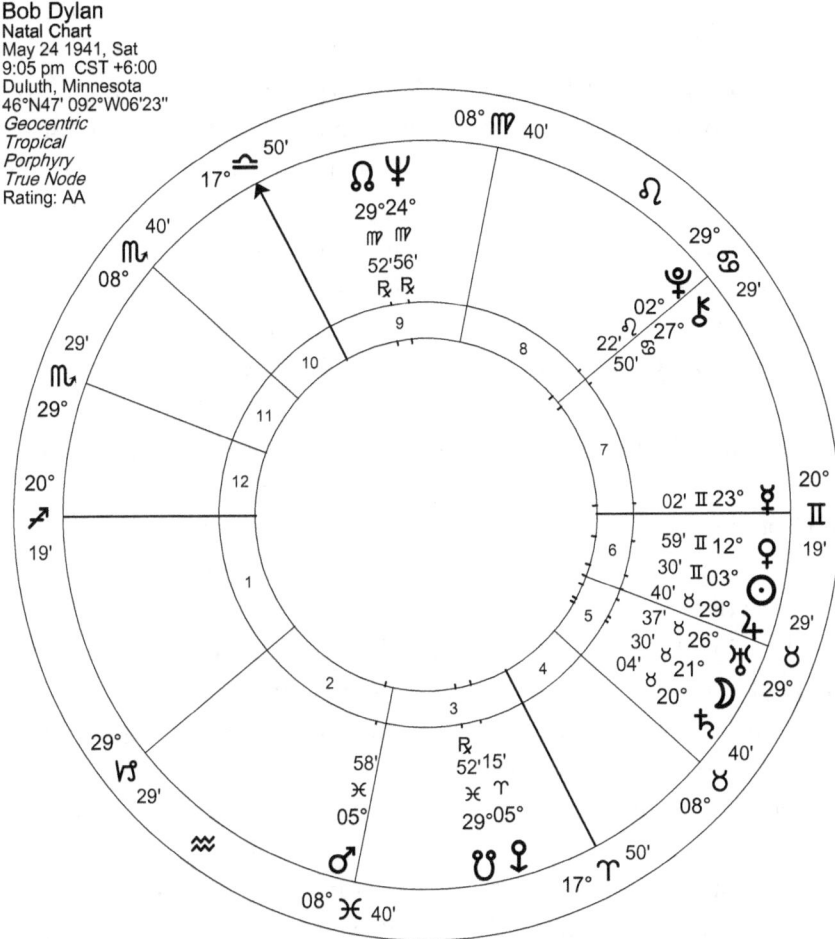

With over 50 albums and hundreds of original songs, Dylan has defied categorization, influencing virtually every major artist since the 1960s. His ability to shift musically while maintaining artistic authenticity has made him a living legend—one whose sound continues to resonate across generations.[44]

Bob Dylan's 3rd house Eris, conjunct his South Node in Pisces, profoundly indicates his karmic and evolutionary journey. The 3rd house, traditionally associated with communication, learning, and articulating ideas, serves as a vital channel for Dylan's soul intentions. With Eris positioned here, there is a fundamental need to disrupt conventional

---

44 Paraphrased from https://bobdylancenter.com/about/biography/

narratives, challenge accepted truths, and use language as a means of transformation. His words, often enigmatic and layered with meaning, possess a disruptive power that reflects the archetypal role of Eris—unraveling illusions, revealing deeper realities, and prompting shifts in consciousness.

The evolutionary significance of this placement is emphasized by Neptune, the ruler of Pisces, conjoining his 9th house North Node. The 9th house symbolizes higher wisdom, philosophy, and the expansive quest for truth, while Neptune dissolves boundaries, enabling Dylan to access vast realms of inspiration, mysticism, and collective consciousness. This configuration suggests that Dylan's life was intended to evolve from the personal and familiar (3rd house) to the visionary and universal (9th house). His music and poetry transcended mere storytelling; they became conduits for a higher message, tapping into the ethereal currents of Neptune's limitless imagination. His ability to lyrically shape-shift and channel a mystical voice that spoke both of and beyond his time reflects this evolutionary imperative.

Born in 1941, Dylan's astrological chart reflects significant dynamics among the outer planets. Pluto was forming a first quarter trine to Eris, while Uranus was distancing itself from a crescent semi-square to Eris. These aspects indicate a profound interaction between individual will, deep transformation, and the desire to break free from previous paradigms. Eris trines his 8th house Pluto in Leo, endowing Dylan with an exceptional ability to merge the unseen facets of reality with raw creative energy. Pluto's position in the 8th house highlights his emotional and psychological depth, his connection to the undercurrents of power, and his capacity for personal regeneration through his art. Dylan's compositions embody this unique synthesis—a knack for distilling complex ideas into potent, symbolic, and archetypal language while channeling an almost prophetic understanding of societal change.

His 6th house Sun in Gemini becomes a vital bridge between his restless, questing spirit and the steady foundation of his chart. The Sun, representing the core of his identity, radiates Gemini's curiosity, adaptability, and lyrical dexterity—qualities that shaped his voice as both a trickster and a truth-teller. This Gemini Sun is anchored by the powerful concentration of planets in the same quadrant—Moon, Uranus, Jupiter, and Saturn—providing durability, persistence, and an instinct for shaping raw vision into something lasting. These energies gave Dylan's creative drive both weight and endurance, allowing his songs to carry not only immediacy but also permanence. Saturn's presence in the cluster underscores discipline and mastery, showing that beneath the improvisational surface of Gemini was a craftsman meticulously constructing his work. In this fusion, Dylan emerges not only as a fleeting voice of his generation but as a cultural architect whose words and music continue to reverberate across time.

Through the activation of Eris in the 3rd house, Dylan's evolutionary path involved probing deeper, questioning established truths, and wielding words as both weapons and revelations. This placement ensured that his music would never be mere entertainment, but instead a catalytic force stirring collective awareness, challenging assumptions, and ultimately altering the trajectory of thought and perception in the modern world.

Sandra Day O'Connor

Sandra Day O'Connor's early years at the remote Lazy B Ranch, situated along the Arizona–New Mexico border, shaped her strong character. Living without electricity or plumbing instilled in her independence, resilience, and a tireless work ethic—qualities that would steer her pioneering journey in law and public service.

At 16, she entered Stanford University and later became one of just five women in her Stanford Law School class, graduating near the top in 1952. Despite her credentials, she faced widespread gender discrimination—rejected by firms unwilling to hire a female attorney. Refusing to accept a secretarial role, she secured a position as deputy county attorney in San Mateo County by offering to work without pay, launching a legal career that would defy precedent.

After relocating to Arizona with her husband John O'Connor, she practiced law while raising three sons. In 1969, she was appointed to the Arizona State Senate, and in 1972, she became the first woman majority leader in any U.S. state legislature. A champion of women's rights, she sponsored laws for equal property management in marriage and co-founded the National Association of Women Judges to expand women's roles in the judiciary.

Her judicial ascent continued with her 1979 appointment to the Arizona Court of Appeals, laying the groundwork for her historic nomination by President Ronald Reagan in 1981 to the U.S. Supreme Court, fulfilling

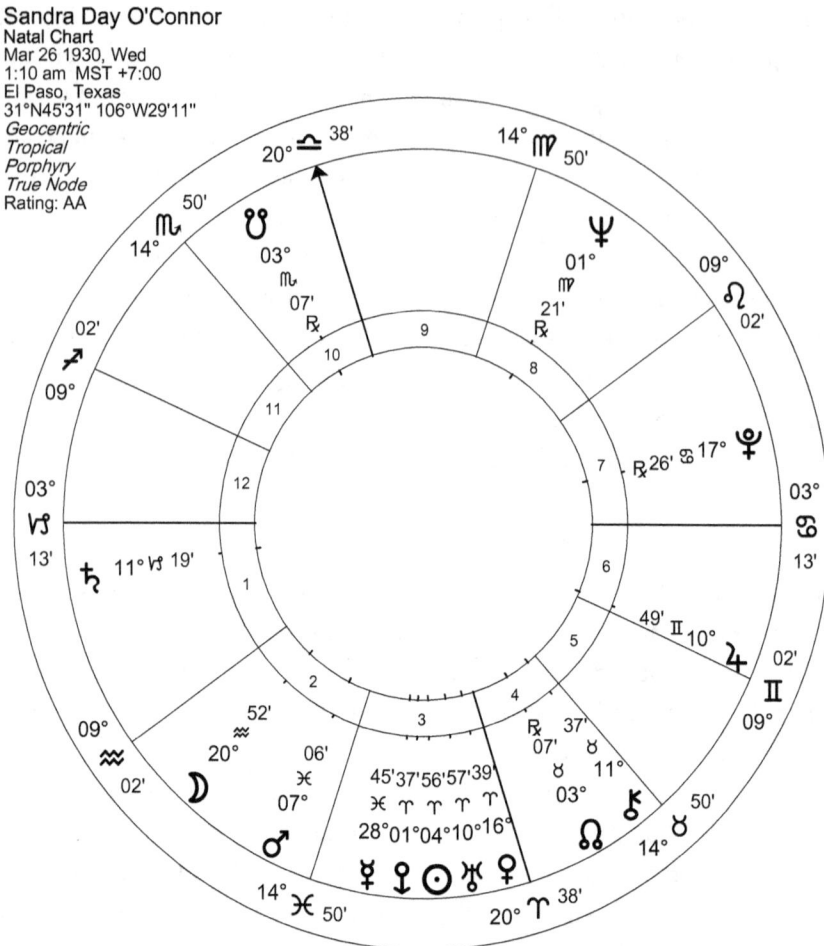

his campaign promise to appoint a woman. Unanimously confirmed, she became the first woman justice in the court's history.

For nearly 25 years, Justice O'Connor played a decisive role in crucial 5–4 rulings. While she resisted being labeled a "swing vote," her pragmatic, case-by-case approach established her as a key voice in cases concerning abortion rights, affirmative action, and the balance of federal and state power.

After retiring in 2006, she founded iCivics in 2009 to promote civic education for young people. That same year, she received the Presidential Medal of Freedom from President Barack Obama, recognizing her influence on American law and society.

Sandra Day O'Connor's legacy is that of a trailblazer, a moderate voice of reason, and a dedicated public servant whose imprint on American jurisprudence endures—from the dusty ranch of her youth to the nation's highest court.[45] Sandra Day O'Connor's birth chart reveals the significant influence of Eris in shaping her path and identity. Born at the end of the Uranus-Eris conjunction of the 1920s, she embodied the energy of revolutionary change and disruption. Her Sun in Aries, separating from a conjunction with Eris, symbolizes a pioneering spirit—someone breaking new ground with an intrinsic drive for self-definition. This separation of her Sun in Aries from Eris anchors the Eris-Sun-Uranus stellium. Mercury in Pisces, applying to a conjunction with Eris, suggests that her thought processes and communication were infused with a deeper, intuitive understanding of the societal shifts occurring around her. Uranus in Aries, also separating from a conjunction with Eris, amplified her radical originality and courage to challenge societal norms.

The Saturn-Eris square in her chart reflects the tension between established systems and her role in dismantling limitations imposed on women in law and leadership. Neptune retrograde in Virgo, forming a inconjunct to Eris, places a visionary and service-oriented demand on her, requiring adaptation and refinement. Her 4th house Taurus North Node highlights her destiny of fostering self-reliance and manifesting her values in a tangible, grounded manner. Meanwhile, her Scorpio South Node reveals the karmic legacy of power dynamics and mastery over life's deeper complexities.

A yod formation, featuring Neptune retrograde in Virgo and her Scorpio South Node aligning with Eris in Aries, indicates a fated imperative for self-actualization. Eris' activation through this "Finger of God" suggests that she is driven to embrace her individuality and assert her presence in a world that resists her inclusion.

Her Sun is in a conjunction with Uranus, indicating an ongoing integration of innovative and rebellious energy into her self-identity. The Sun's separation from a conjunction with Mercury shows that her thoughts and communication have always been infused with the pioneering essence

---

45 Paraphrased from https://www.supremecourt.gov/visiting/exhibitions/SOCExhibit/Section1.aspx#

of Aries, reinforcing her role as a woman who speaks her truth regardless of convention.

The core essence of Eris in Aries within her chart reflects a relentless journey of self-actualization. O'Connor was self-empowered, embodying the archetype of a trailblazer. Her Taurus North Node instilled an early lesson in self-reliance, shaping her ability to navigate a male-dominated legal field with unwavering persistence. The Uranus-Eris conjunction compelled her to assert her intelligence, independence, and originality in areas where women were traditionally excluded.

With the Neptune-South Node yod to Eris, she envisioned manifesting her highest aspirations. The combined influence of her Sun, Uranus, and Eris stellium propelled her into a life of continuous achievement, allowing her to adapt to the rugged rural life as a child and later establish a position of influence in academia and the legal profession.

The Sun in her chart reflects the fire of authenticity that guided her. She navigated paths long blocked to women, unafraid of controversy or opposition. Her 10th house South Node in Scorpio indicates a karmic inheritance of power, status, and social authority—demonstrating that she was well-prepared to reclaim and build upon those achievements in this lifetime.

The activation of her 3rd house Eris played a crucial role in shaping her voice, empowering her to articulate her truth with both precision and defiance. This placement signifies that her words carried a revolutionary charge, dismantling outdated paradigms and asserting perspectives that challenged the status quo. Eris ensured that she would not remain silent, compelling her to express her thoughts and principles irrespective of societal expectations. This was not just a woman speaking her mind; it was the voice of someone destined to transform the discourse, reshaping the very fabric of what was deemed acceptable or possible for women in positions of power.

4th House ~ Self Awareness

In the 4th house we embark on a profound journey of self-exploration, awakening to the depths of our emotional being and establishing a foundation for our personal identity. It is here that we nurture self-awareness, not through the external world's definitions, but through the intimate realm of feeling and emotional truth. This house, associated with Cancer and the Moon, embodies the essence of cardinal water—initiatory, fluid, and deeply personal. While the 1st house signifies the primal spark of existence, the 2nd house represents the physical vessel, and the 3rd house reflects the intellect, the mental body that shapes our interactions with the world. The 4th house is where we fully inhabit the emotional body. In this space, we shift from mere observation and analysis to direct emotional experience, allowing feelings to inform our consciousness in a way that transcends intellect.

Emotions emerge instantaneously, preceding thought, bypassing rationalization, and communicating in a language older than words. They pulse through us with undeniable intensity—poignant, passionate, sometimes harrowing, and other times euphoric, but always visceral. Within these flowing currents, we absorb the world around us, allowing our emotional responses to shape our perception of reality. The 4th house is where we internalize these impressions, forming the subconscious framework from which we navigate life. The emotional scaffolding of this house, particularly shaped by early experiences, serves as the foundation upon which we build our sense of self. It is here that we find echoes of the past resounding into the present, shaping our instincts, reactions, and the emotional filters through which we interpret existence.

The 4th house teaches us the importance of emotional self-reliance. It is where we learn to honor our inner world and hold space for our vulnerabilities without being overwhelmed by them. Authenticity emerges in this house, urging us to embrace the full spectrum of our emotions—our joys and sorrows, our triumphs and wounds. This house illustrates the delicate balance between nurturing and self-protection, allowing us to feel without losing ourselves in the depths of our emotions. In this space, the ego, often criticized in spiritual discussions, reveals its essential purpose. It is not merely an obstacle to be eliminated but a necessary framework that enables us to integrate our emotional experiences into an evolving identity.

The ego, shaped by the currents of the 4th house, provides coherence to our inner world, allowing us to navigate our consciousness with clarity and intention.

The formative influences of the 4th house arise from our early home environment, the emotional imprint of our mother or primary caregiver, and the ancestral and karmic themes we carry across lifetimes. Childhood circumstances are never random; they result from previous emotional experiences, a continuation of unresolved soul memories manifesting in the present. Although we may not consciously recall past lives, their emotional residue lingers, shaping our unconscious patterns. Within this house, we encounter the inherited legacies of family, culture, and lineage, which form the undercurrents of our emotional landscape. Our approaches to seeking comfort, establishing security, forming attachments, and responding to perceived threats—all of these are encoded within the 4th house, woven into the fabric of our subconscious. As we grow, recognizing these patterns provides us the opportunity for healing, enabling us to transmute old wounds and liberate ourselves from cyclical emotional repetitions.

The Imum Coeli, meaning "bottom of the sky," signifies the deepest point of the natal chart, anchoring the soul's need for security and belonging. However, the comfort of the familiar, while providing refuge, can also bind us to outdated emotional constructs. This house is where the work of shadow integration begins, as the subconscious material stored here becomes the very substance we later confront in Scorpio and the 8th house. By the time we reach Pisces and the 12th house, we encounter the dissolution of these deeply rooted patterns, completing a cycle of emotional evolution that starts with recognizing ourselves in the mirror of our feelings.

Cancer, the archetype of the 4th house, forms a natural square with Aries and Libra, highlighting the tension between emotional security and external dynamics. Aries, embodying pure instinct, can challenge the stability of the 4th house with impulsive actions, compelling us to reconcile the need for emotional grounding with the desire for independence. Libra, seeking balance through relationships, presents another challenge—if we look outside ourselves for emotional fulfillment, we risk losing our inner foundation. The opposition to Capricorn emphasizes the struggle between inner and outer security, between the emotional self and the structures we establish to support us. When external frameworks falter, we must turn inward, confronting the raw emotional realities we may have long overlooked.

Ultimately, the 4th house represents the journey of returning home, not to a physical location, but to the sanctuary within ourselves. The path of emotional self-awareness guides us to recognize that true security is not found in the external world but in our ability to be present with ourselves, honor our emotions without becoming enslaved by them, and embrace the full depth of our inner experience. The more we consciously engage with the 4th house, the more we reclaim our personal power, dissolving the unconscious emotional imprints that bind us to the past and stepping into a fuller, more authentic expression of who we truly are.

James Dean

James Dean, despite appearing in only three films, became an enduring cultural icon. His breakthrough role in *Rebel Without a Cause* captured the angst and alienation of postwar youth, making him the face of rebellion for a generation. With his raw emotional intensity, Dean's performances distinguished him from his peers and helped solidify his status as one of Hollywood's most mythic figures.

His film debut came with *East of Eden*, where he played Caleb Trask, a modern Cain figure. His emotional depth earned immediate acclaim. In *Giant*, his final film, he portrayed Jett Rink, a poor ranch hand who turned into a bitter oil tycoon—a performance that reflected Dean's own inner turmoil. Although *East of Eden* was the only film released during his lifetime, the posthumous releases of *Rebel Without a Cause* and *Giant* elevated his legendary status.

Dean's life ended tragically on September 30, 1955, when his Porsche collided with another vehicle. He was only 24. The crash immortalized him as a symbol of lost potential and youthful defiance.

Born into a farming family, Dean experienced personal loss at a young age—his mother passed away from cancer when he was nine. His father, unable to care for him, sent Dean to live with relatives in Indiana. This early abandonment left emotional scars that persisted throughout his life.

Offscreen, Dean embodied the same rebellious charisma he projected onscreen. Known for his disheveled appearance and unpredictable behavior, he often defied Hollywood conventions—showing up

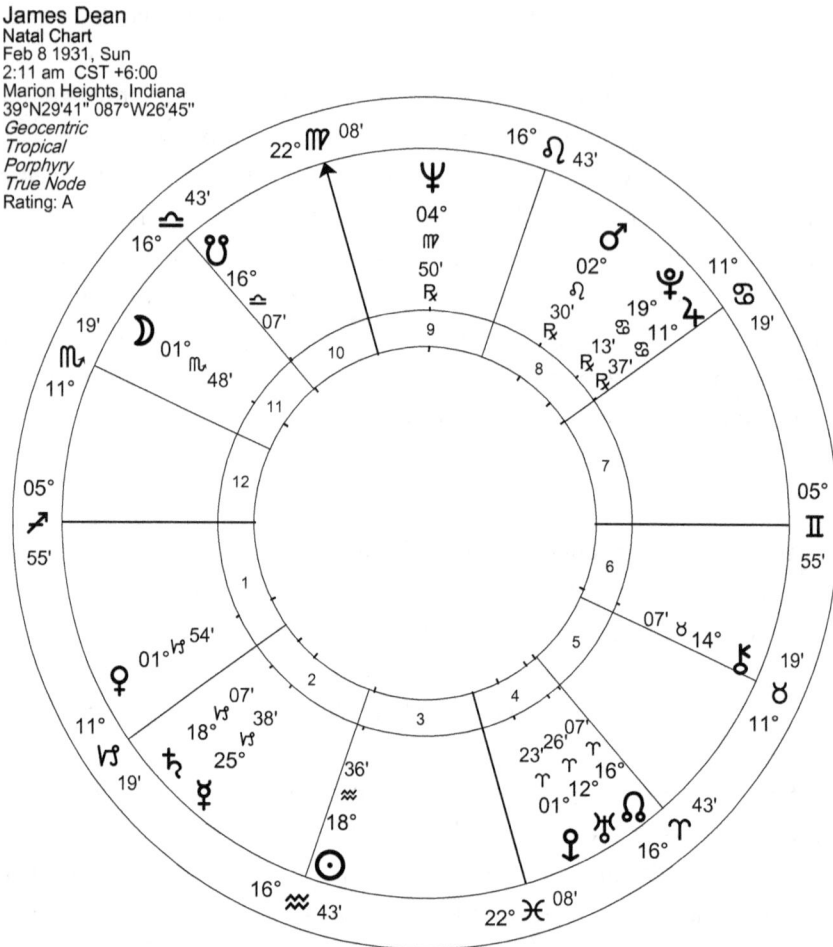

barefoot at formal events and wearing safety-pinned pants to rehearsals. Friends described him as moody and restless, prone to late-night calls or unannounced visits.

He admired Marlon Brando and tried to forge a friendship, but Brando dismissed him. "I referred him to a psychoanalyst, and he attended. At least his work improved," Brando quipped, revealing his indifference.

Dean was captivated by outlaws and misfits, especially Billy the Kid, whom he yearned to portray. His attraction to emotionally complex characters indicated a future rich with roles that challenged traditional norms.

Before achieving film stardom, Dean honed his craft on live television, where his improvisational method acting sometimes clashed with his co-stars. In one instance, he deviated from the script during a scene with Ronald Reagan, leaving the future president confused. One frustrated actor once demanded, "Just make him say the lines as they're written."

Though his career was brief, James Dean left a lasting legacy. He remains a symbol of artistic passion, emotional authenticity, and youthful defiance—forever frozen in time, a rebel who never grew old.[46] With Eris direct at 1° Aries in the 4th house, James Dean's soul entered this life to actively challenge, disrupt, and overthrow the ancestral and familial conditioning that sought to define him. This was not a private struggle buried in the psyche but an outwardly lived defiance. Dean embodied Eris as a raw and unfiltered force of truth, refusing to conform to the emotional expectations of family or society. His rebellion became cultural rather than merely personal: through his art, his presence, and his legend, he exposed the fault lines of mid-20th-century American values. Eris here manifests as a disruptive seed planted in the collective imagination, insisting that what has been denied or suppressed within the family soul—and by extension, the national soul—must be brought into the light.

The North Node at 16° Aries in the 4th house, conjunct Uranus, amplifies the evolutionary drive toward radical self-definition through the reclamation of inner roots and emotional authenticity. This placement demands individuation not just in outer expression but in the very foundations of life: family, belonging, and soul nourishment. Dean's karmic task was to shock the system by breaking free from inherited conditioning, creating a home within himself rather than seeking it externally. Uranus' conjunction to the North Node also squares Pluto in Cancer and the South Node in Libra, marking Uranus as a skipped step. Individuation through disruption was therefore not simply a gift but an unresolved evolutionary mandate: he had to embrace sudden breaks, shocks, and revolutionary impulses in order to progress.

In contrast, the South Node at 16° Libra in the 10th house reflects past-life patterns of performing for the public, shaping identity through external approval, and projecting relationally pleasing personas on the collective stage. The karmic residue here indicates an over-identification with societal expectations and polished appearances, often at the expense of inner authenticity and emotional security. The evolutionary shift

---

46 Paraphrased from https://www.biography.com/actors/james-dean-facts

demanded a move from outer conformity and public image into raw selfhood rooted in personal truth and emotional depth.

A T-square from multiple planets stresses this nodal axis. Most significantly, Pluto at 19° Cancer retrograde in the 8th house squares both nodes, marking it as the evolutionary key that must be resolved before integration can occur. Pluto in Cancer suggests deep unresolved grief, maternal loss (his mother died when he was nine), and complex entanglements around emotional enmeshment, abandonment, or betrayal. The 8th house placement intensifies this into a soul-level crisis of survival and intimacy. Until Dean confronted and transmuted the emotional trauma held here, he could not fully embody the courageous Aries path of individuation.

Jupiter at 11° Cancer retrograde, also in the 8th house and square the nodes, suggests a philosophical or religious worldview shaped by emotional loss and withdrawal. It indicates a past orientation toward emotional idealism, possibly in maternal or nurturing roles, that now requires inner excavation and transformation. Jupiter opposite Saturn at 18° Capricorn in the 2nd house emphasizes the tension between emotional faith and material reality, safety and exposure, nurture and control.

Mercury at 25° Capricorn in the 2nd house loosely conjoins Saturn, and both square the nodes—highlighting the karmic weight of self-worth, language, survival, and internalized authority. Mercury also opposes Mars and Pluto, while squaring the Moon at 1° Scorpio in the 11th house. This intense Mercury configuration reflects a deeply embedded psychic fragmentation: a mind shaped by control, fear of loss, and buried rage, all struggling to find clear, integrated expression. His speech, writing, and presence were unmistakably serious, burdened, and compelling—yet intertwined with inner conflict and volatility.

His 8th house Mars, ruling Eris in Aries, emphasizes the evolutionary need to reclaim self-directed power through confronting buried emotional content and suppressed desires. Its retrograde motion indicates an internalized rage or creative force turned inward, often erupting under pressure. The Moon square both Mars and Mercury reflects emotional turbulence, volatile attachments, and challenges in reconciling instinct and communication. This friction likely manifests in Dean's passionate yet troubled relationships and haunted screen presence.

The Scorpio Moon in the 11th house, suggests profound emotional depth and psychic sensitivity projected into collective ideals and social networks. This placement shows Dean's emotional life channeled into friendships, groups, and—symbolically—his audience. The Scorpio signature reflects a fierce protectiveness and brooding intensity, while the fixed sign tension of the T-square with Mars and Mercury resists exposure. His intimacy with others often played out through surrogate bonds with groups or causes, carrying both magnetism and alienation.

The Sun at 18° Aquarius in the 3rd house adds a clear signature of individuation through mental, verbal, and social disruption. Dean's revolutionary voice—whether as an actor, icon, or outsider—shone through his need to break the mold and speak a truth that had no script. Mercury's opposition to Pluto and Mars, along with its square to the Moon, shows how his intellect was a crucible for this eruption of soul.

Dean rebelled—not from arrogance, but from an evolutionary mandate to shatter the silence of inherited emotional suppression. His 4th house Eris in Aries dared to confront the ghosts of the past, while the Pluto-nodal axis square exposed raw grief and the compulsions of emotional enmeshment. Uranus-North Node in Aries ensured that his path could only unfold through shocking disruption and an uncompromising authenticity. Through his acting, body, and voice, he gave form to the collision between inner trauma and public persona. Yet the skipped steps—the need to process, transmute, and integrate Uranian disruption and Plutonian grief—remained unfinished. Dean became a myth not because he perfected the self, but because he made the fracture visible. That is the work of Eris.

Elvis Presley

Elvis Presley, known as the King of Rock and Roll, rose to fame in the 1950s as a cultural and musical revolutionary. By blending rock, country, gospel, and rhythm and blues, he captivated audiences with a style and energy that defined a generation. More than just a performer, he became an enduring icon whose influence continues to shape music and popular culture. Decades after his death, he remains one of the best-selling solo artists of all time.

Born on January 8, 1935, in Tupelo, Mississippi, Elvis was raised in poverty by his devoted parents, Vernon and Gladys Presley. His twin brother, Jesse, was stillborn, leaving Elvis as an only child. Despite their limited means, Gladys nurtured his love of music, giving him his first

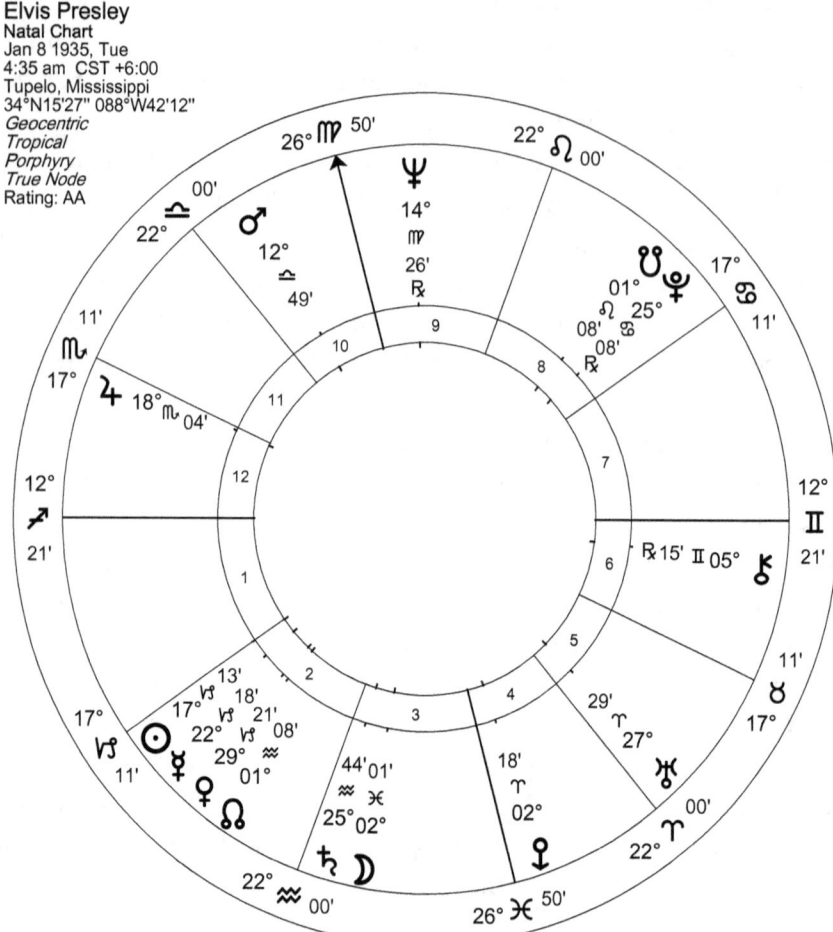

guitar at age ten. The gospel music he heard in church, along with early exposure to country and blues, laid the foundation for his unique sound.

In his teens, the family moved to Memphis, where Elvis absorbed various musical influences, particularly from black artists on Beale Street. Unlike many white musicians of his era, he openly embraced African American music—melding genres in a way that challenged the racial and cultural boundaries of the time.

In 1953, Elvis recorded a song at Sun Records as a gift for his mother, which caught the attention of producer Sam Phillips, who soon signed him. By 1956, after signing with RCA Victor, Elvis had his breakout hit with *Heartbreak Hotel*. His televised appearances—particularly on *The Ed Sullivan Show*—sparked both awe and controversy, as his provocative dance moves were viewed as scandalous by conservative critics but thrilling to fans.

His early success continued with hits like *Love Me Tender* and a series of blockbuster songs and films. While some criticized him for cultural appropriation, others viewed him as a bridge between black and white musical traditions—bringing rhythm and blues into the mainstream and breaking racial barriers in popular music.

Elvis's charisma, emotive voice, and stage presence revolutionized performances. Although his later years were marked by health issues and personal struggles, his impact remained immense. Following his death in 1977, his legend only continued to grow. From humble beginnings to global superstardom, Elvis's legacy endures as a symbol of artistic innovation and cultural transformation.[47]

Elvis Presley's life and career were profoundly influenced by the interplay between his 12th house Jupiter and 4th house Eris, linked through a sesquiquadrate—an aspect that is both challenging and catalytic. Jupiter in Scorpio—deep, magnetic, and emotionally intense—in the 12th house, amplified his aura with an almost mythic mystique. The 12th house represents dreams, dissolution, the collective unconscious, and hidden realms; in Scorpio, Jupiter here endowed Elvis with a deep emotional undercurrent and spiritual depth that magnetized mass attention while concealing vast inner complexity. This was not charisma in the conventional sense—it was archetypal, drawing from something beyond the personal self. His fame had a fated, even sacrificial quality, as though he were channeling something from the deep well of collective longing.

The sesquiquadrate from his 4th house Eris created catalytic friction between his private emotional roots and his vast, often isolating spiritual visibility. In the 4th house Eris stirred up ancestral memory, family trauma, and emotional unrest, while Jupiter in the 12th acted as a broad amplifier of unconscious material—his own and the collective's. Together, they formed a circuit of soul pressure, compelling him to articulate the inexpressible, to embody the chaos and longing of a culture in transition. His performances, often deemed scandalous, were not merely personal expressions—they were eruptions from the mythic underworld of the American psyche. In

---

[47] Paraphrased from https://study.com/academy/lesson/elvis-presley-biography-songs-movies-death.html

this configuration, Jupiter became not just the harbinger of expansion but the priest of a sacred, albeit dangerous, mystery—one that Eris, from the depths of the 4th house, persistently provoked.

This Jupiter-Eris tension stirred the cauldron of his inner world, with Eris in the 4th house agitating the very roots of his being—ancestry, emotional memory, and the private self. The 4th house speaks to the foundation of identity, and Eris here signaled a disruptive force within the personal realm, driving him to challenge societal norms and reinvent cultural archetypes. The sesquiquadrate to Jupiter electrified his stage presence and emboldened him to express his sexuality and passion in ways that were revolutionary for the time.

His performances were not merely acts of rebellion—they were eruptions from the depths of his soul. Scorpio's emotional intensity and the 12th house undercurrents in his chart endowed him with an aura of mystique and spiritual gravity. In this context, Eris in the 4th house did not just reflect personal unrest—it stirred the cultural landscape itself, rendering Elvis's very existence a revolutionary act.

Further amplifying this radical expression, his nodes were direct—an unusual condition that intensified the force of his evolutionary path. With his North Node in the 2nd house in Aquarius, he could forge an independent and entirely unique mode of self-expression, free from conventional expectations. This was intrinsically linked to his South Node in the 8th house in Leo, closely conjunct a retrograde Pluto, compelling him to navigate deep psychological and emotional waters. His past-life signatures, indicated by the South Node and Pluto, suggest a profound familiarity with power, performance, and the captivating force of personal magnetism. The retrograde motion of Pluto made this process deeply introspective, urging him to uncover the layers of his soul's evolutionary journey. Through his art, he participated in this transformational process, exposing raw emotion in a way that resonated universally.

The influence of the 4th house resonated throughout his chart, shaping both his inner world and public persona. His upbringing, closely connected to the energy of Eris here, immersed him in an environment where emotional intensity and turbulence coexisted with a nearly sacred familial bond. This early conditioning laid the foundation for the unshakable confidence and intuitive, emotional connection he later expressed in his music. The 4th house, traditionally linked to roots, home, and personal security, became a stage of its own—one where the disruptive force of Eris ensured that his personal history would not be separate from his public identity but rather a defining aspect of it. His profound connection to his mother, Gladys, shaped the emotional wellspring from which he drew his evocative performances, each note resonating with deep devotion and unresolved sorrow.

This emotional depth was further reflected in his 3rd house Moon, which governed his Pluto in Cancer and formed an exact semi sextile to Eris. This subtle yet powerful relationship heightened his ability to channel emotions into his performances with almost unconscious ease. The 3rd house Moon endowed him with an instinctive understanding of communication, enabling him to connect with audiences on an intimate, visceral level. The semisextile to Eris in the 4th activated this emotional expressiveness, ensuring that his personal and artistic revolutions were inseparable. His voice became an instrument of emotional alchemy, transforming pain and passion into something tangible that the world could feel.

Thus, the activation of his 4th house Eris not only shaped his personal narrative but also became a disruptive force in the collective consciousness. This energy allowed his music to resonate as both deeply personal and universally revolutionary, altering the trajectory of popular culture.

Shirley Temple Black

Shirley Temple was one of history's most iconic child stars, bringing joy and hope during the Great Depression. Born on April 23, 1928, in Santa Monica, California, she was the youngest of three children. Her mother nurtured her talents early by enrolling her in dance classes at three years old—a decision that launched her film career.

Aged three, Temple signed with Educational Pictures and starred in the *Baby Burlesques* short films, which, despite later controversy, showcased her charm and prepared her for stardom. Her big break came when Fox Film Corporation signed her, propelling her into mainstream Hollywood.

By age six, Temple starred in her first feature film, and her 1934 role in *Little Miss Marker* made her a sensation. Her curly hair, dimples, and spirited performances brought comfort to a struggling nation. That same year, she won a special Juvenile Academy Award and performed the

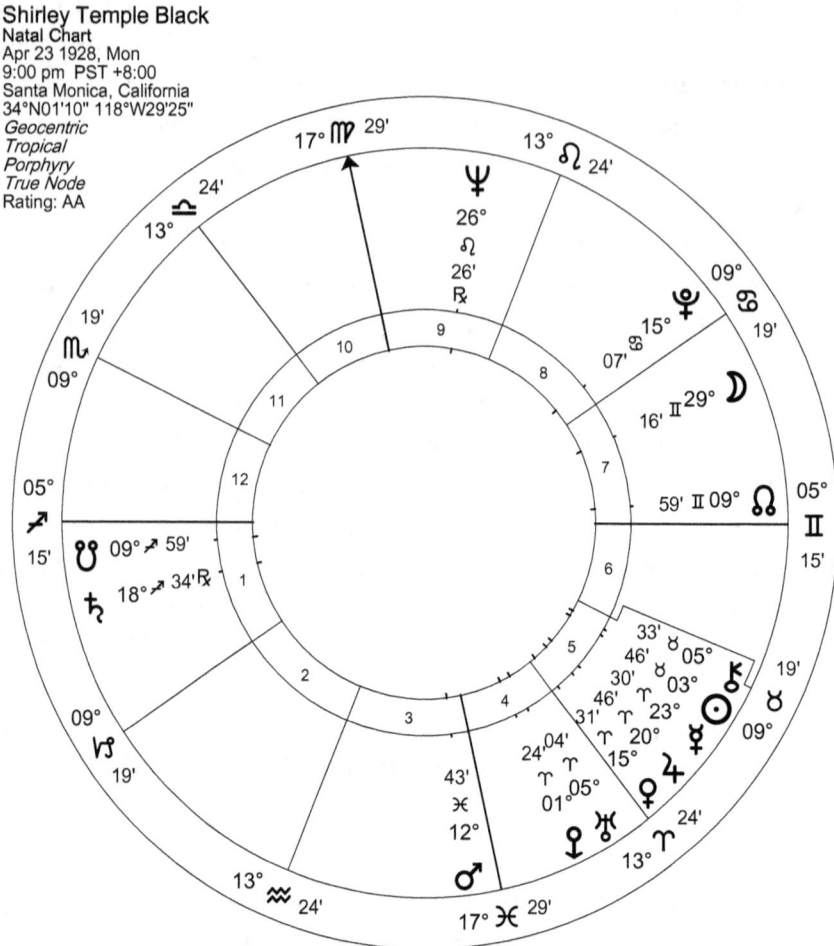

iconic *On the Good Ship Lollipop* in *Bright Eyes*, solidifying her image as America's sweetheart.

Temple became a cultural symbol, with President Franklin D. Roosevelt calling her "Little Miss Miracle." She led the box office for four consecutive years and had starred in 43 films by 1940. However, as she matured, the public struggled to accept her adult image, and her career declined. She retired from acting at just 22.

She then turned to public service, running for Congress in 1967 and later becoming a U.S. delegate to the United Nations in 1969. Her diplomatic career thrived: she served as Ambassador to Ghana (1974–1976), Chief of Protocol (1976–1977), and Ambassador to Czechoslovakia in 1989, earning recognition as the first honorary U.S. Foreign Service officer.

Temple received a Screen Actors Guild Lifetime Achievement Award and a Kennedy Center Honor for her significant contributions to both entertainment and diplomacy. She passed away on February 10, 2014, at the age of 85. Her family remembered her as a loving mother, grandmother, and wife. Shirley Temple's life stands as a testament to resilience, reinvention, and enduring optimism.[48] Eris conjunct Uranus in Shirley Temple Black's 4th house reveals a deep disruption and reinvention of traditional notions of home, family, and personal roots. The 4th house signifies the inner foundation, ancestral inheritance, and emotional security; however, Eris here signifies a soul that could not simply conform to familial or societal expectations—there was a need to challenge established norms and create a unique path. With Uranus, this impulse was electric, unpredictable, and revolutionary, mirroring her early rise to fame as an extraordinary child star who reshaped the entertainment industry's view of children on screen.

Eris square to her 7th house Moon in Gemini indicates a tension between personal emotional needs and the expectations placed upon her by others—especially in partnerships and public relationships. The Moon in Gemini, already a highly expressive, adaptable, and communicative placement, was further energized by the unpredictable force of Eris-Uranus, enhancing her ability to capture the hearts of audiences while also making her acutely aware of the dynamics of performance and expectations in relationships.

Her 5th house Taurus Sun, widely conjunct Mercury in Aries, provided the steady grounding necessary for maintaining her sense of self while being continuously shaped by public attention. The 5th house relates to personal creativity, performance, and joy; with the Sun positioned here, she radiated natural talent, charm, and confidence. Mercury in Aries, ruling her 10th house, indicates an assertive and pioneering approach to her career—she was not merely a passive participant in her rise to fame but an active force of expression, capable of influencing cultural ideals surrounding childhood, femininity, and success.

Her Sagittarius South Node in the 1st house, conjunct Saturn, indicates past-life wisdom and a karmic focus on self-definition and independence. With Saturn positioned here, there is a serious, disciplined quality that implies she entered this life carrying the imprint of leadership and an

---

48 Paraphrased from https://www.biography.com/actors/shirley-temple

ability to manage immense responsibility from a young age. The trine to Eris-Uranus in the 4th suggests a natural talent for navigating disruptive personal circumstances with resilience, preparing her for the next chapter of her life, where she transitioned from Hollywood stardom to diplomatic and political roles, ultimately becoming a leader on the world stage.

Neptune retrograde in Leo in the 9th house adds a mystical and visionary quality to her path. The 9th house is expansive, representing philosophy, worldview, and a search for deeper meaning. In Leo, this placement amplifies the theme of self-expression through performance, while its retrograde motion indicates that much of her idealism and spiritual evolution was driven from within. Neptune trining her Aries stellium of Venus, Jupiter and Mercury in the 5th, adds another dimension to her allure, creativity, and ability to inspire. This connection suggests that she was not only a performer but also a mythic figure in the collective imagination, embodying an idealized form of joy and hope during the Great Depression.

Her Taurus Sun-Chiron conjunction in the 5th highlights the deeper layers of her narrative. The 5th house represents not only joy and performance but also the courage to take risks in order to express one's soul essence. Chiron in this position signifies a journey of wounding and healing related to identity and creative expression. Although she was cherished as a child star, there was also an inherent sacrifice—her childhood was shaped by the pressures of the entertainment industry, compelling her to navigate the complexities of being seen primarily as a public figure. As she matured, she transformed this wound into wisdom, using her experiences to guide others and assume a broader, more impactful role on the world stage.

Ultimately, Eris played a catalytic role in shaping her journey, particularly in disrupting and refining expectations surrounding childhood, performance, and feminine power. Whether in film or diplomacy, she consistently shattered conventions, embodying the revolutionary spirit of Eris-Uranus while staying grounded in the enduring strength of her Taurus Sun.

Alexandria Ocasio-Cortez

Alexandria Ocasio-Cortez (AOC) is a pioneering political figure celebrated for her progressive ideals, grassroots activism, and dynamic presence in both Congress and on social media. As the youngest woman and Latina ever elected to the US Congress, she has transformed the perception of modern political leadership with a bold emphasis on economic and social justice.

Born in the Bronx's Parkchester neighborhood, she grew up in a working-class Puerto Rican family. Her parents' dedication—her father was a small business owner and her mother a domestic worker—shaped her deep understanding of working-class struggles.

AOC excelled early in academia, placing second in microbiology at the 2007 Intel Science and Engineering Fair. An asteroid was even named in her honor. She graduated cum laude from Boston University with a degree in Economics and International Relations. As a college intern in Senator Ted Kennedy's office, she assisted Spanish-speaking constituents with immigration issues, shaping her views on policy and advocacy.

After graduating, she returned to the Bronx, where she worked as an educator and community organizer while also supporting herself as a waitress and bartender. Her involvement in Bernie Sanders' 2016 campaign and her visit to the Standing Rock protests further strengthened her commitment to systemic change and public service.

In 2018, she shocked the political establishment by defeating a long-time incumbent in New York's 14th district through a grassroots campaign driven by volunteers. Her win marked a significant moment for progressive politics and made her the first woman of color to represent the district.

In Congress, she swiftly emerged as a leading advocate for policies such as Medicare for All, a living wage, and progressive taxation. She co-sponsored the Green New Deal, an ambitious plan to tackle climate change and economic inequality, which solidified her role as a key proponent for climate justice.

AOC is also a founding member of The Squad, alongside Rashida Tlaib, Ilhan Omar, and Ayanna Pressley, later joined by Jamaal Bowman and Cori Bush. Together, they have pushed for legislative reform and highlighted the need for diverse representation and grassroots leadership in government.

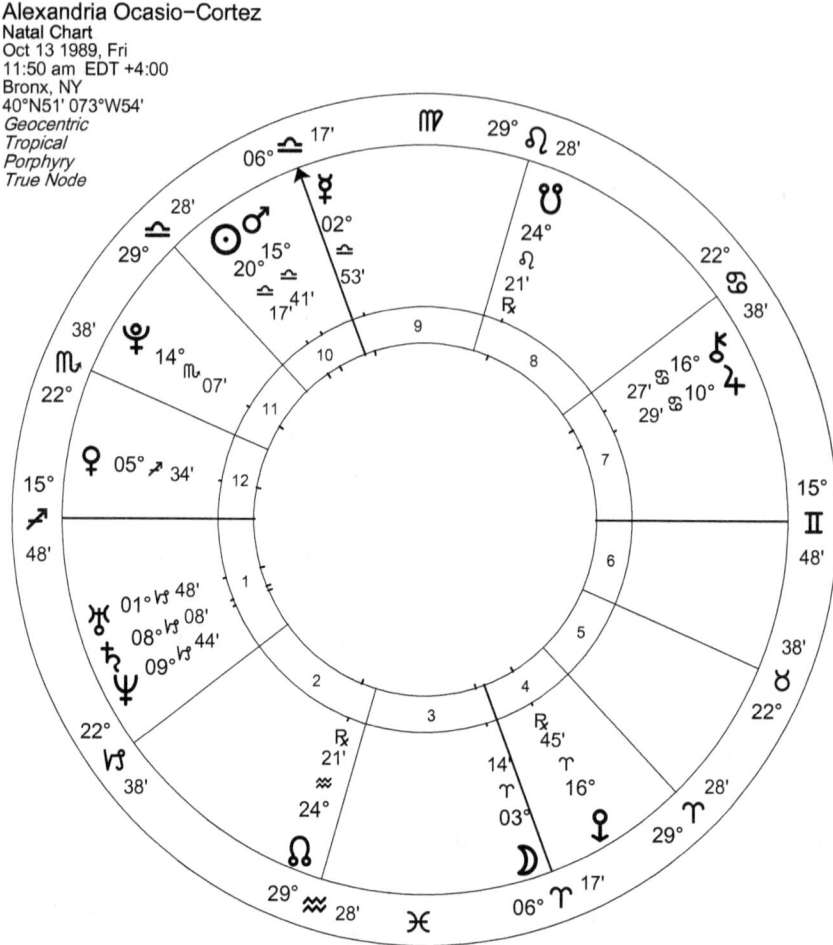

Beyond policy, AOC has transformed political communication by utilizing social media to engage the public and enhance the transparency of politics. Her authenticity and accessibility have inspired a new generation to get politically involved.

In 2022, Olympic soccer star Megan Rapinoe said Ocasio-Cortez "single-handedly transformed our idea of what a politician can be." Through her advocacy, legislative efforts, and public engagement, AOC continues to shape the future of American politics and challenge the status quo.[49]

---

[49] Paraphrased from https://www.womenshistory.org/education-resources/biographies/alexandria-ocasio-cortez

Ocasio-Cortez's 4th house Eris retrograde is the apex of a powerful cardinal grand cross, opposing her 10th house Sun-Mars conjunction in Libra while squaring her 1st house Saturn-Neptune conjunction in Capricorn and her 7th house Jupiter-Chiron conjunction in Cancer. This intense configuration amplifies the tension between personal roots, public destiny, individual authority, and relational responsibility, forging a life path defined by action, struggle, and the will to challenge entrenched structures. The 4th house, which represents ancestry, home, and the emotional foundation of the self, serves as the crucible for transformation, internalizing the tension of the Grand Cross before externalizing it through decisive, pioneering efforts. The cardinal nature of these placements emphasizes relentless movement, as if the very ground beneath her being fuels the necessity to initiate change.

The 1st house Saturn-Uranus-Neptune stellium in Capricorn grounds her vision in discipline and determination, creating a rare synthesis of structure and radical reform. This blend enables her to maintain the momentum of her efforts in both pragmatic and revolutionary ways. Her 4th house Eris, the disruptor within her core self, carries the resonance of ancestral wounds and historical injustices, urging her to carve out a space where the marginalized find representation and empowerment.

The 10th house Sun-Mars conjunction in Libra, which rules her Eris, underscores her destiny as a warrior for justice, with her personal drive inseparable from a mission to restore balance in society. The opposition between Eris and this solar force creates unrelenting tension between personal identity and collective responsibility, a dynamic that fuels her rise as a powerful advocate for reform.

The influence of the 7th house Jupiter-Chiron conjunction in Cancer deepens her commitment to those she serves, defining her sense of family as an inclusive, extended community united by shared struggles. This aspect highlights the healing power of relationships, where emotional intelligence and a profound understanding of collective wounds shape her leadership. Her 8th house South Node in Leo, trining Eris, connects her current mission with a rich reservoir of ancestral memory and karmic inheritance. The past is not merely a reference point but an active force propelling her forward, as though she is tapping into the strength of those who came before her to kindle the fire of her work.

Pluto supports the core intensity of her chart in Scorpio in the 11th house, where personal power transforms into a relentless force for societal change. Pluto, supported in its own sign, gives her the ability to handle power struggles, withstand ongoing opposition, and turn crises into collective progress. Eris in Aries introduces the archetype of disruption and a demand for truth, strengthening her role as a challenger of established hierarchies. Together, Pluto offers depth and resilience, while Eris injects a raw insistence on exposing discord as a catalyst for change. Within her cardinal grand cross, this synergy charts a life journey driven by crisis and the ability to turn tension into collective strength. The 4th house foundation of the grand cross ensures her public influence is rooted in more than policy—it's also about reclaiming dignity and agency for those long denied a voice.

5th House ~ Self Actualization

In the 5th house, the ego radiates outward as personality, transforming the inner self-image into the external persona consciously presented to the world. This personality is not a singular, static construct but rather an evolving integration of emotional, intellectual, and physical dimensions, embodying the totality of self-perception. Here, the initial spark of instinctual self-expression, ignited in the 1st house and Aries, expands into a more self-aware and purposeful manifestation of identity. The individual, now fully engaged in the ongoing journey of personal evolution, participates in the active process of self-actualization, refining and broadening the scope of their creative and expressive potential.

The 5th house signifies the fundamental drive to imbue life with meaning, shaping experiences that not only affirm identity but also serve as pathways for exploration, self-discovery, and transformation. This area of the natal chart is where the raw energy of self-expression gains structure and purpose, allowing the individual to consciously engage in the creative process of crafting their destiny. The sign positioned on the 5th house cusp, the condition and placement of its ruling planet, and any planets residing within its confines illustrate the intricate and personalized approach to creativity, self-expression, and personal fulfillment.

As an archetypal seat of creative energy, the 5th house is closely tied to artistic expression, the joyful process of creation, and the generative power of life itself. It naturally aligns with matters concerning children, both literal and metaphorical, as well as how individuals express themselves in the world through their works, passions, and romantic connections. The square relationship between the 5th house and the 2nd and 8th houses underscores its deep ties to sexuality, vitality, and the essential drive toward procreation and self-perpetuation. This tension reveals the intricate dance between self-worth, desire, and transformation, showcasing the complex dynamics through which individuals channel their creative life force.

With Leo as its archetypal expression, the 5th house externalizes the emotional depth and security nurtured in Cancer and the 4th house, transforming inward care into outward confidence and vibrant self-expression. Leo represents a crucial stage in the journey toward self-realization, emphasizing the conscious assertion of identity in a way that seeks recognition, impact, and legacy. Here, personal creativity serves as a means of showcasing one's individuality, a process that requires both courage and authenticity. When functioning at its highest expression, this house empowers the manifestation of the self in ways that are not only personally fulfilling but also inspiring to others.

The interplay between the 5th house and the 1st and 9th houses through the trine aspect enhances qualities of spontaneous action and expansive vision. The unfiltered impulse of Aries in the 1st house fuels the drive to assert oneself without inhibition, while Jupiter's wisdom-seeking nature and the 9th house infuse this expression with a sense of grand purpose and adventure. This potent combination often results in boundless enthusiasm for life, a hunger for experiences that affirm one's creative potential, and an unshakable belief in one's own importance. However, without sufficient grounding such an alignment can tip into excess, causing self-expression to shift into unchecked ego inflation. The allure of admiration and validation can lead to overindulgence in personal grandeur, sometimes at the expense of deeper authenticity. It is in these moments that the evolutionary journey naturally propels the individual toward a necessary phase of refinement, often initiated through crisis, humility, and the critical self-examination inherent in Virgo.

The experiences formed in the 5th house create a foundation that helps the individual develop their understanding of themselves as a creative force. It serves as a space for learning through direct experience, where both triumph and failure serve as catalysts for deeper self-awareness. Those who effectively integrate the lessons of this house cultivate a sense of personal radiance that is both magnetic and meaningful. Their expressions of self become not merely displays of ego but authentic embodiments of their inner truth.

The dynamic interplay of forces within the 5th house reveals an extraordinary range of self-expression. It manifests in individuals who, through their unique evolutionary paths, harness these energies to achieve profound levels of creativity and personal fulfillment. Whether through artistic brilliance, leadership, performance, or the deeply personal act of shaping one's life as a creative endeavor, the journey of the 5th house illuminates the self, radiates outward, and ultimately leads to the joy of being fully, unapologetically alive.

Grace Kelly

Grace Kelly was born into privilege as the daughter of a self-made millionaire and Olympic gold medalist. Her mother, Margaret Majer, was the first female athletic coach at the University of Pennsylvania. Despite her family's skepticism toward acting, Kelly pursued her passion by moving to New York City after high school to study at the American Academy of Dramatic Arts. To support herself, she modeled for advertisements and appeared on magazine covers.

After graduating, Kelly struggled to gain traction on Broadway. One of her teachers doubted her stage potential, though he acknowledged her striking beauty. Her breakthrough came in Hollywood when Gary Cooper helped cast her in *High Noon* (1952), launching her film career.

Her role in *Mogambo* (1953) opposite Clark Gable earned her a Golden Globe and an Oscar nomination, which led to a contract with MGM that permitted her to continue stage work every other year. She became a favorite actress of Alfred Hitchcock, starring in *Dial M for Murder*, *Rear Window*, and *To Catch a Thief*, embodying the cool, elegant femme fatale.

In 1954, she won the Academy Award for Best Actress for *The Country Girl*, proving her depth beyond glamorous roles. At the height of her success, Kelly met Prince Rainier III of Monaco during the 1955 Cannes Film Festival. They married the following year in a lavish ceremony, and

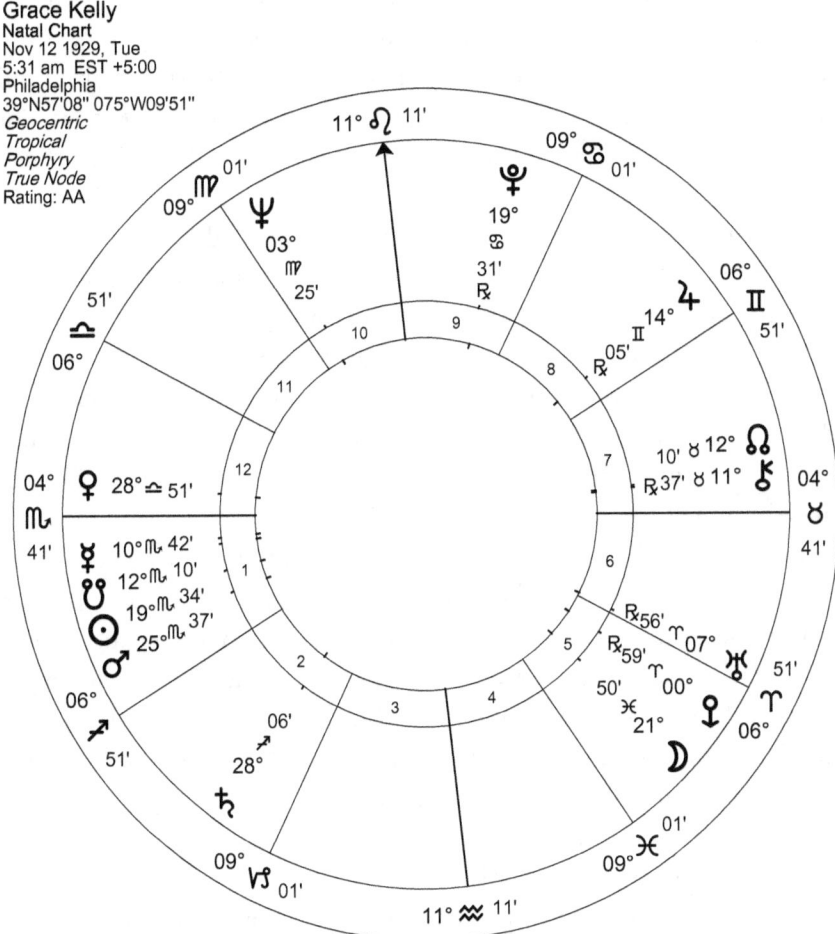

she retired from acting to become Princess of Monaco. The couple had three children, and she became involved in philanthropy and cultural affairs.

Though she contemplated returning to acting—most notably in Hitchcock's *Marnie*—she ultimately declined. In 1976, she joined the board of Twentieth Century Fox.

On September 13, 1982, Grace suffered a stroke while driving, which led to a tragic car accident near the Côte d'Azur. She passed away the following day, while her daughter Stéphanie survived. Grace Kelly is remembered as both a Hollywood icon and a beloved royal.[50] With Eris retrograde in Aries

---

50 Paraphrased from: https://www.britannica.com/biography/Grace-Kelly

in the 5th house, Grace Kelly bore the karmic imprint of a woman born into roles shaped by others, yet destined to break the mold from within. The 5th house, traditionally associated with performance, creativity, romance, and the sovereign self, turns into a battlefield when Eris occupies it in warrior Aries. The retrograde motion signifies an internal rebellion: a life defined by the pressure to embody perfection clashing with a deeper, evolutionary need to rupture the script and reveal a raw, unfiltered identity.

This Eris placement evokes the paradox of someone in the global spotlight, crowned by both Hollywood and royalty, yet inwardly driven to reclaim authorship over her narrative. Eris conjunct her Moon in Pisces, also in the 5th house, emphasizes emotional sensitivity, receptivity, and idealization. Her Scorpio stellium in the 1st house—Mercury, South Node, Sun, and Mars—indicates a soul shaped by intensity. The 1st house amplifies personal magnetism and survival instinct, while Scorpio grants her the composure, secrecy, and inner depth that make her appear untouchable. This stellium suggests karmic residues around identity, power, and performance; lives where survival demanded total control of one's image. Her evolutionary work in this life involved moving from manipulation or defensiveness (Scorpio South Node) toward peace, embodiment, and relational simplicity through her Taurus North Node in the 7th house, conjunct Chiron. That conjunction reveals the wound: a deep yearning for unconditional love and trust in partnership, set against the fear of losing herself in another's expectations.

Uranus in Aries in the 6th house, separating from Eris, injects a spark of disruptive originality into her daily life and work. It fosters Eris' desire for individuation, challenging conventional expectations of service and routine. Together, Uranus and Eris suggest someone who was not meant to be a passive participant in her fate but to confront it—subtly, behind the veil of elegance.

Her Saturn in Sagittarius in the 2nd house reflects themes of duty, restraint, and moral philosophy that shape her relationship with material stability and personal values. It signifies someone whose sense of self-worth may have been defined by societal expectations or inherited beliefs—perhaps limiting, perhaps dignified, but always heavy. It also indicates someone learning to discover her own truth, even under the pressures of public life.

Pluto retrograde in Cancer in the 9th house adds a profound current of ancestral and cultural transformation. It suggests a soul revisiting deep emotional themes through motherhood, nationhood, and identity. From American actress to European princess, her life became a bridge between continents, cultures, and emotional worlds. However, Pluto retrograde also hints that the true transformation remained private—less about public roles and more about inner reclamation.

Eris did not make her a rebel in the typical sense. It transformed her into a disruptor through her presence, beauty, and myth. In evolutionary terms, Grace Kelly's Eris demanded that she break free—not through scandal or revolt, but by daring to embody poise without surrendering her essence. Hers was a life of archetypal magnitude, but the deeper drama was not cinematic—it was the soul's quiet defiance, hidden behind the eyes of a princess.

Julian Assange

Julian Assange, born in July 1971 in Townsville, Australia, was an exceptionally talented computer programmer. In 1995, he pleaded guilty to hacking-related charges and received a fine. He later studied mathematics and physics at the University of Melbourne.

In 2006, Assange founded WikiLeaks, a secure platform for whistleblowers. The site gained global attention in 2010 with the release of classified US military footage showing a helicopter attack in Baghdad that killed several civilians, including two Reuters journalists. That same year, WikiLeaks released over 90,000 classified documents related to the Afghanistan war and nearly 400,000 from the Iraq war—among the largest military leaks in US history. In 2011, it published around 250,000 U.S. diplomatic cables in collaboration with outlets like *The New York Times* and *The Guardian*.

The disclosures sparked global debate and a strong backlash from US officials, who claimed the leaks endangered lives. Chelsea Manning, the source of many documents, was sentenced to prison and later pardoned. WikiLeaks resurfaced in 2016 by publishing emails from Hillary Clinton's campaign, fueling controversy during the U.S. presidential race.

In late 2010, Sweden pursued Assange's extradition over sexual misconduct allegations, which he claimed were politically motivated. To

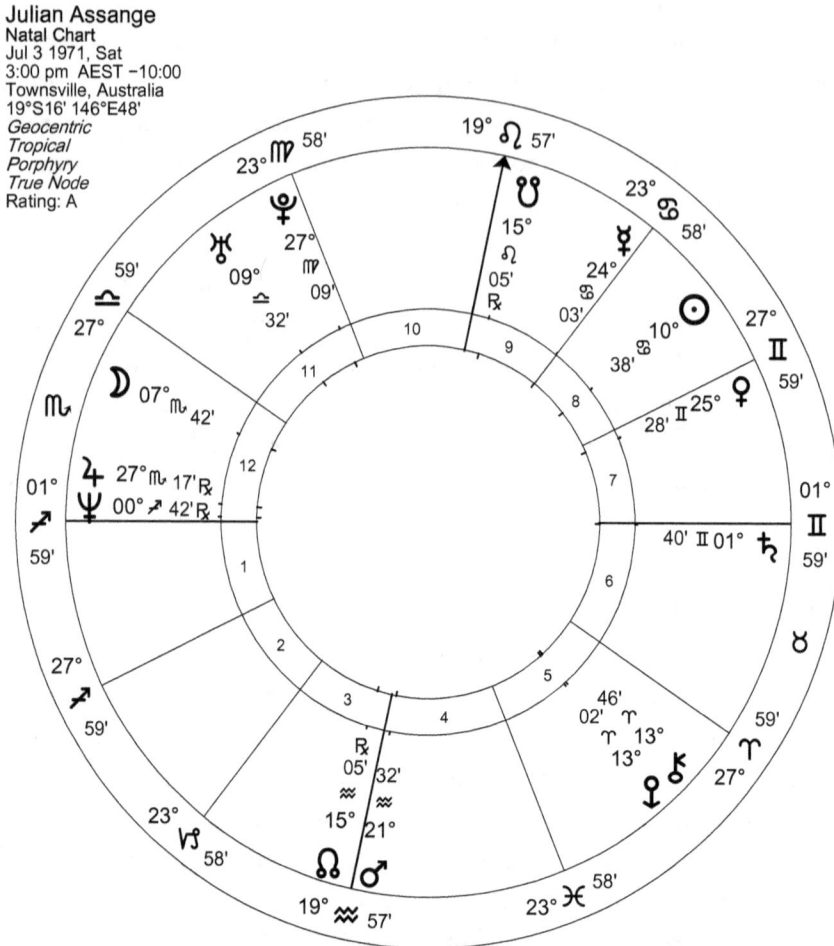

avoid being extradited he sought asylum in Ecuador's London embassy in 2012.

In 2022, the UK approved Assange's extradition to the US. After legal appeals, his team argued that the charges threatened press freedom and expressed concern that he could face the death penalty. The court required assurances from the US to protect his First Amendment rights and exclude capital punishment.

In June 2024 Assange reached a plea deal with the US, pleading guilty to one charge and was able to return to Australia as a free man.[51]

---

51 Paraphrased from https://www.biography.com/activists/julian-assange

Julian Assange was born with Chiron in Aries, conjunct Eris in the 5th house, ruled by his 4th house Mars in Aquarius. Chiron symbolizes both the wounded healer and the archetype of deep vulnerability; both being roles that Assange vividly embodies. With this conjunction, his wounds and healing impulses merged powerfully with Eris' disruptive, truth-revealing nature. This planetary combination strongly influenced his pursuit of radical transparency, catalyzing his efforts to expose hidden abuses of power.

His natal chart reveals an opposition between Chiron and Eris in Aries and Uranus in Libra, located in the 11th house. This polarity intensified Assange's revolutionary tendencies, driving him to break social conventions and radically challenge authority. Uranus in Libra motivated him to address injustices through unconventional methods, continually seeking balance through disruption.

Assange's Sun in Cancer forms a tense square to Eris, emphasizing the personal cost and emotional turmoil inherent in his rebellious path. This alignment highlights the profound internal and external struggles he faced, reflecting his choice to risk isolation and persecution in pursuit of greater transparency and societal transformation.

His 11th house Pluto further emphasizes his outsider identity, compelling him to operate on the fringes of society. Pluto's presence here indicates an inherent urge to transform collective consciousness from behind the scenes, aligning with Assange's underground lifestyle and clandestine operations through WikiLeaks.

Assange's Scorpio Moon in the 12th house heightened his willingness to explore morally ambiguous territory, navigating dark, hidden realms to uncover suppressed truths. The emotional depth and intuitive sensitivity of this placement strengthened his determination to expose concealed corruption, despite the personal risks involved.

His 12th house Jupiter clearly illustrates Assange's visionary tendencies and expansive commitment to truth in Scorpio, which is conjunct retrograde Neptune at 0° Sagittarius, both conjunct his Sagittarius Ascendant. This potent alignment amplified his idealism, providing him with boundless passion and courage to uncover and disseminate the truths he viewed as essential humanitarian actions. Jupiter-Neptune here also denotes his almost mystical belief in the transformative power of truth, fueling his relentless crusade against secrecy and injustice.

Jacqueline Kennedy Onassis

Jacqueline Lee Bouvier was born in Southampton, New York, to John and Janet Bouvier and was primarily raised in Manhattan alongside her sister, Caroline Lee. Her childhood reflected a strong emphasis on culture—she became fluent in French, studied ballet, and enjoyed horseback riding.

In 1947, she began her studies at Vassar and later studied abroad in Paris, immersing herself in French culture. She earned her degree in French literature from George Washington University in 1951. After graduation, she worked as a photographer and reporter for the *Washington Times Herald*.

In 1952, she met Congressman John F. Kennedy and they married the following year. As he advanced in politics, Jacqueline played a crucial role, particularly in his successful 1960 presidential campaign. During her tenure as First Lady (1961–1963), she became renowned for her elegance and commitment to the arts and history. She restored the White House, established the Fine Arts Committee, founded the White House Historical Association, and published the first official guidebook. Her televised tour of the White House in 1962 reached more than 80 million viewers and earned her an Emmy Award.

Jacqueline brought the arts to the White House by hosting performances and promoting American culture. Her time as First Lady ended tragically with President Kennedy's assassination in 1963. She planned her husband's funeral with historical reverence, consciously evoking that of his predecessor Abraham Lincoln, who was also assassinated.

In 1968, she married Aristotle Onassis. Later, she played a role in establishing the JFK Presidential Library and worked as an editor at Doubleday Publishing. She also advocated for historic preservation, including efforts to save Grand Central Station.

Jacqueline Kennedy Onassis passed away on May 19, 1994, at the age of 64. She is interred next to President Kennedy in Arlington National Cemetery, remembered for her grace, cultural impact, and commitment to preservation.[52]

Jacqueline Kennedy Onassis was born at the beginning of the Eris Aries ingress, near the end of the dwarf planet's conjunction of Uranus, both retrograde in her 5th house. Her 9th house Leo Sun conjoined

---

[52] Paraphrased from https://www.whitehousehistory.org/bios/jacqueline-kennedy

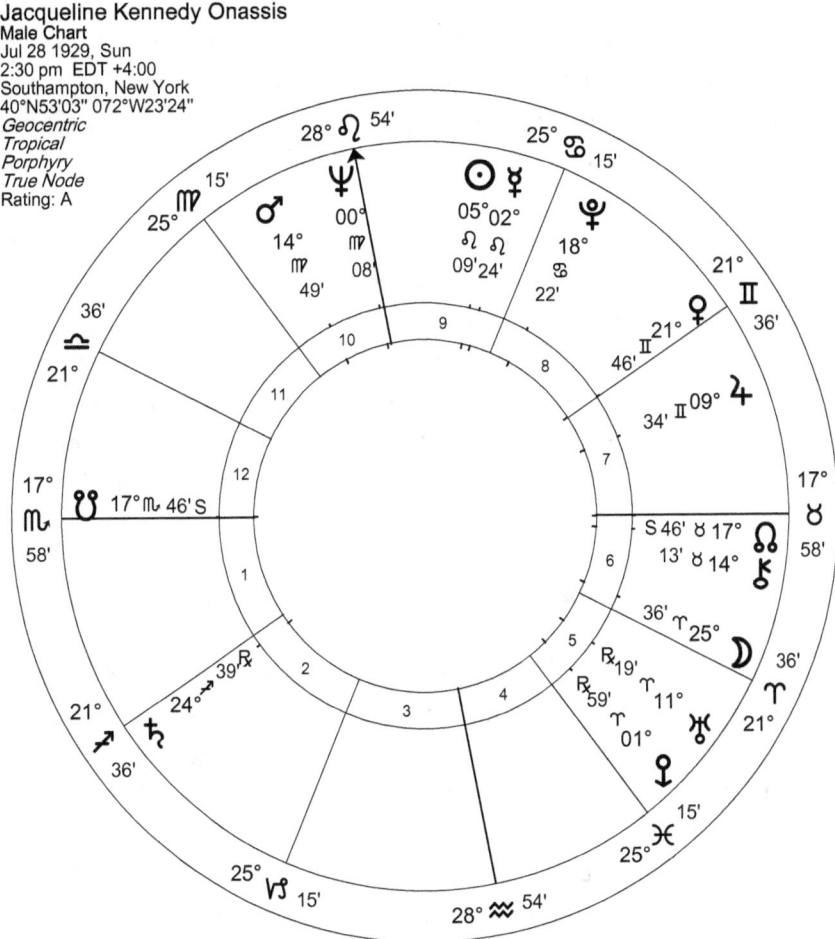

Mercury, creating a harmonious trine to Eris. Her lunar nodes were stationed retrograde, indicating deeply karmic themes that influenced her life path. The 12th house South Node formed a sesquisquare aspect to Eris, highlighting unresolved past-life tensions and challenges that manifested as subconscious drives. Her 6th house North Node formed a semisquare aspect to Eris, suggesting a destined push toward resolving karmic patterns through practical service, refinement, and healing. The South Node, which is conjunct her Ascendant, further emphasizes a life marked by hidden depths, profound sensitivity, and karmic encounters. Her North Node, conjunct Chiron in Taurus, underscored a soul purpose deeply connected to healing, self-worth, and overcoming personal wounds to achieve spiritual and practical integration.

Her 2nd house Saturn retrograde in Sagittarius instilled essential self-reliance, resilience, and an emotional foundation that enabled her to endure devastating tragedies. Saturn's influence provided her with innate strength and determination, allowing her to transform personal suffering into tangible achievements through creative individuality and a personal vision.

Her fiery Aries Moon in the 6th house, ruled by a meticulous and ambitious 10th house Mars in Virgo, endowed her with emotional courage, fierce independence, and unwavering dedication to pursuing her personal goals and aspirations. Her 10th house Neptune enhanced her public persona and professional accomplishments with exceptional strength, creative vision, and spiritual purpose, amplifying her ability to inspire and captivate the world through her unique presence and resilient spirit.

6th House ~ Growth Through Crisis

Ruled by Mercury and infused with the yin, mutable earth energy of Virgo, the 6th house represents a domain of introspection, refinement, and transformation through disciplined effort. It acts as a threshold, a liminal space that links the subjective self—developed through the first five houses—and the external world of service and duty that emerges in the 7th house and beyond. Here, consciousness transitions from the self-centered confidence nurtured in Leo to the humbling acknowledgment of imperfection, laying the groundwork for essential refinement and evolution.

The developmental arc of the zodiac progresses from Aries to Leo, fostering an increasingly individualized and self-expressive identity. Aries ignites the fire of self-discovery, Taurus grounds it in material stability, Gemini broadens awareness through curiosity and connection, Cancer deepens emotional intelligence, and Leo culminates this phase with the full radiance of personal expression. The experience of Leo, in particular, can evoke an intoxicating sense of being special, of being the center of one's own universe. Yet, as the soul transitions into Virgo, the reality of limitation becomes apparent. The subjective self, once so confident in its own significance, now encounters a sobering truth: there is work to be done. Virgo introduces feelings of inadequacy—not as punishment, but as a call to growth. It is a sign that inherently understands the tension between what is and what could be, between imperfection and the persistent urge toward improvement.

This is where Mercury's analytical function turns inward, honing the mind's capacity to discern, critique, and refine. Unlike Gemini, where Mercury's energy is directed outward in an experiential exploration of knowledge, in Virgo, it becomes methodical and precise, striving to identify flaws, inefficiencies, and imbalances. Virgo intuitively senses an idealized state, echoed in its opposition to Pisces, the sign of ultimate transcendence, unity, and spiritual perfection. Yet, rather than dissolving into that ideal, Virgo confronts the painful reality of how far one remains from it. The work of the 6th house is thus a practice of devotion to improvement, bridging the aspirational and the practical, the divine and the mundane.

Here, crisis acts as a catalyst. The experience in the 6th house is rarely easy, as it involves confronting one's weaknesses, whether through personal struggles, health issues, work challenges, or a pervasive sense of inadequacy. However, this crisis is not random; it serves as a necessary mechanism for evolution. Growth requires discomfort, and Virgo intuitively understands this. While Pisces may yearn to dissolve suffering through surrender, Virgo approaches it methodically, embracing discipline, structure, and the gradual changes needed to refine both the self and one's craft. The idea of "chopping wood and carrying water" epitomizes the 6th house journey: enlightenment is not discovered through grand gestures but in the quiet, daily commitment to self-improvement.

The 6th house carries a deeply karmic undertone, representing the realms of service, humility, and purification. It implies a recognition that the self, as it currently exists, is insufficient. Not in a way that diminishes, but in a manner that propels one forward. Through the struggles of the 6th house, the individual is compelled to shed egoic illusions, refine their skills, and cultivate a deeper understanding of their role in the greater whole. This process of refinement prepares the soul for the transition into Libra, where self-awareness expands to encompass relationships with others.

The sextile relationship between Virgo and Scorpio enhances this transformative function, reinforcing the evolutionary pressure that characterizes the 6th house. Pluto, as the ruler of Scorpio, amplifies the call for purification and surrender, ensuring that the Virgoan process of refinement is not superficial but profoundly alchemical. There is no option to stagnate—only to advance through dedicated self-improvement.

Stagnation, when it occurs, often presents itself as obsessive self-criticism, perfectionism, or cycles of anxiety that emerge when the lessons of the 6th house are resisted rather than integrated.

The way this process unfolds in an individual chart depends on several factors. The sign at the cusp of the 6th house, the placement and condition of Mercury—the planetary ruler of the house—and Virgo's position in the chart all provide insights into the nature of the crises faced, the methods of self-correction needed, and the ultimate path to mastery. These elements reveal where one's weaknesses lie, as well as where one's greatest potential for skill, service, and spiritual growth can be found. Through patience, discipline, and a willingness to confront the discomfort that accompanies growth, the 6th house offers a pathway to true self-actualization—not through external validation, but through the quiet, persistent refinement of both body and soul.

Paloma Picasso

Paloma Picasso, a renowned French jewelry designer and businesswoman, is celebrated for her bold designs with Tiffany & Co. as well as her signature fragrance, *Paloma*. As the daughter of legendary artist Pablo Picasso, she was immortalized in his paintings and sculptures yet sought her own creative path, influenced by a childhood steeped in art and culture in Paris and southern France.

Early in her career, Picasso gained recognition in Paris as a costume designer and stylist for avant-garde theater. Her innovative rhinestone necklaces, made from flea market finds, received critical acclaim and prompted her to formally study jewelry design. A pivotal moment occurred when Yves Saint Laurent commissioned her to create accessories for his 1971 collection, leading to the launch of her first jewelry line through his Rive Gauche boutiques.

After her father's death in 1973, she paused her design work to help catalog his estate and played a significant role in establishing the Musée Picasso in Paris.

In 1980, she began her landmark partnership with Tiffany & Co., where her sophisticated designs became iconic. Tiffany's design director emeritus John Loring described her work as "aggressively chic and uncompromisingly stylized." Her creative vision extended to fragrance in 1984,

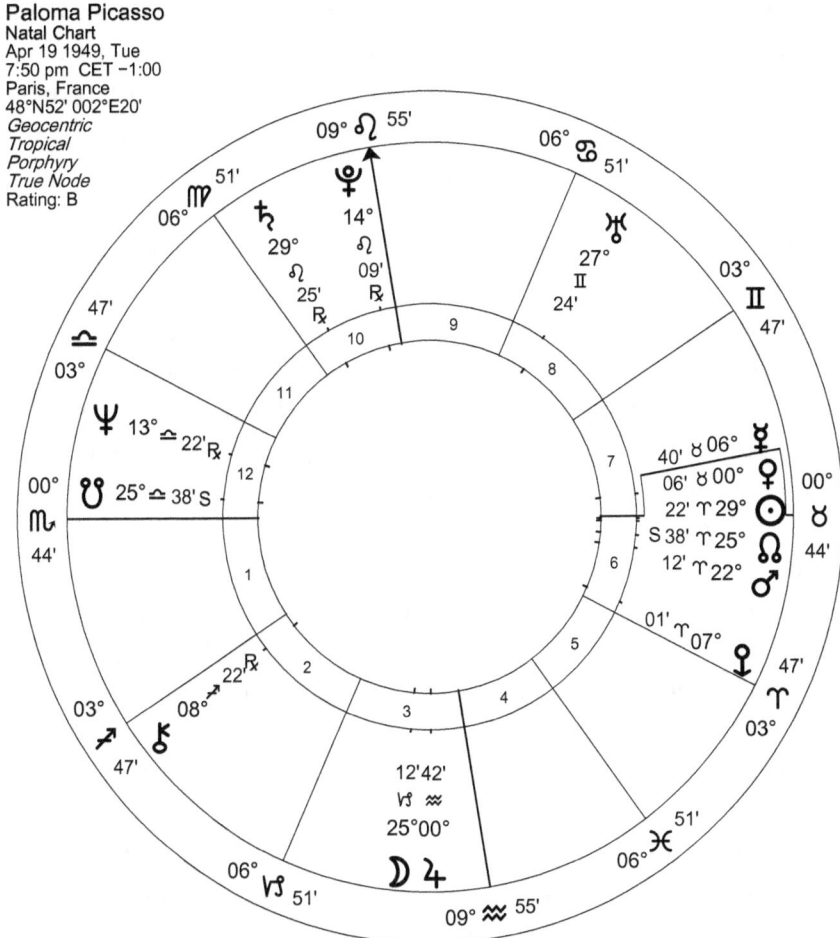

when she released her bold perfume *Paloma* with L'Oréal, targeting strong, confident women.

Her jewelry is permanently displayed at two U.S. institutions: a 396.30-carat kunzite necklace at the Smithsonian and a 408.63-carat moonstone bracelet at The Field Museum in Chicago.

A fashion icon known for her elegance, Picasso has been on the International Best Dressed List since 1983. Her signature red lipstick has become a defining part of her image—so much so that makeup artist François Nars dubbed it her "trademark" and "the designer's red period," a nod to her famous lineage.[53]

---

53 Paraphrased from https://en.wikipedia.org/wiki/Paloma_Picasso

Paloma Picasso was born with Neptune in the 12th house in Libra, opposing Eris in the 6th house. This placement endowed her with a rich imagination and profound intuitive sensitivity, fueling her exceptional creative talents. Her artistic vision reflects the balancing, harmonious nature of Libra while simultaneously harnessing the transformative and unconventional energy of Eris.

Her assertive 6th house Mars, placed prominently in its home sign, rules Eris. Mars is also conjunct her vibrant Aries Sun, the evolutionary North Node in Aries, and is harmoniously aligned with Venus in Taurus. This dynamic Aries stellium highlights her passionate, pioneering spirit and emphasizes her courage and independence in artistic expression. The Venus placement in Taurus adds a sensual elegance and material richness to her work, which is perfectly reflected in her acclaimed jewelry designs.

With Scorpio on the Ascendant, Paloma projects an aura of mystery, intensity, and self-containment. Individuals with Scorpio rising often exude a compelling presence that can be somewhat intimidating yet often magnetic. This placement suggests a strong-willed and intensely private personality who does not easily reveal herself—yet channels tremendous emotional and psychological depth into her creations.

Creativity for people with Scorpio rising is often not just aesthetic—it's alchemical. The raw materials of life (grief, desire, eroticism, memory, legacy) are transformed through symbolic and artistic expression. In Paloma's case, this is evident in her bold, architectural jewelry—often featuring primary colors, heavy gold, crosses, and mythic motifs. Her style doesn't aim to please—it claims space, often reflecting power, sensuality, and protection.

Paloma Picasso's Uranus in the 8th house adds a powerful, disruptive, and visionary dimension to her creativity and life path—especially considering her Scorpio Ascendant, which highlights the 8th house in her psyche. Uranus in the 8th is never satisfied with the surface of things; it penetrates, liberates, and transforms the deeper layers of psyche, power, intimacy, and legacy. In Paloma's case, it speaks directly to her creative independence, personal revolution, and how she has redefined her inheritance.

Her ambitious 10th house Pluto retrograde in Leo forms a harmonious trine with her 6th house Eris, reinforcing a potent triple Leo signature. This energetic alignment significantly amplifies her natural creativity and magnetism, facilitating powerful career advancement and public recognition. Additionally, disciplined Saturn retrograde in Leo occupies her 10th house, reflecting an authoritative validation of her artistic accomplishments and signifying her inherited status as the distinguished daughter of a legendary artist.

Paloma's independent and emotionally resilient nature stems from her 3rd house Moon conjunct Jupiter in Aquarius. This powerful conjunction has endowed her with emotional self-reliance, intellectual depth, and visionary individuality, fueling her innovative approach to design and supporting her significant professional achievements.

Robin Williams

Robin Williams grew up as a lonely boy amid midcentury wealth—his father was a Ford executive, and his mother was a charming but neglectful Southern belle. He attended expensive boarding schools and developed a manic sense of humor, reflecting both his isolation and vitality. His comedy revealed our own national madness: to be American meant to be wildly alive, chaotic, and endlessly expansive. We wanted to believe in him—his energy gave us hope and made us feel that life could be limitless and painless. His suicide, then, came as a shock.

This contradiction—between joy and despair—defines both Williams' legacy and the American experience. The HBO documentary *Robin Williams: Come Inside My Mind* captures this duality. While the first half celebrates his brilliance, the second half takes a darker turn, suggesting that the ending was always foreshadowed. It frames his death not as suicide but as the result of Lewy body dementia, a condition beyond his control.

Williams' film roles often revealed his inner shadows—portrayals of men hollowed by the cost of freedom. He cleaned up his life after partying with John Belushi the night he died, another icon of manic energy and chaos. Surviving that moment, Williams evolved from comic oddball to beloved mentor, shouldering the weight of decades in his comedy. Beneath the jokes lay sharp insights into a fractured culture.

In middle age, he took up long-distance biking—perhaps a metaphor for his restlessness, a constant motion concealing a deeper search for peace.[54]

---

54 Paraphrased from https://www.pbs.org/wnet/pioneers-of-television/pioneering-people/robin-williams/

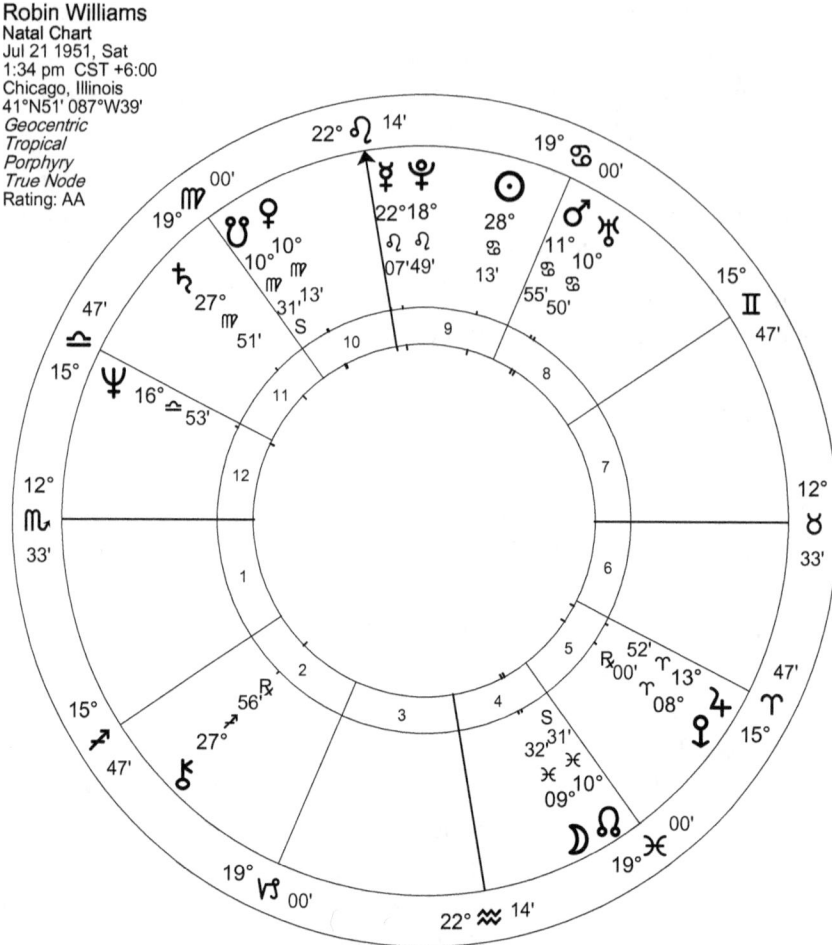

Eris retrograde at 8° Aries in the 5th house, conjoined with Jupiter, is the fiery core of Robin Williams' chart. Here the Soul erupts with uncontainable creative force, compelled to disrupt consensus reality through performance, parody, and play. Eris in Aries insists on absolute authenticity, and in the 5th house she demanded that Williams express himself with unfiltered spontaneity, even chaos. Jupiter magnified this signature into mythic proportion: the archetypal trickster, the clown as truth-teller, the improviser who shattered conventions with volcanic laughter. Yet retrograde, Eris turned her disruption inward as well, generating a private battleground of alienation and self-division. The very same force that liberated others became a source of torment within, as if the chaos he unleashed onstage could not be silenced inside him.

This Erisian fire did not exist in isolation. With a Scorpio Ascendant, Williams entered this life cloaked in intensity, compelled toward transformation and confrontation with shadow. Scorpio rising gave his presence magnetic depth, while demanding ongoing metamorphosis. It is no accident that his comedy often touched taboo, death, sex, or pain—he instinctively carried Pluto's underworld into the spotlight, forcing others to laugh at what they feared.

The Moon conjunct the North Node in Pisces in the 4th house shows the evolutionary intention behind this intensity: to grow through compassion, vulnerability, and emotional transparency. Williams' genius was not merely comic but deeply empathic. He was a vessel for collective feeling, dissolving boundaries as he blurred laughter and tears, channeling the raw emotional currents of humanity. The cost of this gift was exposure; his openness to others' suffering amplified his own.

Mercury conjunct Pluto in Leo in the 9th house intensified his mind into a furnace of thought, communication, and performance. His words were compulsive, transformative, volcanic—erupting in manic torrents of voices and characters. Yet beneath the comedy lay Mercury–Pluto's relentless demand for truth. His improvisations were not random; they were eruptions of the underworld disguised as humor, demolishing illusions with every punchline.

Robin Williams' Venus in Virgo in the 10th house, conjunct the South Node, symbolizes a karmic pattern of seeking validation and love through public recognition and professional achievement. The Soul carries over habits of equating worth with service, productivity, and the critical eye of authority. In the evolutionary journey, this placement suggests that his artistry, career, and public roles were arenas where old relational dynamics and values resurfaced. The task was to move beyond over-identification with external approval and instead evolve toward a deeper integration of love and self-value, not dependent on professional image.

These archetypal dynamics converged in his friendship with John Belushi. Belushi's sudden death was more than personal tragedy; it was karmic confrontation. Through Belushi, Williams was forced to face the abyss—addiction, denial, mortality—echoing the Scorpio Ascendant's evolutionary demand for transformation and Eris' ruthless exposure of truth. Belushi's fate mirrored the dangers Williams himself skirted, a skipped step made visible in another's life, leaving him no choice but to see the razor's edge he lived upon.

In Robin Williams, Eris' archetype is unmistakable. She made him disruptor and healer, clown and mystic, liberator and sufferer. His gift was to tear away the mask of consensus reality, to show the rawness beneath, to make us laugh at the very chaos we fear. And yet the same chaos lived in him, demanding confrontation without rest. He embodied Eris' golden apple in human form: tossing it into the banquet of culture, shattering illusions, and leaving behind both laughter and truth.

Jeffrey Dahmer

Jeffrey Dahmer was an American serial killer who murdered 17 men and boys between 1978 and 1991. He lured victims—mostly black men—from gay bars, malls, and bus stops with promises of money or sex, drugged and strangled them, then performed sex acts on their corpses. He dismembered the bodies, kept body parts as souvenirs, and photographed the process to relive the murders. Captured in 1991, he was sentenced to 16 life terms and was killed by a fellow inmate in 1994.

Born in 1960, Dahmer was initially an energetic child, but after a painful hernia surgery at the age of four, he became withdrawn. His behavior worsened following the birth of his brother and the family's frequent relocations. Fascinated by bones from an early age, he collected animal remains and preserved them in jars.

By adolescence, he was tense, isolated, and began drinking heavily. He later claimed that his urges toward necrophilia and murder began at age 14. His parents' troubled marriage and eventual divorce may have intensified these compulsions. At 18, he committed his first murder.

Dahmer continued to struggle with alcoholism and was arrested multiple times, including for indecent exposure and child molestation. In 1989, after a molestation conviction, he was sentenced to a year in prison on "day release," allowing him to work by day and return to jail at night. During and after this period, he killed 12 more victims.

As his crimes progressed, Dahmer developed rituals involving chemical disposal and cannibalism. He chose vulnerable victims whose disappearances were less likely to draw attention.

Eris Through The Houses   159

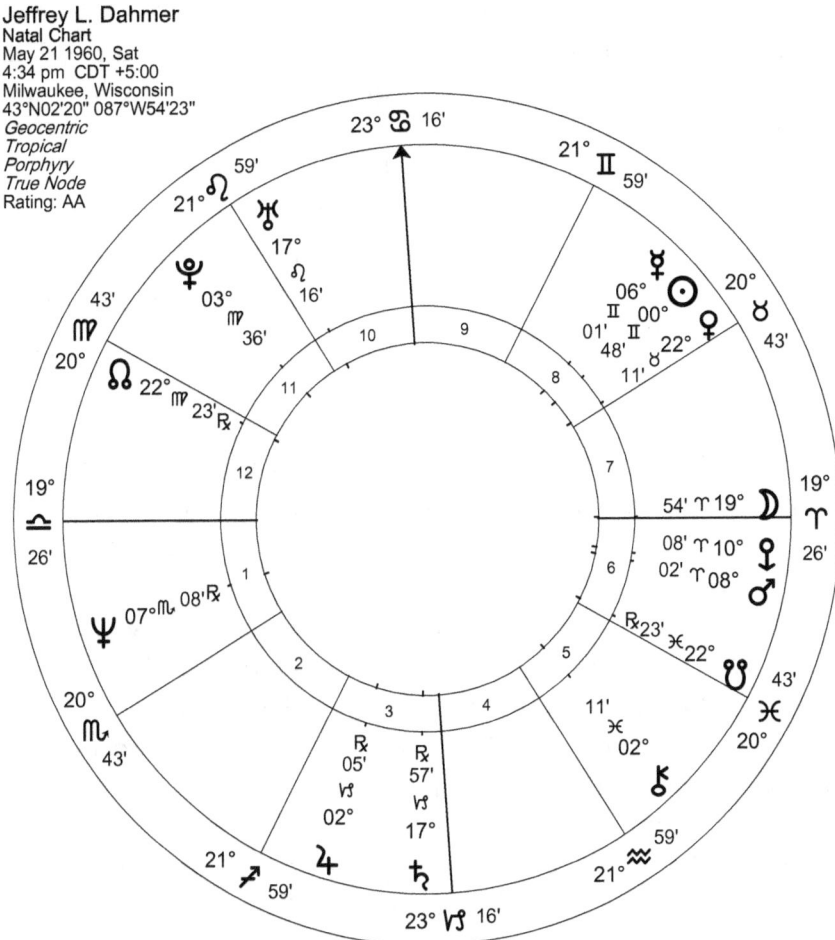

His arrest on July 22, 1991, followed the escape of a potential victim. Police found body parts and disturbing photos in his apartment, confirming the extent of his crimes.

At his 1992 trial, Dahmer pleaded guilty by reason of insanity, but the jury found him sane and fully aware of his actions. He was sentenced to 15 life terms, with a 16th added later. His life ended violently when fellow inmate Christopher Scarver killed him in prison.[55] Jeffrey Dahmer was born with the Moon in his 7th house in Aries, separating from his 6th house Eris. Eris was in close conjunction its ruler Mars, also in Aries. The

---

55 Paraphrased from https://www.biography.com/crime/jeffrey-dahmer

depression and anxieties of his early childhood served as the emotional vehicles that later shaped his severe dystopian behavior and outlook on life.

The Moon and Mars formed a trine with 10th house Uranus in Leo and squared retrograde Jupiter and Saturn in Capricorn. As he grew older, he became the monster he had internalized.

Dahmer's nodal axis from the 6th house Pisces to the 12th house Virgo further distorted his perception of reality. His 1st house Neptune retrograde in Scorpio amplified the delusions, painting a horrific image of the world for Jeffrey Dahmer.

Coretta Scott King

Coretta Scott King was born in Marion, Alabama, and was recognized early for her talents in singing, violin, and civil rights activism. She graduated as the valedictorian of her high school and earned a Bachelor of Arts in music and education from Antioch College.

After receiving a fellowship to the New England Conservatory of Music in Boston, she met Martin Luther King Jr., who was then pursuing his doctorate at Boston University. They married in 1953 and relocated to Montgomery, Alabama, where Martin became the pastor of Dexter Avenue Baptist Church. Coretta supported his work and embraced the traditional responsibilities of a pastor's wife.

During the 1950s and '60s, she played a vital role in the civil rights movement—taking part in the Montgomery Bus Boycott, celebrating Ghana's independence in 1957, traveling to India in 1959, and advocating for the Civil Rights Act of 1964.

Although she was often seen alongside her husband, Coretta cultivated a strong activist identity of her own, serving as a mediator and advocate for peace and justice.

After Martin Luther King Jr. was assassinated in 1968, Coretta led the Memphis march he had planned and went on to establish the Martin Luther King Jr. Center for Nonviolent Social Change, where she served as its longtime leader. She also played a key role in creating the King National Historic Site in Atlanta.

She continued to engage in global causes, protesting apartheid and writing as a syndicated columnist. In 1983, she witnessed the official establishment of Martin Luther King Jr. Day as a federal holiday.

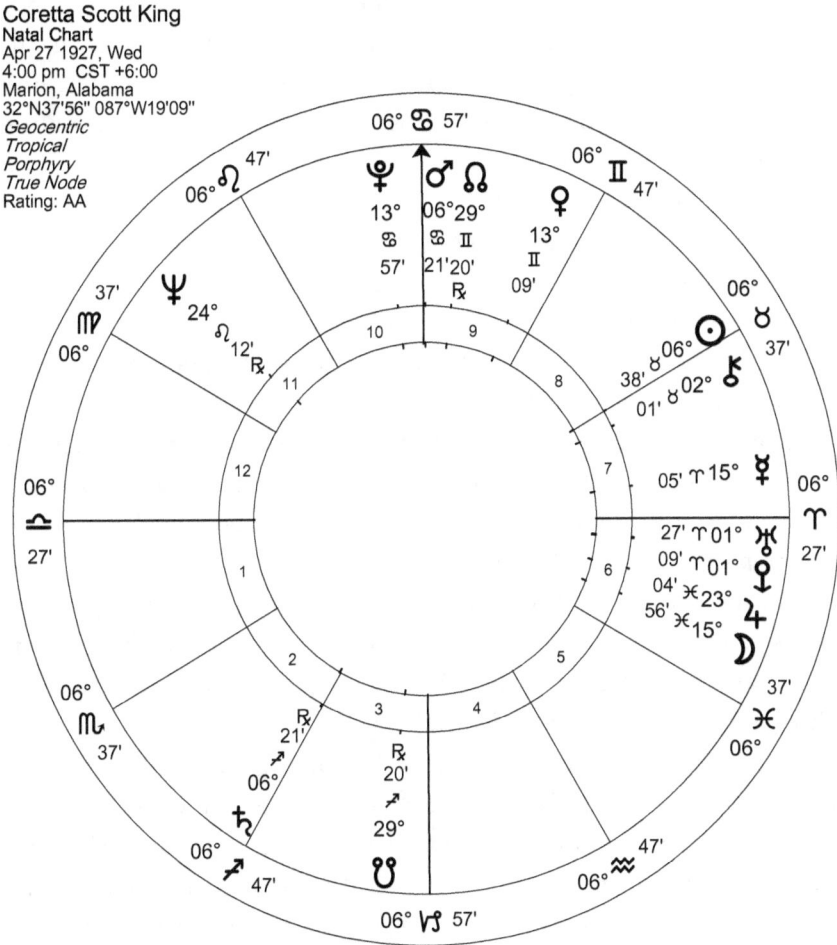

Coretta experienced a heart attack and stroke in 2005 and passed away on January 30, 2006, at the age of 78, while receiving treatment for ovarian cancer in Mexico.

Her funeral on February 7, 2006, at New Birth Missionary Baptist Church in Georgia, drew over 14,000 attendees, including Presidents George W. Bush, George H.W. Bush, Jimmy Carter, and Bill Clinton, along with Senator Barack Obama. Her daughter, Bernice King, delivered the eulogy.[56]

In the chart of Coretta Scott King, Eris at 1° Aries in the 6th house, conjunct Uranus, signifies the evolutionary imperative to embody fierce

---

56 Paraphrased from https://www.biography.com/activists/coretta-scott-king

authenticity in the service of justice. Although physically placed in the 6th, in Aries, Eris here resonates like a 1st house presence—raw, initiating, and unwilling to remain silent or invisible in the face of systemic injustice. This placement reveals a soul who must disrupt the normalized, the routine, and the roles assigned—especially where conformity is expected in service, gender, race, or the labor of care. Her very presence in daily life became a revolutionary act, particularly in the context of oppression.

The conjunction with Uranus electrified this signature, amplifying Eris' demand to rupture false peace and reframe what it means to be of service. She was not here to assist quietly in the background, even though she may have often seemed to do so. Instead, her deeper soul function was to awaken others by example, demonstrating that liberation begins in how we live, work, and uphold our integrity. The body, the voice, the daily ritual—everything became part of a larger movement. There's something evolutionarily explosive about the way she enters spaces, holds her presence, and moves through systems with dignity and rebellion intertwined. This intensity was amplified by Eris' balsamic conjunction with Jupiter in Pisces, and the presence of the Pisces Moon, which saturated her work with compassion, vision, and dedication.

Eris squares the nodal axis—with the South Node at 29° Sagittarius in the 3rd house and the North Node at 29° Gemini in the 9th. The South Node initiates a new karmic chapter rooted in Sagittarian archetypes, including truth, justice, worldview, moral principles, and the spiritual quest. However, as this is the beginning degree, her soul is newly exposed to both the shadow and light of Sagittarian energy—possibly facing challenges related to belief systems, the temptation to preach instead of engage, and the need to distinguish between universal truth and culturally or ideologically constructed certainty.

The North Node calls her soul into Gemini's evolutionary field of curiosity, multiplicity, storytelling, and listening. At the initiating degree, this indicates a soul just beginning to experiment with a new way of learning, teaching, and connecting—more dialectical than declarative, and more rooted in shared language and everyday truths than in grand philosophical visions.

In Evolutionary Astrology, when a planet squares the lunar nodes, it is known as a "skipped step" condition. Something from the past or a requirement for the future has been left unfulfilled. In this scenario, the focus centered on the North Node. The evolutionary demand was urgent. The soul was not gently easing into this new Gemini path; rather, it was being thrust into it. This created a sense of urgency, intensity, and initiatory force, not because the nodes were concluding something, but because a new karmic layer was breaking open, and Eris refused to let that process remain theoretical or private. She made it palpable. Through Gemini, she insisted that entering Gemini involves voicing the unspeakable, challenging inherited truths, and creating space for the voices that history has attempted to erase.

In the 7th house, Chiron at 2° Taurus indicates that relationships serve as both a balm and a wound—especially the connection with the Other in its broadest sense: lovers, the public, and even the concept of peace itself. Chiron here reflects the pain caused by disrupted stability and the ache of trying to maintain beauty and groundedness amidst chaos. Her marriage to Martin Luther King Jr. exemplifies this wound—an intense soul bond marked by a shared vision and profound loss. However, Chiron also acted as a channel; she carried the people's wounds, those excluded from the American promise, and transformed them into collective healing. The semi-sextile proximity to Eris suggests a sacred tension: how do we love in a world that wounds us? How do we create peace when peace is used to silence?

The Sun at 6° Taurus in the 8th house imparted depth and rooted strength to the chart. The loss and hardship of the conjoined Chiron cast shadows in its essential brilliance. Its light emerged through endurance, navigating profound loss and transformation with grace.

The Moon and Jupiter in Pisces in the 6th house symbolize devotion—spiritual, compassionate, and inclusive—but these qualities can be easily exploited or overlooked. The presence of Eris alongside these placements was crucial: the compassion of Pisces in service had to be sharpened by Eris' sword, or it risked collapsing into martyrdom. She had to learn to fuse spiritual service with revolutionary fire.

Mercury at 15° Aries in the 7th house embodies the voice of the warrior: direct, unyielding, and truthful, particularly in relationships. It bestowed upon her the courage to speak out, even when faced with those who preferred her silence. Her mind was alight with clarity. Mercury in Aries synchronized her voice with the evolutionary drive of Eris, even if not in direct aspect; it empowered her to embody the fierce yet graceful expression of what needed to be said, even at a personal cost.

Mars and Pluto, located in Cancer in the 9th and 10th houses respectively, indicate an energy of sacred protection aimed at the collective: the nation, the family, and the ancestral lineage. Pluto in the 10th house represents transformative public power, especially concerning themes of home, safety, motherhood, and race. Mars, positioned near the North Node, encouraged courageous movement toward reclaiming voice and depth in the narrative of liberation.

Saturn at 6° Sagittarius retrograde in the 2nd house brought karmic lessons around self-worth, values, and security. This placement reflected a past-life imprint of constriction in relation to resources—both material and inner—along with the need to build a solid foundation of self-reliance and integrity. Retrograde Saturn internalizes this struggle, suggesting that Coretta's sense of worth and stability had to be claimed from within, often against external limitations or the weight of inherited expectations. In Sagittarius, the work involved aligning personal values with universal truth, lifting survival concerns into the realm of moral and spiritual conviction. Her ability to sustain herself and her family, especially in the wake of profound loss, testifies to this Saturnian discipline: turning restraint into resilience, scarcity into purpose, and values into a guiding compass for justice.

In the 11th house, Neptune in Leo retrograde reflects her dream of a beloved community—a spiritual vision of collective joy, dignity, and creativity. However, Neptune retrograde must cut through illusion; the dream have been rooted in truth, not fantasy. Eris assisted here by serving as the ruthless midwife, tearing the veil away so that Neptune's vision could shine without delusion.

Coretta Scott King's evolutionary signature through Eris represents radical integrity. It was not loud, but unwavering. It was not reckless, but untamable. Her Eris, wedded to Uranus and squared to the nodes, carries the DNA of revolution through service—not merely the helper behind the hero, but the indispensable embodiment of justice's fierce, feminine edge. She taught us that peace is not just the absence of conflict, but the presence of truth, spoken and lived, daily and collectively.

7th House ~ The Dating Game

As we traverse the western horizon of the natural zodiac, we enter the realm of the 7th house, where the energy of yang cardinal air begins the journey of relationships, engagement, and reflection. Libra, the archetype governing this house, is the second sign ruled by Venus. However, the Venusian expression here transitions from the internal domain of Taurus to an outward focus, influencing how we interact with the world around us. In Taurus and the 2nd house, Venus teaches us about self-worth, personal values, and nurturing our inner resources. These qualities establish the foundation of attraction—what we embody within ourselves inevitably radiates outward, generating the magnetism that shapes our experience of relationships in the 7th house.

Every relationship we encounter within this archetype acts as a mirror, revealing aspects of our inner nature through the people, situations, and dynamics we attract. The glyph of Venus, resembling a hand mirror, offers profound insight into this dynamic. Just as we look into a mirror to see our external reflection, the people we interact with reflect deeper truths about our inner world. Whether through romantic partners, friendships, or even brief encounters, each connection presents an opportunity to view ourselves from various perspectives—who we are, who we think we are, and who we aspire to be. Relationships become a path to self-awareness, a process through which we refine our identity by engaging with diverse perspectives, temperaments, and experiences.

Libra and the 7th house represent the evolutionary purpose of teaching balance, harmony, and fairness, emphasizing the importance of equality in relationships. This is where the skills of negotiation, compromise, and diplomacy are cultivated, allowing one to hold space for another's reality while staying true to one's own. An inherent duality exists here, as Libra aims to create equilibrium between opposing forces, harmonizing the self with others. The ability to see through another's eyes fosters a deeper appreciation for human complexity, encouraging us to respond with authenticity and grace rather than through control or imposition. The aim of this house is not merely to form relationships but to achieve a deeper understanding of oneself through the act of relating, mastering the delicate dance of giving and receiving, asserting and accommodating.

One of the most misunderstood aspects of the 7th house is its presumed connection to marriage. While traditional astrology often associates this house with committed partnerships, its true essence aligns more closely with the exploration of relational dynamics before solidifying a commitment. The 7th house represents the "dating game," a phase of trial and error in which individuals interact with various types of partners, discovering their desires, needs, and boundaries through experience. This house revolves around attraction and interaction, emphasizing self-understanding through diverse encounters rather than permanence or deep entanglement. True commitment, where relationships evolve beyond mere attraction into deeper emotional and psychological merging, is more closely related to Scorpio and the 8th house, where bonds are formed through intimacy, vulnerability, commitment, and shared transformation.

The 7th house, in its purest form, represents a space where we learn the dynamics of engagement without the burden of entanglement. It is a realm for exploring various expressions of partnership, discovering what resonates and what does not. Some relationships flow effortlessly, while others challenge us, forcing us to confront projections, unconscious expectations, and hidden aspects of our psyche. Each connection, no matter how brief, leaves an imprint, shaping our understanding of both love and ourselves. Attraction in this house is not arbitrary; it responds to the energetic frequency one embodies. The relationships formed here reflect our inner state, sometimes bringing joy and growth, while at other times revealing insecurities or wounds that must be addressed before deeper bonds can form.

Beyond romantic or personal partnerships, the 7th house also governs broader relational experiences. Some individuals form meaningful connections with their communities, belief systems, or even entire generations. These relationships shape identity as profoundly as one-on-one interactions, influencing how a person engages with the world at large. Whether through mentorship, social influence, or collaboration, the way one navigates relationships on a larger scale reflects the lessons learned through personal engagement.

Understanding the 7th house in a natal chart provides insight into how individuals approach relationships, what they seek in others, and how they integrate reflections from those they attract. The placements and aspects of planets within this house reveal specific themes and challenges regarding partnerships, highlighting patterns of attraction, interpersonal dynamics, and the evolutionary lessons that emerge through connection. For some, this house may indicate ease in forming relationships, while for others, it may present lessons in balance, boundaries, or self-awareness before healthy, fulfilling relationships can fully manifest.

Ultimately, the 7th house represents a realm of exploration, where the self engages with the other in an ongoing dialogue of reflection and growth. It is the space where the dynamics of attraction and interaction unfold, shaping the journey of self-awareness within the expansive and intricate world of human connections.

Caesar Chavez

Cesar Chavez was a Latino civil rights leader, farm labor activist, and a deeply religious and spiritual figure. He was also a community organizer, social entrepreneur, champion of nonviolent social change, and a crusader for environmental and consumer rights.

His deeply spiritual faith guided his activism. He was a dedicated community organizer, a visionary social entrepreneur, and a steadfast advocate for nonviolent social change. His work extended beyond labor rights; he also championed environmental justice and consumer protections, recognizing the interconnectedness of human dignity, ecological responsibility, and economic fairness.

As a first-generation American, Chavez was born near his family's small homestead just outside Yuma, Arizona. At the age of 11, during the Great Depression, his family lost their farm and was forced into a life of migrant labor, moving from place to place in search of work. He left school after the eighth grade to work full-time in the fields, helping to support his family. This nomadic life—harvesting crops in California's fields, orchards, and vineyards—exposed him firsthand to the harsh conditions, exploitation, and profound injustices faced by farm workers. These experiences planted the seeds of his lifelong mission: to organize a union that would empower and protect those who, like him, had endured the dehumanization of migrant labor.[57]

In Chavez's natal chart, Eris at 0° Aries in the 7th house, conjunct Uranus, signals a soul whose evolutionary journey hinges on relational

---

57 Paraphrased from https://chavezfoundation.org/about-cesar-chavez

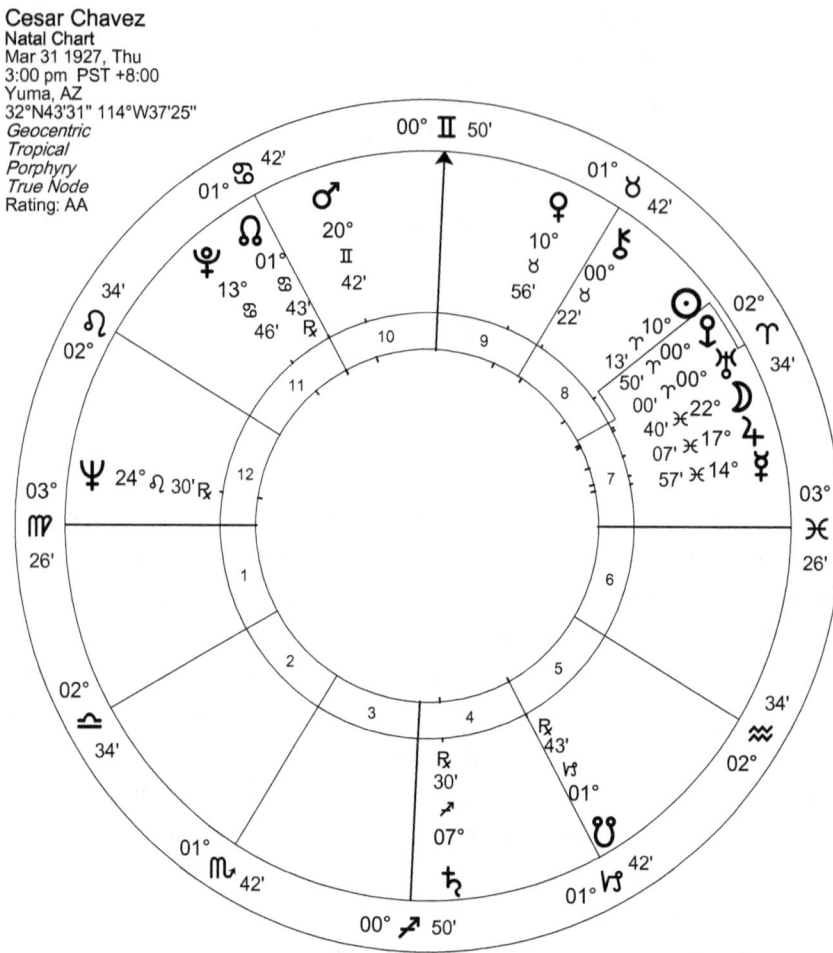

rupture. This conjunction at the first degree of the zodiac initiates a radical rebirth—not only for the self but for the collective. The 7th house placement reveals that disruption is not personal—it happens in the field of contracts, justice, and social power. Eris here exposes false harmony and reveals buried injustices in human relationships; Uranus electrifies the process, calling for immediate, visible change.

The Sun at 10° Aries in the 8th house deepens the theme of systemic confrontation. In Aries, the Sun initiates; in the 8th, it regenerates through encounters with power, loss, and transformation. Chavez's identity was forged in collective trauma and healed through collective struggle. His solar will was not driven by ego, but by the soul's necessity to reveal what was hidden—and to challenge the deeper mechanisms of control.

The Eris–Uranus conjunction squares the nodes—South Node at 1° Capricorn in the 5th house and North Node at 1° Cancer in the 11th—marking a classic skipped step. The South Node suggests a karmic past where leadership and visibility may have been exercised through performance, control, or rigid identity roles. The evolutionary mandate now lies with the Cancer North Node in the 11th: building emotional safety and solidarity within community, nurturing collective purpose, and stepping into protective, inclusive leadership.

The skipped step—Eris and Uranus in the 7th house—reflects unresolved past-life crises around relational rupture, social rebellion, and principled conflict. This lifetime demands not only disruption, but the integration of that disruption into a broader vision of justice. Chavez could not remain private or passive; his soul's evolution required public confrontation.

In the 7th house, a stellium in Pisces—Mercury (14°), Jupiter (17°), and Moon (22°)—offers emotional sensitivity and spiritual compassion. These planets square the Eris–Uranus conjunction, creating powerful evolutionary tension. His communication (Mercury) and beliefs (Jupiter) were steeped in universal values and mysticism; his empathy (Moon) ran deep. But these qualities were not enough on their own. The nodal square to Eris demanded that internal knowing become external action—vision had to erupt into voice.

Chiron at 0° Taurus in the 8th house represents wounding around value, trust, and survival—especially in collective and economic contexts. While not in close aspect to Eris, Chiron's placement echoes the pain of shared suffering and the call to heal through courageous exposure of systemic harm.

Venus at 10° Taurus in the 9th house reveals a love for the Earth, for beauty grounded in natural law, and for justice as a spiritual principle. Her sextile to Pluto at 13° Cancer in the 11th house supports evolutionary transformation rooted in values: protecting the people, honoring the land, and fostering inclusive, soul-centered leadership. Chavez's fight was philosophical and embodied—it was about rights, but also about reverence.

Mars at 20° Gemini in the 10th house provided the skill, stamina, and strategic intelligence to engage publicly. He was a warrior of words, persuasion, and mobility—nimble in thought, tireless in cause.

Neptune retrograde at 24° Leo in the 12th house suggests a hidden current of mysticism and divine guidance. Chavez's devotion, sacrifice, and endurance flowed from this wellspring. He fasted not only as protest but as prayer. His leadership came from within—a quiet, powerful source of spiritual alignment.

Cesar Chavez's chart centers around a skipped step: the Eris–Uranus conjunction at 0° Aries in the 7th house, square the nodal axis. This evolutionary pattern demands resolution through courageous, disruptive action in the field of human relationships—facing what is unjust, naming it, and transforming it through direct engagement.

The South Node in Capricorn (5th house) suggests prior roles in elite, visible leadership; the North Node in Cancer (11th) points toward a future of collective care, emotional authenticity, and grassroots solidarity.

David Koresh

David Koresh, born Vernon Wayne Howell in Houston, Texas, in 1959 to a 15-year-old single mother, was raised by his grandparents. He described his childhood as lonely and was teased by peers who called him "Vernie." Struggling with dyslexia, he dropped out of high school; however, he displayed musical talent and developed a profound interest in the Bible, memorizing large portions by the age of 12.

At 20, he joined his mother's Seventh-Day Adventist Church but was expelled for being a negative influence. He briefly pursued a music career in Hollywood before joining the Branch Davidians in Waco, Texas, in 1981. He had an affair with prophetess Lois Roden, who was decades older than him, and traveled with her to Israel. After Roden's death, a power struggle erupted between Koresh and her son George. In late 1987, Koresh and seven followers, armed with multiple weapons, returned to Mount Carmel, leading to a gunfight that left George Roden injured. Charged with attempted murder, Koresh claimed they were investigating corpse abuse and was acquitted after a mistrial.

By 1990, Koresh had risen to a leadership position within the sect and legally changed his name, citing "publicity and business purposes." He chose the name Koresh, the Hebrew transliteration of Cyrus, after the Persian king who liberated the Jews from Babylon. He believed he was the head of the biblical House of David.

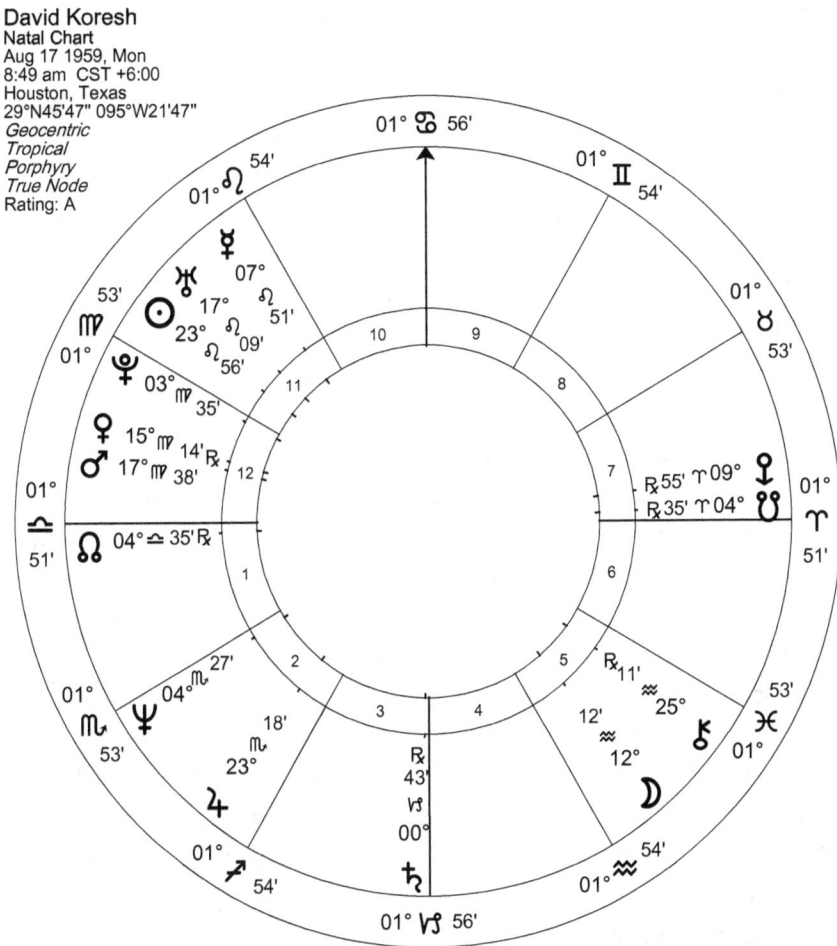

Koresh died during the famous siege of the sect's headquarters, in which 76 people were killed in April 1993.[58]

In David Koresh's natal chart, the nodal axis spans the 1st and 7th houses, with the North Node at 4° Libra in the 1st house and the South Node at 4° Aries in the 7th, conjoined by Eris at 9° Aries, which is retrograde. This axis reflects a profound evolutionary journey from defining oneself through others to fostering autonomous self-awareness. However, with Eris involved, the path is far from linear, often characterized by rupture, confrontation, and the demand for radical honesty

---

58 Paraphrased from https://www.pbs.org/wgbh/pages/frontline/waco/davidkoresh.html

in relationships. The presence of Eris conjunct the South Node amplifies the karmic past, emphasizing themes of exclusion, conflict, and identity formed through relational rupture.

The South Node in Aries in the 7th house suggests a karmic history marked by conflicted partnerships, likely involving domination, the assertion of will, or identity enmeshment through the reflection of "the other." This may indicate lifetimes where Koresh's soul learned to define itself through combative or heroic engagement with others—whether as a challenger, martyr, or warrior for a cause. The 7th house highlights relational projection and contractual dynamics, suggesting that Koresh may have repeatedly faced evolutionary crises surrounding autonomy versus enmeshment or individuality versus submission.

Eris, retrograde and conjunct the South Node, adds complexity to the situation. She signifies unresolved wounds of exclusion, displacement, or moral outrage, often manifesting through disruption of collective norms or relational betrayals. Eris in Aries is uncompromising, insurgent, and fiercely individuated; her position here implies that Koresh harbored an unconscious, perhaps mythic grievance from previous lifetimes—a feeling of being cast out or silenced, fueling a desire to defy social contracts and reclaim a voice at any cost. In the 7th house, this manifested in the domain of relationships, potentially creating a past pattern of projecting chaos, rebellion, or blame onto others, or serving as a vessel for others' projections of similar issues.

His evolutionary task was to evolve toward the North Node in Libra in the 1st house—a movement toward self-reflection, balance, and conscious relationships that do not rely on conflict or polarity to define identity. This Libra North Node encourages the soul to learn inner harmony and integrate both self and others in a way that fosters just leadership and social responsibility. However, the 1st house emphasizes individuation—he was meant to embody a balanced self, not just ideologically, but also personally and relationally. The tragedy is that his path seems to have become ensnared in the very distortion he sought to transcend: polarization, extremism, and opposition identity.

The 3rd house Saturn at 0° Capricorn retrograde forms a square to the nodal axis, marking a classic skipped step. In Evolutionary Astrology, this configuration reveals a karmic impasse: the soul has previously tried to integrate the lessons of Saturn—authority, structure, responsibility, and voice—but has not succeeded. In Capricorn, Saturn symbolizes systems of control, discipline, and ambition, but the retrograde condition and square indicate deep inner doubt and unresolved trauma surrounding mental authority, communication, and possibly dogma.

The 3rd house position reveals thought patterns, early environment, language, and learning. This may indicate a soul with past experiences of being either oppressed or oppressive in speech, education, or ideology—perhaps as a preacher, teacher, or ruler whose words were either repressed or misused. This karmic inheritance can manifest as a compulsive need to assert one's truth, particularly when combined with the South Node in Aries: "I must speak because I was silenced." However, without evolving the skipped step of Saturn, the mind may become a prison of distorted logic and authoritarian control.

The chart's 12th house stellium in Virgo—Pluto (3°), Venus (15°), Mars (17°)—reinforces themes of hidden compulsions, spiritual crises, and unconscious patterns. Pluto in this position suggests deep karmic residues stored in the unconscious, particularly concerning purity, service, and control. Mars and Venus in Virgo may indicate an intense, even obsessive drive for perfection or spiritual purity, expressed through distorted acts of service or submission to a higher "plan." In Koresh's case, this may have transformed into fanaticism disguised as devotion, where sexuality, power, and spiritual authority became intertwined in a subterranean struggle for self-purification and control over others.

His Leo stellium with the Sun at 23° in the 11th house, Uranus at 17° and Mercury at 7°, signifies a radically individualistic identity shaped by concepts of destiny, revolution, and self-appointed leadership. The 11th house represents visionary ideals and group identity; however, in Leo, this expression can become egocentric or absolutist—especially when evolution is obstructed. This placement may indicate a deep desire to be part of a divine plan and to guide others toward spiritual awakening, yet with Uranus's distortion, along with the unintegrated Saturn square, the outcome appears as alienation from consensus reality and a compulsion to assume the role of the chosen one or martyr.

The Moon in Aquarius in the 5th house reflects an emotional life shaped by themes of detachment, individuation, and visionary longing. Aquarius suggests a psyche that doesn't easily conform to emotional norms—someone who may feel like an outsider in matters of the heart or who channels their emotional energy into creative or ideological expression. In the 5th house, the Moon seeks recognition, self-expression, and love, but Aquarius adds an impersonal quality, indicating a need to be seen as unique, even exceptional, in emotional or creative arenas. This placement can reflect someone who expresses emotions through ideals rather than intimacy and who may have felt misunderstood or emotionally alienated in early life.

Chiron retrograde at 25° Aquarius, also in the 5th house, introduces a distinct yet thematically linked wound: a profound psychic imprint concerning a sense of not fitting in, especially in the realms of creativity, romantic connections, and the capacity to feel joy and spontaneity. While it is not conjunct the Moon, Chiron in the same house implies that self-expression has historically been wounded, potentially through rejection, ridicule, or a lack of validation from others. This may lead to a soul attempting to heal through performance, ideology, or attracting followers, compensating for the pain of not being genuinely seen or accepted in their unguarded authenticity.

Although not in aspect, the Moon and Chiron in Aquarius in the 5th house reflect a soul with profound evolutionary lessons about creative individuation, emotional authenticity, and the right to exist as one's true self. However, if wounded and unconscious, this individual may seek external validation through ideological performance, leadership, or visionary martyrdom.

David Koresh's chart reveals a volatile karmic mix: an unresolved skipped step (Saturn square the nodes) concerning mental and ideological authority; a South Node-Eris conjunction in Aries that points to past patterns of relational rupture, rebellion, and projected blame; and a powerful unconscious drive (12th house stellium) to combine spiritual control with personal power.

His evolutionary direction was Libra in the 1st house: to learn equanimity, self-awareness, and relational balance. However, the unresolved past took the wheel instead. The voice of the skipped step transformed into doctrinal certainty, the wound of Eris evolved into a war against exclusion, and the Leo-Uranus energy in the 11th house made him the center of a self-defined apocalypse.

Koresh was born with the potential to challenge systemic norms. His unresolved trauma and distorted Saturn confined him to the shadow of his mission: a self-styled messiah seeking vindication whose refusal to evolve became the very fire that consumed him and those who followed.

Paul McCartney

Paul McCartney is a British vocalist, songwriter, composer, bassist, poet, and painter whose influence on popular music is unmatched. His innovative work with The Beatles during the 1960s transformed rock and pop from mere entertainment into a sophisticated and commercially successful art form. Besides his iconic time with The Beatles, McCartney has enjoyed one of the most successful solo careers in history, characterized by record-breaking album sales and sold-out concerts worldwide.

Born in Liverpool, McCartney was the son of James McCartney, a cotton salesman, and Mary McCartney, a devoted midwife who tirelessly rode her bicycle to deliver babies. Her untimely death from breast cancer in October 1956, when McCartney was just 14, profoundly affected him and later inspired the Beatles' poignant ballad, *Let It Be*.

In 1957, McCartney's life changed forever when he met John Lennon at the Woolton Village Fête. Shortly after, he joined Lennon's skiffle group, The Quarrymen, which eventually evolved into The Beatles. The two formed a deep bond, especially after Lennon's mother was tragically killed by a speeding police car in 1958. With his own grief still fresh, McCartney offered emotional support to Lennon, forging a partnership that would become one of the most celebrated songwriting duos in history.

By 1962, McCartney and Lennon had established themselves as the primary songwriters for The Beatles, creating an unprecedented catalog of music that defined an era. With 60 gold records and over 100 million singles sold throughout his career, McCartney is widely regarded as one of the most commercially successful musicians of all time. His 1965 classic *Yesterday* remains one of the most frequently played songs on American radio and television, with an estimated six million broadcasts.

Over the decades, McCartney has received numerous accolades that highlight his artistic achievements and cultural influence. In 2010, he was awarded the U.S. Library of Congress Gershwin Prize for Popular Song, and later that year, he was celebrated by the Kennedy Center. In 2018, he was appointed a Companion of Honour, one of the United Kingdom's most esteemed distinctions.

Paul McCartney
Natal Chart
Jun 18 1942, Thu
2:00 pm BDST −2:00
Liverpool, England
53°N25' 002°W55'
Geocentric
Tropical
Porphyry
True Node
Rating: A

Beyond music, McCartney is a passionate advocate for vegetarianism and animal rights, as well as humanitarian efforts like debt relief for developing countries, landmine removal, and opposition to seal hunting. More than just a rock legend, he has become a national treasure—an enduring symbol of British culture, as classic as warm beer and cricket, woven into the very fabric of the nation's identity.[59] Paul McCartney's chart reveals the signature of a soul shaped by the dynamic tension between self and other, spirit and form, myth and embodiment. At its center is Eris at 5° Aries in the 7th house, a placement that demands the emergence of a bold, autonomous identity—not in solitude, but in the reflection of

---
59 Paraphrased from https://www.britannica.com/biography/Paul-McCartney

relationships. This is not Eris as an outsider or an exile. Here, she serves as a catalyst within the relational field, provoking growth, confrontation, and individuation through the charged terrain of intimacy, partnership, and collaboration. Her presence in Aries is primal: the soul must learn to say "I am" even in the face of love, even when the world would prefer harmony over truth. This Eris insists on presence, not appeasement; on authenticity, not accommodation.

Opposite Eris, Neptune at 27° Virgo rises in the 1st house, forming a wide yet significant opposition. Although the aspect spans just under 8°, it resonates like a low-frequency hum—ambient, persistent, shaping the inner landscape. Neptune here suffuses the self-image with idealism, spiritual yearning, and subtle self-effacement. It suggests a karmic history of playing roles for others, becoming who others needed, merging into collective dreams, or disappearing into service. In this lifetime, the soul may be drawn to perfectionism in appearance or purpose, hoping to earn worth through purity or usefulness. However, Eris resists this dissolving impulse. She demands emergence—not as an ideal, but as a fully embodied, raw, and sometimes uncomfortable truth. The Neptune–Eris polarity describes a fundamental evolutionary dilemma: whether to remain lovable in the eyes of others or to become real in one's own.

This axis reflects a deep evolutionary passage from defining oneself through others to cultivating autonomous self-awareness—but with Eris involved, the path is far from linear, often marked by rupture, confrontation, and the demand for radical honesty in relationship.

Saturn in Gemini in the 9th reflects a deep karmic imprint of dogma, rigid thought, and inherited paradigms. It speaks to a soul shaped by external authorities—religious, cultural, or philosophical—that defined truth and morality in limiting ways. These frameworks may have shaped past lives devoted to intellectual mastery or spiritual service, but now function as evolutionary blocks. Saturn here demands discipline, yet also exposes where the mind has become a prison. Uranus, conjunct Saturn, throws sparks into this structure. It seeks liberation, mental revolution, the breaking of old patterns and the awakening of new perspectives. In Gemini, this fusion of order and upheaval points to language, songwriting, and narrative as evolutionary tools—but only if the voice can be claimed on one's own terms.

The South Node in Pisces, positioned in the 6th house, further illuminates the soul's past: lifetimes immersed in service, sacrifice, and systems that demanded invisibility or spiritual subservience. There may have been beauty and compassion present, but also avoidance—a bypassing of the personal self in favor of the ideal. The North Node in Virgo, located in the 12th house, is an intricate invitation: to bring awareness into the unconscious, to develop discernment within the spiritual realm, and to become precise in compassion. It does not demand withdrawal but rather purification of the inner life, enabling service to be offered without self-erasure. Yet, the square from Saturn and Uranus in Gemini to both nodes guarantees that this evolution will not proceed gently. The path forward is only accessible through rigorous re-examination of belief, thought, and mental conditioning. The soul must choose awareness over illusion, truth over tradition, and voice over silence.

This nodal axis reflects an evolutionary journey from the fluid, idealized world of creative fusion (Pisces South Node) toward Virgo's clarity, discernment, and personal integration. For McCartney, this meant evolving beyond mythic partnerships and emotional enmeshment—especially in songwriting and love—toward a more grounded, self-defined voice. With Eris in Aries in the 7th house, the skipped step points to relational disruption as a catalyst: the break with Lennon, the backlash to Linda, and the unraveling of The Beatles myth were not detours but initiations. His soul was tasked with separating fantasy from function, learning how to honor deep connection without losing inner coherence.

Although Eris does not directly aspect the nodal axis or the Gemini conjunction, her role is thematically and evolutionarily intertwined. She exists at the frontier between self and other, activating the same core struggle: asserting identity in the face of internalized pressures and projected roles. Her opposition to Neptune brings the struggle for selfhood into relational and public arenas, where mythologizing and projection are constant. In McCartney's life, this dynamic manifested not only in romantic partnerships but also in creative and cultural relationships—most famously in his collaboration with John Lennon and the broader phenomenon of Beatlemania. The world projected an image onto him; Eris demanded that he burn through it.

Pluto at 4° Leo in the 11th house, conjunct Mars and trine Eris, offers the evolutionary engine that empowers this individuation. Pluto in Leo seeks transformation through authentic self-expression, creative risk, and emotional leadership. In the 11th house, it signifies the power to influence the collective and ignite the evolution of the group through personal radiance. The trine to Eris provides a clear evolutionary channel: when the soul steps fully into its fire—unapologetic, self-created, creatively sovereign—it unlocks generational change. McCartney's chart, then, is not just the map of a gifted artist, but of a cultural transformer whose voice shaped the collective dream even as he wrestled with it privately.

This nodal axis describes Paul McCartney's evolutionary path from emotional idealism and creative fusion (Pisces South Node) toward clarity, discernment, and self-definition (Virgo North Node). His soul came from a place of merging—musically, romantically, and mythically—but in this life, he was learning to separate, to refine, and to know himself outside of the roles others projected onto him. With Eris in Aries in the 7th house acting as a skipped step, relational conflict became the trigger for growth. The breakup with Lennon, public judgment of his partnership with Linda, and the collapse of The Beatles myth weren't just personal crises—they were necessary disruptions, forcing him to reclaim his voice, identity, and purpose on his own terms.

McCartney's chart is an evolutionary crucible. Eris in Aries challenges Neptune's dreams; Saturn and Uranus fracture old beliefs; the nodes maintain an open bridge between sacrifice and clarity. The tension between projection and presence, myth and reality, conditioning and awakening weaves through every dimension of his life. Yet, through that tension, a new kind of voice emerges—one that carries truth, melody, disruption, and grace all at once.

This is not a chart of escape or quietude; it is a chart of artistic revolt and spiritual reintegration, challenging inherited structures while remaining open to wonder. Here, the soul is not learning to disappear—it is learning to exist fully, in a world that would prefer the mask. Through relationships, creativity, and vision, Paul McCartney's soul writes its way out of illusion and into evolutionary fire.

8th House ~ The Sacred Commitment

"Until you make the unconscious conscious, it will direct your life, and you will call it fate."

—Carl Jung

The 8th house symbolizes the yin fixed expression of the water triad, representing the profound undercurrents of existence where transformation is inevitable. This realm belongs to the underworld, the domain of Pluto and Scorpio, where we confront the unseen forces that shape our lives. Within the depths of this house, we encounter our shadow, the repository of our unprocessed traumas, desires, and emotional remnants. Pluto governs this sphere, revealing the hidden patterns and psychological imprints that remain unacknowledged and unresolved. Through its challenges, we face the primal forces of our unconscious, urging us toward transformation.

Scorpio symbolizes the archetype through which we confront the truth of our identity and the irrevocable reality of who we are not and cannot become. In this confrontation, we shed illusions and face our deepest fears, desires, and compulsions. There is no superficial engagement with life here; the 8th house demands total surrender. It serves as an initiation into the mysteries of existence, a descent into the crucible where the soul evolves through the fire of experience.

The 8th house symbolizes the alchemical potential of deep relationships. It is through our interactions with others, especially regarding shared resources, intimacy, trust, and power dynamics, that we are drawn into the transformative crucible. Love and loss, betrayal and loyalty, surrender and resistance all unfold within this house, with each experience acting as a catalyst for self-discovery and rebirth. The magnetic allure of this house is undeniable, pulling us toward the elements that mirror our unconscious desires and unresolved wounds. Whether through passion, psychology, esoteric studies, or life-changing events, the 8th house requires total immersion into the depths of existence, where we are either consumed by our attachments or liberated by surpassing them.

Evolutionary Astrology teaches that the soul evolves through emotional integration. Merely intellectualizing experiences or detaching from them is insufficient; true growth arises when we allow ourselves to feel, process, and embody the lessons that life offers. The water trinity—Cancer, Scorpio,

Pisces—illustrates this process of involution: Spirit (Neptune) differentiates into Soul (Scorpio) and Ego (Cancer), representing a natural sequence in the zodiacal order of evolution. The shift from the 4th house Ego/Cancer to the 8th house Soul/Scorpio signifies the journey from personal security toward the soul's deeper evolutionary purpose, culminating in the 12th house Spirit/Pisces, where dissolution into the greater whole occurs. Within this framework, the 8th house serves as a vital bridge, a realm where the soul must confront its karmic entanglements and learn to navigate the intricate interplay between power, vulnerability, and surrender.

When an individual resists the transformative lessons of the 8th house, spiritual bypass can occur. Without genuine shadow integration, the illusion of transcendence creates distortions in spiritual identity. This is the trap of spiritual glamour, where enlightenment is proclaimed yet remains disconnected from the deeper, unresolved aspects of the psyche. The 8th house demands authenticity; it does not allow for half-truths or evasions. Its lessons are often challenging, but they are essential for true spiritual maturation.

This house symbolizes a sacred commitment to evolution, an agreement made at the soul level to fully engage with the depths of existence. Those who enter its realm willingly, surrendering to its initiatory process, emerge with an unshakable wisdom forged in the depths of their own being. Each individual examined in this study stands as a testament to the success or failure of embracing the transformative potential of the 8th house. Their journeys illuminate the essential truth that only by descending into the depths can we rise into the fullness of our becoming.

Marilyn Monroe

On June 13, 1926, Gladys Baker left her 2-week-old daughter, Norma Jeane Mortenson, in a foster home in Hawthorne, California, marking the beginning of a lifelong, fragile bond between mother and daughter. Despite a challenging start, Monroe's early years in a devoted foster home were her most stable, characterized by visits from her mother, who made an effort to stay involved.

Baker, however, exhibited signs of mental instability. On one occasion, she attempted to take her daughter by force, stuffing her into a duffel bag before being stopped. Nevertheless, when Monroe turned seven, Baker brought her home. Initially, she tried to provide a stable life, but a series of losses—including the death of a long-lost son and her grandfather's suicide—triggered a breakdown. Diagnosed with paranoid schizophrenia, Baker was institutionalized.

Monroe later found some peace while living with "Aunt Ana," a family friend who introduced her to Christian Science. During that time, she discovered she had a half-sister, which sparked a lifelong bond through letters and visits.

In 1946, as Monroe's modeling career gained momentum and her marriage to Jim Dougherty faltered, Baker returned to live with her. For a brief time, family life felt hopeful again. However, Baker soon vanished, claiming she was moving to Oregon—only for Monroe to discover that she had married a man who already had a family. Studios pressured Monroe to maintain a narrative that both her parents were dead.

Trouble resurfaced when Baker, still alive and manic, was hospitalized again after showing up at Monroe's home. Despite her rise to stardom in *Gentlemen Prefer Blondes* and *The Seven-Year Itch*, Monroe's life was unraveling—rocky marriages to Joe DiMaggio and Arthur Miller, and increasing dependence on pills and doctors mirrored her mother's path.

In 1961, Monroe was briefly admitted to a New York sanatorium. Soon after, Baker attempted suicide. During a tense reunion, Monroe urged her to take medication, while Baker insisted that prayer was enough. As she left, she told her daughter, "You're such a good girl, Norma Jeane," and disappeared again.

Later that year, Monroe's life ended—her body succumbing to years of drug abuse, echoing the legacy of instability and pain passed down from mother to daughter.[60]

With Eris at 1° Aries in the 8th house, Marilyn Monroe bore an evolutionary mandate to disrupt inherited power structures surrounding intimacy, sexuality, and control. This Eris placement signifies a soul driven to reveal what lies beneath the surface—both within herself and the collective. Her life was characterized by a battle to assert agency over her own body and image in a culture that imposed fantasy and desire upon her, often at the cost of her humanity. The 8th house placement suggests

---

60 Paraphrased from https://www.biography.com/actors/marilyn-monroe-mother-relationship

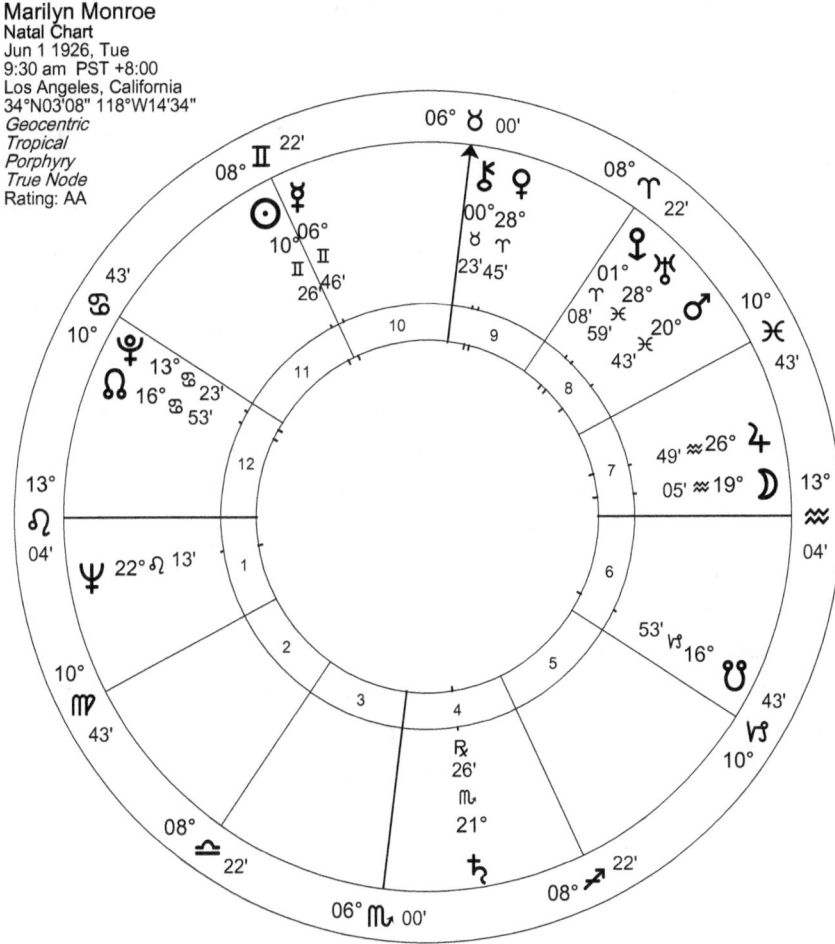

that transformation, trauma, and taboo were not merely themes—they were initiatory gateways.

Uranus at 28° Pisces in the same house, just behind Eris, adds a dimension of psychic volatility, sudden breaks, and destabilizing awakenings in the realm of trust and shared vulnerability. Uranus's presence amplifies the unpredictable and isolating nature of Monroe's emotional life—relationships brought both intensity and upheaval, often awakening deeper wounds instead of healing them.

Mars at 20° Pisces, also in the 8th house, indicates an instinctive drive influenced by dissolution, empathy, and the unseen. Mars here reflects a tendency to act through emotional osmosis, often absorbing collective projections of desire and surrendering to them at a cost to the self. The combination of Eris, Uranus, and Mars in the 8th suggests a karmic pattern involving exploitation, disempowerment, and eventual resistance at the soul level.

Venus at 28° Aries in the 9th house introduces an evolutionary thread around the feminine principle in relationship to truth, belief, and higher knowledge. This placement speaks to a soul seeking to define its philosophy of love—raw, brave, and unfiltered—and not shaped by external expectations. Venus in Aries desires to lead in love, yet in the 9th house, that leadership is spiritualized: it becomes a quest for authenticity through desire. Monroe's Venus here suggests her beauty and sensual magnetism were not just personal traits, but vehicles for deeper teachings about autonomy, projection, and the disillusionment of idealized love.

Chiron at 1° Taurus in the 9th house introduces the theme of wounding through belief systems, value frameworks, and the quest for meaning. Her soul carried a wound around self-worth, likely stemming from early abandonment and cultural narratives that defined her worth through others' perspectives. Chiron here suggests that Monroe sought truth and healing through education, philosophy, or spiritual exploration—but found these paths equally fraught with pain.

Her Moon at 19° Aquarius and Jupiter at 26° Aquarius in the 7th house place a strong emphasis on relational evolution—balancing freedom and intimacy, belonging and detachment. The Moon in Aquarius reflects emotional eccentricity and a deep yearning to be understood as unique, while Jupiter expands her role as a cultural mirror, offering the collective a reflection of its own longings and contradictions.

Saturn at 21° Scorpio retrograde in the 4th house indicates profound karmic patterns rooted in the family system—particularly concerning secrecy, abandonment, and shame. Its square to the Moon signifies a fundamental tension between emotional vulnerability and internalized judgment. Saturn retrograde represents lessons left uncompleted in past lives, now requiring inner restructuring and facing survival fears and feelings of powerlessness.

The Sun at 10° Gemini in the 11th house, conjunct Mercury at 6° Gemini in the 10th, describes a brilliant communicator whose identity was shaped in the public eye. The 11th house Sun symbolizes a soul aligned with collective themes, while Mercury in the 10th indicates a public role in shaping discourse, image, and perception. Her iconic status grew from this dynamic—she became both messenger and message, embodying an archetype larger than life.

Her Pluto at 13° Cancer, conjunct the North Node at 16° Cancer, both positioned in the 12th house, reveals deep soul work: recovering emotional security, ancestral memory, and inner nurturance through surrender, spiritual solitude, and ego dissolution. Opposing this is the South Node at 16° Capricorn in the 6th house, which reflects a karmic inheritance of striving, service, and control—often at the expense of emotional fulfillment. The Eris square to this axis challenges the polarity: it calls for a break from performance and repression, demanding truth from the underworld.

Neptune at 22° Leo in the 1st house gave Monroe the aura of a dream incarnate. It bestowed glamour, mystique, and psychic permeability—but also blurred her identity, leaving her vulnerable to projection and erasure. Neptune's rulership of Mars and Uranus in Pisces connects personal agency and sexual awakening to a larger mythic and sacrificial narrative.

Monroe's life embodied the paradox of Eris in the 8th: the power to transform through vulnerability, the cost of being desired, and the enduring wound of being seen but not known. Her chart speaks of a soul whose disruption was as much internal as cultural—who, even in tragedy, revealed the deeper truth of feminine complexity behind the screen.

Maya Angelou

Maya Angelou, born Marguerite Ann Johnson on April 4, 1928, in St. Louis, Missouri, led a life marked by both challenges and remarkable accomplishments. At the age of seven, during a visit to her mother in St. Louis, she experienced a traumatic sexual assault by her mother's boyfriend. In a heartbreaking turn of events, her uncles took justice into their own hands and killed him. Overwhelmed by the trauma, young Maya fell into silence, refraining from speaking for nearly five years.

When she was very young, her parents separated, and she and her brother Bailey went to live with their grandmother in Stamps, Arkansas. Bailey lovingly gave her the nickname "Maya," which she kept for the rest of her life.

Maya Angelou
Natal Chart
Apr 4 1928, Wed
2:10 pm CST +6:00
Salcedo, Missouri
36°N53'20" 089°W41'
Geocentric
Tropical
Porphyry
True Node
Rating: A
From Birth Certificate (CAH, AA

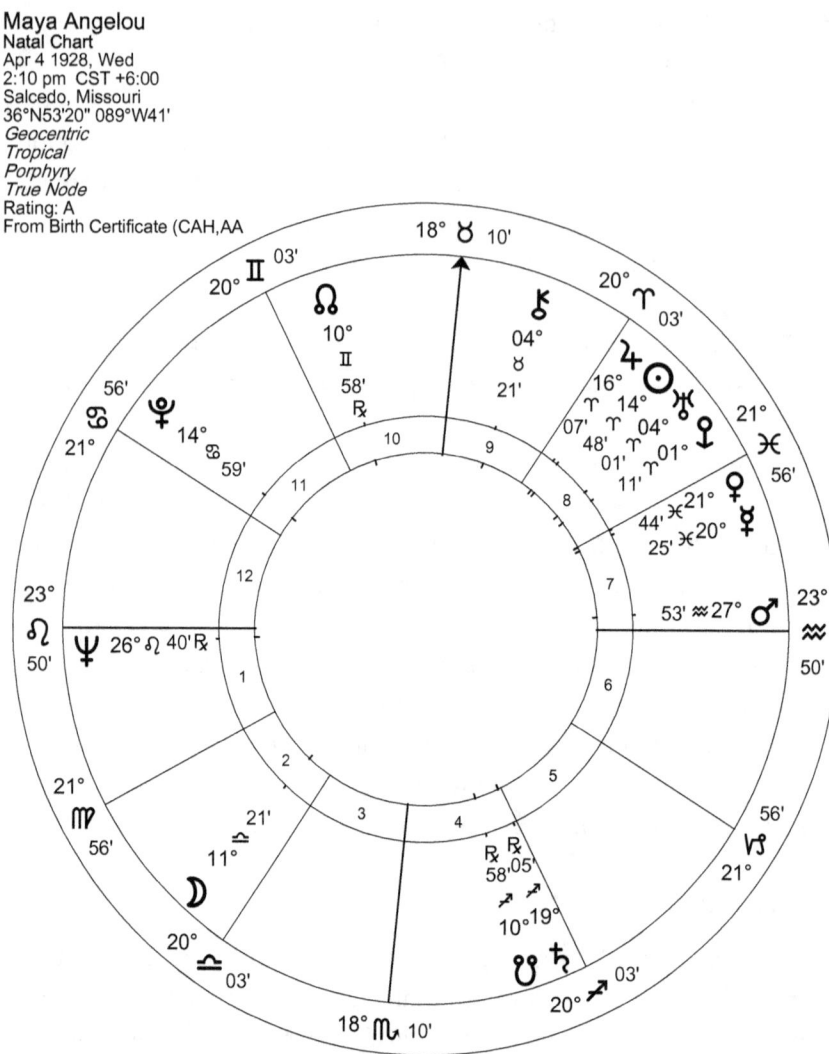

    Growing up in the segregated South, Maya experienced unfair treatment because of the color of her skin. During that quiet time when she stopped speaking, she developed a deep love for reading and writing.

    At the age of 16, Maya became a mother to her son, Guy, and worked hard to care for him. In the 1950s, she embarked on a successful career in the performing arts—singing, dancing, and acting on stage. She even toured internationally with a production of *Porgy and Bess* and later earned an Emmy Award nomination for her role in the TV series *Roots*.

Maya was a powerful advocate in the Civil Rights Movement. She collaborated with leaders such as Dr. Martin Luther King Jr. and Malcolm X to advocate for equality and justice. She played a key role in organizing events and utilized her writing and performance skills to support significant causes.

In the 1960s, Maya lived in Africa, where she worked as a teacher and a writer. She learned more about history and culture, which helped shape her powerful voice as a storyteller and leader.

In 1972, Maya made history by becoming the first black woman to have her screenplay adapted into a movie, *Georgia, Georgia*. However, it was her writing that catapulted her to global fame. Her book *I Know Why the Caged Bird Sings*, published in 1969, recounted the story of her early life and became a bestseller, inspiring millions.

Maya also wrote many beautiful poems, including *Still I Rise*, *Phenomenal Woman*, and *On the Pulse of Morning*. In 1993, she read *On the Pulse of Morning* at President Bill Clinton's inauguration, winning a Grammy Award for her powerful performance.

Throughout her life, Maya Angelou received many honors, including the Presidential Medal of Freedom, which is the highest award a civilian can receive in the United States. She passed away on May 28, 2014, at the age of 86.

Maya Angelou will always be remembered as a trailblazer, a talented writer, and a courageous voice for justice and hope. Her words continue to inspire people of all ages around the world.[61]

Eris at 1° Aries in Maya Angelou's 8th house manifests through the intense crucible of transformation, trauma, and profound encounters with power and survival. In Aries, Eris embodies the evolutionary drive of a spiritual warrior who must reclaim her voice and agency through the fires of deep emotional and psychological initiation. The 8th house amplifies this placement by necessitating the confrontation of the soul's core wounds—especially those related to betrayal, abandonment, sexual violation, and collective ancestral trauma. Eris in this house is never about comfort; she represents the fierce force of reconstitution after everything else has been burned away.

Eris is conjunct Uranus at 4° Aries, also in the 8th house, infusing this placement with disruptive, liberating energy. The evolutionary intention

---

61 Paraphrased from https://www.biography.com/authors-writers/maya-angelou

here is revolution at the deepest level of the psyche—not just for the individual, but on a collective scale. Uranus and Eris in the 8th symbolize a soul born to shatter taboos and expose systemic oppression, particularly regarding race, gender, and trauma. Maya Angelou's life testifies to this: her bold self-revelation, her poetic testimony of childhood trauma, and her refusal to be silenced all reflect this initiatory Uranus–Eris force. These planets mark a soul that cannot hide; it must erupt in authenticity. Their presence in the 8th house links directly to the nodal story—what was inherited in silence and suppression must be spoken, taught, and brought into the world as living truth.

The South Node at 10° Sagittarius is widely conjunct Saturn retrograde at 19° Sagittarius in the 4th house, while the North Node sits at 10° Gemini in the 10th. This polarity highlights the evolutionary movement from ancestral memory, moral conviction, and cultural inheritance (South Node–Saturn in the 4th) toward a public path of communication, teaching, and storytelling (North Node in Gemini in the 10th). Eris in Aries in the 8th resonates with this nodal axis, supplying the courage to transform private trauma into public truth. The task is translation: to carry wisdom and hard-won experience from the ancestral depths into language that can reach, teach, and liberate others.

Saturn retrograde in Sagittarius in the 4th house reinforces the karmic weight of ancestral memory and cultural responsibility. Though not in aspect to Eris, Saturn resonates strongly with her Sun–Jupiter conjunction in Aries, symbolizing the discipline and inner authority that enabled her to transform private wounds into public testimony. Saturn in the 4th suggests that her voice was forged in the crucible of lineage and loss, while its retrograde motion shows how deeply internalized these lessons were across lifetimes. In this incarnation, she was called to break through that weight, transforming it into resilience and moral authority.

The Sun at 14° Aries conjunct Jupiter at 16° Aries in the 8th house gave Angelou a bold creative force and radiant self-expression. When the Sun and Jupiter fuse here, the soul is driven to seek meaning, growth, and truth by facing life's most intense passages of transformation — trauma, intimacy, loss, regeneration, and empowerment.The 8th house demands immersion in experiences that strip away false layers of identity. For Angelou, the Sun–Jupiter conjunction means her growth and creative vitality emerged not despite suffering, but through it. Her art, poetry, and autobiography bear witness to transformation of pain into wisdom.

Jupiter in the 8th intensifies the urge to speak the unspeakable — sexuality, race, trauma, power, death. With the Sun here, her personal identity became inseparable from this mission. She embodied the 8th house courage to shine light on hidden truths. Jupiter expands the Sun's life force, but here this faith is tested again and again. The evolutionary message is that spiritual wisdom is not found in avoidance, but in embracing shadow and transmuting it into light. Angelou's resilience and her repeated self-reinventions reflect this cycle of death and rebirth of identity.

A cardinal T-square deepened this dynamic: the Moon at 11° Libra in the 2nd house opposes the Sun–Jupiter conjunction in Aries, while both square Pluto at 14° Cancer in the 11th house. The Moon longed for peace and stability, but the Aries Sun–Jupiter demanded bold assertion. Pluto at the apex compelled transformation through community, activism, and collective empowerment. This configuration fueled her poetry and public presence, making her private struggles inseparable from her collective mission.

Mercury at 20° Pisces conjunct Venus at 21° Pisces in the 7th house gave her the voice of the mystic and poet. This union softened Aries' fiery edge with lyrical empathy, enabling her to express the inexpressible. It allowed her to turn raw trauma into words that resonated universally, merging personal experience with the collective emotional field.

Mars at 27° Aquarius in the 7th house added rebellious clarity to her partnerships and activism, echoing Uranus's disruptive signature and underscoring her refusal to conform.

Chiron at 4° Taurus in the 9th house represents a wound in belief, value, and voice, but also a profound teaching gift. Out of this pain came wisdom, which she offered to others through education, writing, and mentorship.

The North Node in Gemini in the 10th defined her evolutionary aim: to claim her public voice, not through abstract proclamation, but through accessible communication—storytelling, dialogue, poetry, and testimony. This was her destiny: to turn life into language and to offer that language as liberation.

Maya Angelou's chart tells the story of a soul compelled to break silence. Eris conjunct Uranus in the 8th house demanded truth at the deepest levels; Saturn on the South Node in the 4th carried ancestral weight that could not be ignored; the Sun–Jupiter conjunction in the 5th transmuted survival into artistry; and the North Node in Gemini in the 10th called her to bring all of it into the public sphere. Her legacy reveals the power of Eris in Aries in the 8th: to make visible what is hidden, to turn fracture into strength, and to speak the unspeakable so that others may find their own liberation.

Andy Warhol

Born Andrew Warhola, Andy Warhol was the youngest of three boys in a family of poor Czechoslovakian immigrants. His strict father, Andrei, saw promise in him early on. Before dying of peritonitis when Andy was 13, Andrei said to his eldest son, "You're going to be very proud of Andy."

Andy's mother, Julia, was deeply devoted to him. Believing he needed extra care, she stayed close to him throughout her life—cooking, cleaning, and taking care of his many cats, all named Sam. She frequently encouraged him to find a good wife.

As a child, Andy was small, sensitive, and often bullied. He later described himself as a "sissy" and "momma's boy." At the age of eight, he contracted rheumatic fever, which caused tremors and required extended bed rest. A relapse left him bedridden once more, and the illness made him pale and self-conscious about his appearance.

Though introverted, Andy's artistic gifts stood out. In high school, he kept to himself, saying, "I wasn't very close to anyone." However, at Carnegie Institute of Technology (now Carnegie Mellon University), he found his place. Classmate Martha Sutherland recalled his magnetism: "He gathered people around him... He was different... and good. His drawing was marvelous."

Despite his talent, Andy struggled academically. In his first year, he failed "Thought and Expression," a writing course. He often submitted unconventional work—rushed assignments, sliced paintings displayed as multiple pieces, and experiments that perplexed his professors.

Warhol's unique style divided the faculty. Fellow student Sidney Simon remarked, "They couldn't teach him anything, and he couldn't learn anything." Faculty reviews of student work were decided by committee, and he often advanced by just a single vote. One professor later admitted,

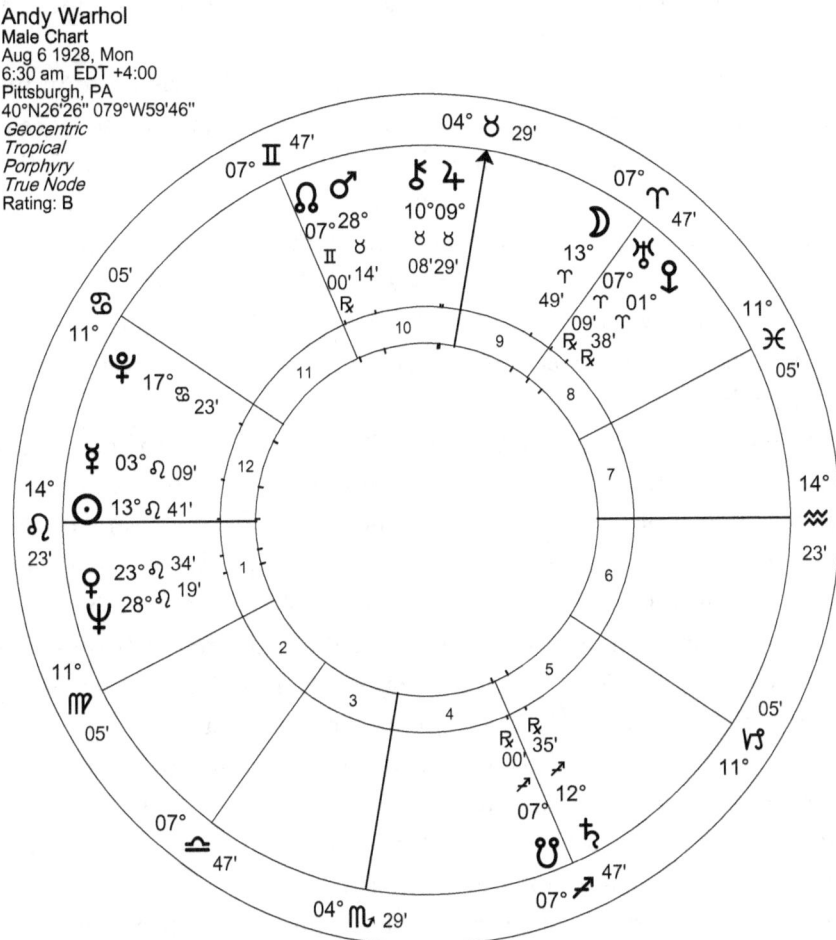

"If anyone had asked me who was least likely to succeed, I would've said Andy Warhola."[62]

With Eris retrograde at 1° Aries in the 8th house, Andy Warhol's chart opens with a soul signature forged in the crucible of confrontation and disruption. In Aries, Eris burns with the fire of radical self-definition, and in the 8th house, she expresses through deep psychological transformation—especially in areas that society prefers to keep hidden: power, death, sex, money, and vulnerability. Warhol didn't provoke through overt rebellion. His disruption came through aestheticized stillness, repetition,

---

62 Paraphrased from https://crystalbridges.org/blog/early-life-andy-warhol/

and stylized detachment. He disturbed the cultural unconscious by reflecting it—flattened, silkscreened, multiplied.

Her wide conjunction to Uranus retrograde at 7° Aries, also in the 8th, amplifies this evolutionary drive. Though not tight, their resonance is unmistakable: a revolutionary impulse aimed at unearthing the collective shadow. This suggests a karmic history shaped by rupture, alienation, and trauma—now returned in this life not to be repeated, but to be transformed into cultural confrontation. Warhol's work—electric chairs, suicides, car crashes, endless Marilyns—invited viewers to see what they normally turn away from. He didn't explain the violence of modern life; he aestheticized it until it became impossible to ignore.

Beneath this eruptive pair, Pluto at 17° Cancer in the 12th house holds the deeper evolutionary wound. Pluto in Cancer suggests soul memory shaped by emotional control, familial imprinting, and the ancestral residue of abandonment or enmeshment. The 12th house placement hides these dynamics under layers of unconscious defense. Warhol's compulsive visual production, emotional opacity, and stylized identity reflect this hidden karmic legacy. He did not express emotion—he ritualized it, embalming feeling into form, repeating imagery until it no longer hurt.

The South Node at 7° Sagittarius in the 4th house, conjunct Saturn retrograde in the 5th, points to a karmic inheritance of belief systems, isolation, and culturally defined identity—possibly linked to religion, exile, or tradition. Saturn intensifies this signature, suggesting that Warhol brought in rigid structures: inner walls built from inherited truths that once kept him safe, but now limit the soul's evolution. His early life—marked by immigrant Catholic roots, childhood illness, emotional dependency on his mother, and closeted sexuality—echoes this karmic insulation. Sagittarius here may also imply moral or philosophical certainty from the past, now serving as an outdated inner compass.

The soul's evolutionary task lies with the North Node at 7° Gemini in the 10th house, which calls for public communication, cultural participation, and intellectual fragmentation. Gemini dismantles certainty. It reflects contradiction, multiplicity, and surface. In the 10th house, this evolutionary arc demands expression through career, media, and collective engagement—not from the pedestal of authority, but from the mirror of pop culture. Warhol met this precisely. He didn't define truth—he fractured it into endlessly reproducible symbols.

Mars at 28° Taurus, conjunct the North Node, empowers this evolutionary agenda with will, endurance, and repetition. Mars in Taurus builds by doing the same thing again and again, transmuting form through fixation. Warhol's silkscreens, his obsession with surface and commodity, his cold precision—these all reflect Mars working steadily toward evolutionary goals. Conjunct the North Node, this Mars indicates a soul that evolves through action in the public sphere. Warhol didn't merely think about culture—he materialized its contradictions and sold them back to it.

The nodal axis is further shaped by the Chiron–Jupiter conjunction in Taurus, close to the North Node. With Chiron in Taurus, the soul carries a deep imprint of insecurity around worth, survival, and belonging. Conjunct Jupiter, this wound expands into a lifelong search for meaning through art, beauty, and the commodification of creativity. Warhol's obsession with consumer products (*Campbell's Soup, Coca-Cola*) shows how he both confronted and elevated questions of value.Warhol transformed his personal alienation (awkward physical appearance, outsider status, illness in childhood) into a Jupiterian message about the nature of value, fame, and consumption in modern society. Warhol blurred the line between the sacred and profane, turning ordinary objects into icons.

His Sun at 13° Leo in the 12th house, widely conjunct Mercury at 3° Leo, underscores his mythic function. The Sun in the 12th does not shine personally—it radiates symbolically, unconsciously. Warhol's identity was not fixed; it was projected, elusive, and archetypal. He did not perform himself—he performed culture's projection of the self. Mercury here trines Eris, linking language to disruption, image to fracture. His famously evasive interviews and deadpan wit were not evasions of personality—they were his method of deconstructing identity.

Layered over this is the Venus–Neptune conjunction at 23° and 28° Leo in the 1st house—his public mask. This pairing made Warhol both object and subject of glamor. Venus gave allure, aesthetic instinct, and desire; Neptune infused mystique, idealization, and erasure. In Leo, these forces crave recognition, but with Neptune involved, what is seen is never what is real. Warhol wore beauty like armor, projected sexuality as abstraction, and transformed intimacy into image. His queerness is here—romanticized, hidden, stylized, yet never fully embodied. Love, for him, was distance. Identity, a costume. Intimacy, an illusion curated by the artist and consumed by the viewer.

Andy Warhol's chart reveals a soul born to fracture the cultural mirror, not by breaking it, but by flattening its depth. Eris in the 8th stirred from beneath, challenging what society refuses to see. Pluto in the 12th buried feeling so deep that only repetition could safely express it. The nodal axis moved from karmic withdrawal and rigid belief to public fragmentation and symbolic detachment. He became a mirror of the world—not as it wished to be, but as it truly was.

9th House ~ What Is Greater Than Self?

The 9th house embodies the yang mutable expression of the fire triad, representing a dynamic phase of expansion and exploration governed by Jupiter and associated with Sagittarius. Here, personal ideas and beliefs originally formed in the 3rd house converge with the broader currents of collective thought. It is a realm where the quest for meaning extends beyond the immediate environment, drawing individuals toward religion, philosophy, metaphysics, and higher education. The 9th house is where one strives to understand life from a broader perspective, driven by an intrinsic curiosity about the workings of the universe and a desire to uncover its underlying truths.

This house embodies the pursuit of personal philosophy, a way of interpreting existence that infuses life with purpose. Here, belief systems take shape, influenced by both subjective experiences and exposure to collective teachings. The beliefs fostered in the 9th house affect how an individual perceives reality, guiding their approach to challenges, opportunities, and the unknown. Yet, these interpretations are not absolute. Truth, as viewed through Jupiter's domain, is inherently personal, tinted by the lens of one's conditioning, education, and cultural influences. In the 12th house, through Pisces and Neptune, the individual ultimately faces the ineffable, all-encompassing Truth—one that transcends human constructs and dissolves all separateness.

Jupiter, Sagittarius, and the 9th house are closely linked to the concept of Natural Law, which posits that fundamental truths are self-evident in nature and can be accessed through direct experience rather than imposed doctrine. This archetype embodies an intrinsic sense of justice and order, distinguishing between wisdom that arises organically and belief systems dictated by societal structures. In its highest form, the 9th house nurtures intuitive, right-brain awareness—the ability to perceive reality beyond linear logic. It serves as a domain for the teacher, rather than the student, where lived experiences are transformed into knowledge that can be shared with others. In contrast to laws established by human institutions, the 9th house resonates with a greater, universal rhythm—one that speaks to a deeper sense of moral and spiritual alignment.

The expansive nature of Jupiter, however, presents its own challenges. Sagittarius, Jupiter's archetype, forms a natural square with Virgo and Pisces, creating an inner tension between discernment and faith, humility and grandiosity, and service and spiritual idealism. When distorted, Jupiter's enthusiasm and conviction may harden into self-righteousness, where belief in one's personal truth overrides the understanding that truth itself is vast and multifaceted. The opposition to Gemini, the sign of curiosity and multiplicity, further illustrates this potential for imbalance. When an individual overly identifies with their beliefs, they may resist alternative viewpoints, becoming rigid or dogmatic. There is a risk of intellectual arrogance, where the urge to share knowledge transforms into an unchecked desire to be right.

Yet, the core lesson of the 9th house is that wisdom is not static; it evolves as an individual's consciousness expands. Through travel, education, and direct experience, the boundaries of understanding continue to stretch, revealing that truth is never confined to a single perspective. When functioning at its highest expression, this archetype fosters an ever-deepening connection to something more significant than the self—a source of meaning that is both personal and universal. This is the house of the seeker, the pilgrim, and the philosopher, who understands that the journey is as vital as the destination.

Pope Francis

Pope Francis was the head of the Catholic Church and sovereign of the Vatican City State from March 13, 2013, until he died in 2025. He was the first Jesuit pope, the first Latin American pope, and the first pope born or raised outside Europe since the 8th-century Syrian pope Gregory III. Known for his humble, informal style, Francis earned praise for his accessibility and "no frills" approach. Born Jorge Mario Bergoglio in Buenos

196 Eris

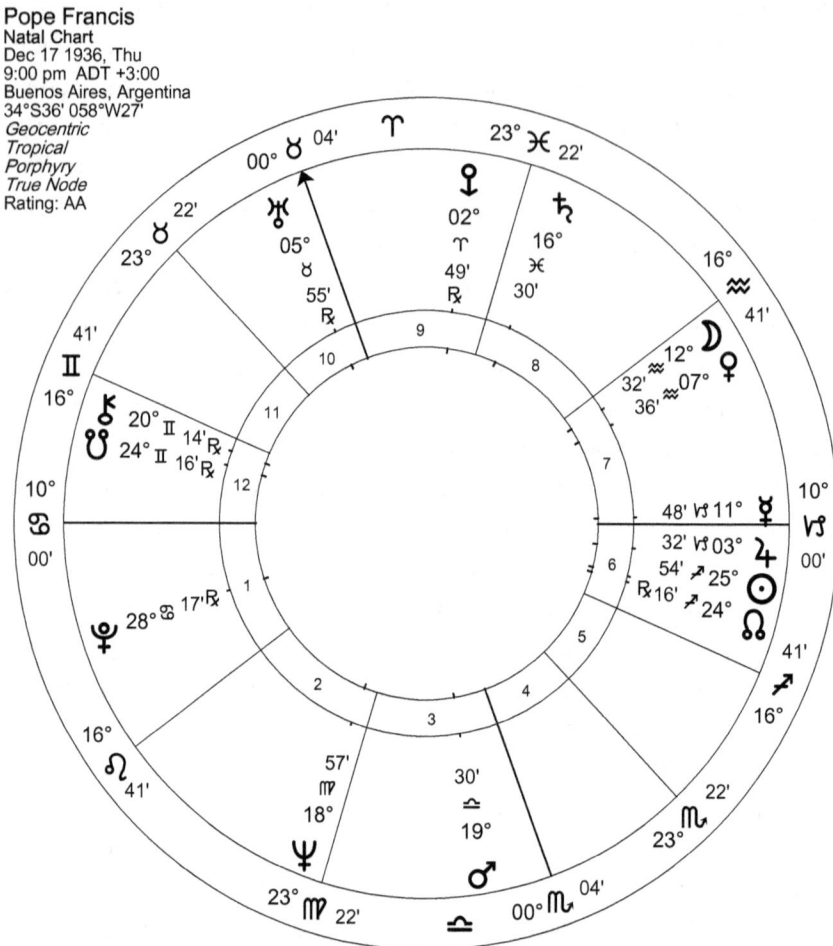

Aires, Argentina, he had a modest early life, working as a bouncer, janitor, and food lab technician before a serious illness led to a spiritual awakening. This experience prompted him to join the Jesuits and eventually become their leader in Argentina.

As Archbishop of Buenos Aires, he led Argentina through an economic crisis and was later made a cardinal by Pope John Paul II. After Pope Benedict XVI's resignation, Bergoglio was elected pontiff and chose the name Francis, honoring St. Francis of Assisi for his dedication to the poor and the environment.

Francis consistently emphasized mercy, compassion, social justice, and interfaith dialogue. He enhanced the role of women in Vatican leadership, promoted pastoral care for marginalized groups, including LGBT individuals, and emphasized the importance of environmental protection by highlighting the impact of consumerism and ecological damage.

A strong opponent of the death penalty, Francis called it an affront to human dignity. His diplomatic efforts include helping to restore US–Cuba relations, negotiating with China over bishop appointments, and urging compassion in immigration policies. He also apologized for the Church's role in the cultural genocide of indigenous peoples in Canada.

Before his passing in 2025, he released *Hope*, the first memoir by a pope, offering personal reflections and reinforcing his message of hope, reconciliation, and compassion.[63]

In Pope Francis's natal chart, Eris retrograde at 2° Aries in the 9th house signifies a soul with a long evolutionary history of confronting and disrupting entrenched belief systems, religious dogmas, and culturally sanctioned truths. This placement reflects a life mission rooted in transforming collective worldviews. In Aries, Eris manifests as a fiery, bold, and self-initiating force, unwilling to passively accept inherited philosophies and feeling compelled to forge a path toward spiritual authenticity through action. Her retrograde motion adds depth, representing lifetimes of inwardly held rebellion and suppressed confrontation, maturing into a capacity to disrupt the outer consensus from a place of integrated experience.

Eris forms an out-of-sign trine to Pluto at 28° Cancer retrograde in the 1st house, revealing a core dynamic of empowered transformation through truth-telling. Pluto in the 1st house indicates a soul undergoing a profound evolutionary metamorphosis of identity. In Cancer, this Plutonian journey is deeply emotional and rooted in karmic attachments to safety, family, and tribal affiliations. The trine from Eris in Aries brings volcanic courage to this process, catalyzing the shedding of conditioned identities that once sought refuge in tradition. For Pope Francis, this aspect reflects the empowerment to confront not only the ideological frameworks of the world but also the inherited emotional structures that have historically defined him. The trine flows as a natural inner alignment between his transformative self-expression and the bold challenge to ideological systems. It empowered him to disrupt with emotional depth and to reform belief structures without losing his center. This evolutionary strength enabled

---

63 Paraphrased from https://en.wikipedia.org/wiki/Pope_Francis

him to remain in the institution of the Church while radically challenging its limitations from within.

Eris' role in this chart cannot be fully understood outside the intense evolutionary crucible represented by the mutable grand cross, which features the Sun at 25° Sagittarius, the North Node at 24° Sagittarius, the South Node at 24° Gemini, Chiron at 20° Gemini, Saturn at 16° Pisces, and Neptune at 18° Virgo. The conjunction of the Sun and North Node in the 6th house reveals a karmic identity shaped through lifetimes of spiritual service, religious authority, and the embodiment of ethical and philosophical principles. There is wisdom here, but also a history of over-identification with belief systems—an attachment to righteousness or hierarchical spiritual structures. The opposition to the South Node and Chiron in Gemini in the 12th house introduces a new evolutionary direction: the relinquishment of certainty, the embrace of paradox, and the healing of the soul through surrender to divine intelligence rather than imposed doctrine. Chiron in Gemini suggests a core wound regarding communication, fragmentation of thought, or past silencing—now becoming a gateway for healing through dialogue, listening, and the sacred transmission of inclusive truth.

Yet Eris' evolutionary pressure does not unfold quietly. She squares Chiron at 20° Gemini in the 12th house, as well as the South Node at 24° Gemini, the North Node at 24° Sagittarius, and the Sun at 25° Sagittarius. These aspects form a dynamic cross between the 9th, 6th, and 12th houses—linking the axes of truth, service, and spiritual surrender. The square to Chiron and the South Node in Gemini reflects a karmic imprint of fragmented thinking, wounds around communication or voice, and intellectual strategies of avoidance or over-rationalization. With Chiron in the 12th, there exists a soul memory of being silenced, cast out, or spiritually exiled—perhaps for speaking inconvenient truths or being a messenger in an era that could not receive it. The Eris square to Chiron confronts these wounds directly, demanding that the voice be reclaimed, not merely for personal healing but in service to collective evolution.

The square to the North Node and Sun in Sagittarius adds further tension—one that shapes the very direction of the soul's growth. The Sun-North Node conjunction in the 6th house reflects an evolutionary journey of becoming: embodying moral clarity, living truth through humble service, and aligning the personality with a higher principle. However, the square from Eris raises the question: *Whose truth? Whose morality?* There is no smooth path here. Eris in Aries challenges this conjunction to ensure that any truth claimed must be personally fought for—stripped of pretense, severed from dogma, and reborn through confrontation with both internal and external authority. This is not about preaching inherited doctrine; it's about igniting truth from within and expressing it through work, words, and example.

Eris serves as a warrior gatekeeper, applying pressure on the nodal axis to evolve beyond outdated paradigms. The square to the South Node in Gemini highlights the karmic temptation to intellectualize or retreat into abstract arguments and duality. The square to the North Node in Sagittarius demands boldness, faith, and the courage to speak the whole truth—even when it contradicts orthodoxy or institutional policy. The square to the Sun brings everything home to the core of identity: the very purpose of this lifetime involves stepping into the fire of ideological conflict, not to dominate, but to initiate renewal.

This Eris-driven T-square is embedded within the larger grand cross, which includes Saturn at 16° Pisces in the 8th house and Neptune at 18° Virgo in the 2nd. Saturn in Pisces adds karmic gravity to the spiritual path, particularly around surrender, grief, and emotional maturity. Neptune in Virgo highlights the evolutionary need to purify values, strip away illusions, and spiritualize material life through humility. The entire cross functions as an evolutionary crucible: Pope Francis must reconcile service and surrender, truth and sacrifice, humility and spiritual authority—all while being pulled between karmic memory and future calling.

Saturn in Pisces in the 8th house anchors this cross in the deep waters of surrender, karmic accountability, and the transformation of power. This placement of Saturn brings a heavy legacy, possibly rooted in institutional control or spiritual repression, which now demands a more compassionate and transcendent form of authority. It challenges individuals to hold space for loss, grief, and the death of outdated identities or systems in order to build something more inclusive and soulful. Neptune in Virgo in the 2nd house completes the grand cross by drawing attention to the dissolution of false values and ego attachments. It calls for humility in one's relationship to self-worth and for the purification of what one truly considers sacred. This configuration places Pope Francis at the center of a profound karmic mandate—to transform not just himself but also the values and structures of a global institution through the tension of opposing principles.

Counterbalancing this crucible of growth is a grand trine in air signs linking Mars at 19° Libra in the 3rd house, Chiron at 20° Gemini in the 12th house, and the Moon at 12° Aquarius in the 7th house. Mars in Libra promotes strategic, justice-oriented action through communication. In the 3rd house, it reflects a sharp and refined ability to articulate ideas with precision and fairness. Trining Chiron in Gemini, this Mars can serve as a healing voice—asserting truth in ways that invite reflection instead of defensiveness. The trine to the Moon in Aquarius enhances emotional clarity, objectivity, and a concern for collective evolution. The Moon in the 7th house emphasizes an emotional orientation toward relationships, diplomacy, and humanitarian ideals. This grand trine creates an inner triangle of relational intelligence, intellectual grace, and emotional attunement—tools that support Pope Francis in speaking and acting with humility, balance, and resonance across divergent worldviews.

Eris, though not directly a part of these significant configurations, interacts synergistically with them. Her trine to Pluto acts as an ignition point, ensuring that the transformations prompted by the grand cross and supported by the grand trine are not merely intellectual but are instead embodied and actualized. Eris in the 9th house amplifies the voice of Mars in the 3rd, reflects the healing intelligence of Chiron in the 12th, and provides ideological space for the Moon's Aquarian vision. Through her, the chart gains its edge—the willingness to defy what is false, to speak when silence is complicit, and to challenge sacred cows not out of rebellion but because truth demands it.

In this context, it is also significant that Pluto resides at 28° Cancer, just one degree from the threshold of Leo, while Eris is positioned at 2° Aries, only two degrees beyond Pisces. These near-threshold degrees imbue their roles with an initiatory quality—both planets balanced on the brink between archetypes, propelling the soul toward new dimensions of evolutionary experience. Pluto is prepared to emerge from the emotional womb of Cancer into the vibrant self-expression of Leo; Eris is charging out of the collective unconscious of Pisces and into the assertion of sovereign will in Aries. This transitional energy further amplifies the theme of spiritual rebirth—of becoming a voice for truth at the edge of an old world and the threshold of a new one.

Eris in the 9th house in this chart is not a background player. She acts as the guardian at the gate of truth, the evolutionary firebrand that challenges the spiritual authority of empire from within its own walls. Her placement early in Aries, trine to the late Cancer Pluto, suggests that this is a lifetime on the cusp of great transition—where identity and ideology must be reborn together. Pope Francis, viewed through this lens, emerges not merely as a reforming pope but as a vessel through which a deeper evolutionary truth demands to be heard, acted upon, and lived out loud.

Her presence signifies that Pope Francis's life encompasses not only compassion, humility, and spiritual service; it embodies audacity—the audacity to name what is corrupt, to challenge the systems that have weaponized faith, and to restore sacredness where it has been distorted. With Pluto's power behind him, and the pressure of the grand cross transforming his soul from all directions, Eris guarantees that his truth will not remain theoretical; it will be lived.

Stephen King

Stephen King is a renowned American author who helped redefine modern horror fiction. With a career spanning decades, his storytelling has influenced not only literature but also film, television, and pop culture.

Born on September 21, 1947, in Portland, Maine, King faced early family struggles after his parents separated. Raised primarily by his mother, he developed a love for storytelling as a means of coping and expressing himself. After high school, he enrolled at the University of Maine, graduating in 1970 with a degree in English and a teaching certificate.

In 1971, King married Tabitha Spruce, a fellow writer whose support proved essential to his career. To make ends meet, he held various jobs, including teaching and laundry work, while writing short stories. His first major break came in 1967 when he sold a short story to a mystery magazine. His work steadily gained recognition in men's magazines.

His breakthrough novel, *Carrie* (1974), was inspired by his time as a janitor and a magazine article about telekinesis. Initially discarded, the manuscript was rescued by Tabitha, who encouraged him to finish it. The novel's success launched his career and led to a successful film adaptation in 1976.

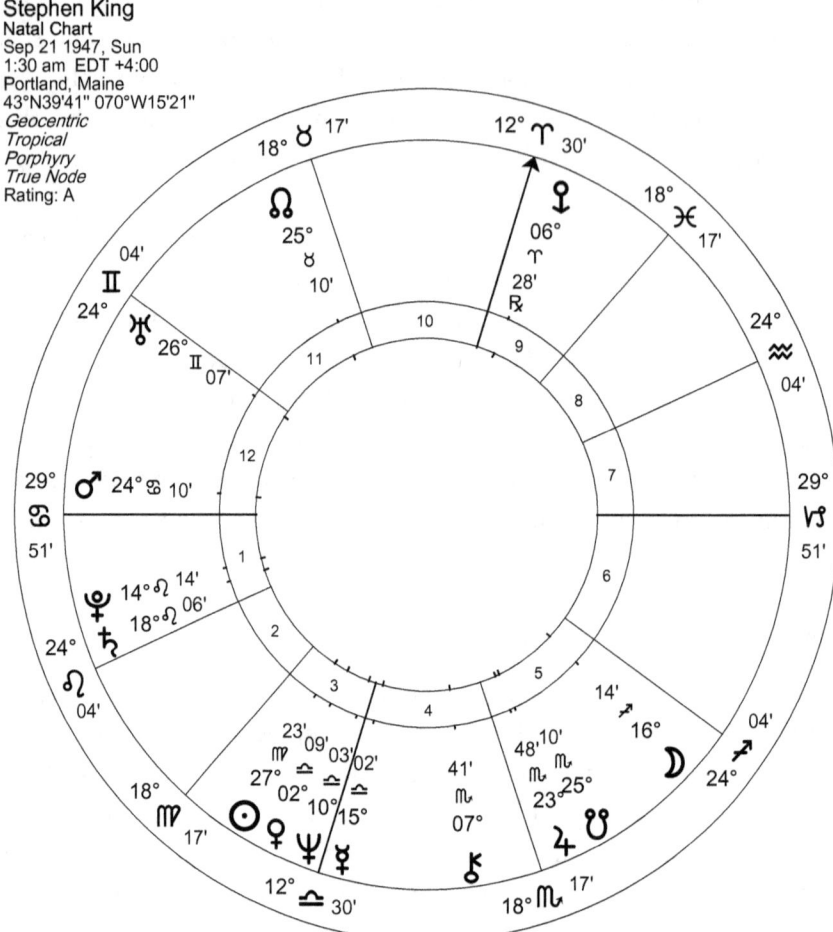

King followed with a series of bestselling novels that blend horror, fantasy, suspense, and sci-fi, including *The Shining* and *The Stand*, both of which were adapted for the screen. By the 1990s, he had sold over 100 million copies, becoming nearly synonymous with horror literature. His stories feature everything from vampires and haunted hotels to telekinesis and killer cars.

Later in his career, King began exploring psychological horror and character depth, as seen in *Dolores Claiborne* and *Gerald's Game*, which feature emotionally complex female leads. By the 1980s, screen adaptations of his work became commonplace, resulting in a vast library of film and TV versions of his novels.

Stephen King is one of America's most influential authors, celebrated for his prolific output, vivid imagination, and ability to terrify and move readers alike.[64]

In Stephen King's natal chart, Eris at 6° Aries in the 9th house symbolizes a position of ideological transformation and philosophical exploration. The 9th house in Evolutionary Astrology reflects the soul's evolving worldview—its beliefs, truths, and moral compass—and Eris here functions as a revolutionary force that disrupts consensus realities, challenges inherited dogma, and pierces through cultural delusions. King's storytelling serves as a vessel for this evolutionary function. Through horror, suspense, and the macabre, he reveals the underbelly of belief systems, highlighting the monsters that arise when truth is denied or suppressed.

Eris forms a powerful grand trine in fire with Pluto at 14° Leo, which conjoins Saturn at 18° Leo in the 1st house, and the Moon at 16° Sagittarius in the 5th house. This configuration marks a profound evolutionary integration of instinct, power, and vision. Pluto and Saturn in Leo in the 1st house convey a soul that has shaped its identity through lifetimes of confronting authority, asserting creative sovereignty, and integrating karmic lessons about power and responsibility. Saturn disciplines the self-assertive intensity of Pluto, grounding it in structure and endurance. The trine from Eris injects ideological fire into this identity—an uncompromising force that speaks truth to power, especially when that power is cloaked in righteousness.

The 5th house Moon in Sagittarius adds emotional and creative vitality to the grand trine. This Moon seeks meaning through expression, adventure, and myth-making. It carries the evolutionary memory of expansive emotional landscapes and philosophical longing. The trine with Eris reflects an emotional compass that instinctively challenges cultural norms and expresses truth through creative risk. King's characters often undergo harrowing initiations that mirror the soul's journey toward emotional liberation and ideological clarity—refracted through the mythic lens of the horror genre.

The Sun at 27° Virgo conjunct Venus at 2° Libra in the 3rd house highlights an identity shaped by precision, discernment, and relational

---

64 Paraphrased from https://www.britannica.com/biography/Stephen-King

intelligence. Virgo fosters a commitment to craft and detail, while Venus in Libra enhances his mental and verbal expression with artistic balance and a refined sense of justice. This conjunction strengthens his literary voice: structured, meticulous, and emotionally resonant. Venus, in her own sign, also forms a square with Uranus at 26° Gemini in the 12th house, introducing a current of creative disruption. This square suggests aesthetic originality and a restless drive to break with convention. Uranus in the 12th links his genius to the collective unconscious—King's inspirations may come like electrical surges from hidden realms, revealing buried fears and forbidden knowledge.

Venus is widely conjunct Neptune at 10° Libra, while Neptune also conjuncts Mercury at 15° Libra, forming a subtle chain of conjunctions that connects aesthetics, imagination, and thought. Neptune in the 3rd lends a dreamlike, intuitive quality to how he perceives and processes information, while Mercury in the 4th expresses it through the lens of domesticity, and emotional roots. Mercury in Libra adds balance and justice to his narrative voice, while the Neptune-Mercury conjunction reveals a mind attuned to the symbolic and the surreal. His ability to write horror with compassion, lyricism, and psychological depth arises from this Libran triad in the 3rd and 4th houses—providing structure to what is ephemeral and beauty to what is terrifying.

Jupiter at 23° Scorpio is conjunct the South Node at 25° Scorpio in the 5th house, indicating a profound karmic imprint related to creative intensity, emotional depth, and encounters with the taboo. King's soul recalls lifetimes of deep psychological exploration, possibly as a mystic, healer, or even a feared outsider. This placement reflects a natural attunement to the hidden currents of human experience—obsession, desire, death, and rebirth. His creativity flows from this Scorpio wellspring, carrying the potential for both personal and collective catharsis. The evolutionary task is to channel this intensity into stability and integration, as indicated by the North Node at 25° Taurus in the 11th house—establishing enduring values that benefit the community and transforming emotional complexity into socially relevant structures.

Mars at 24° Cancer in the 12th house adds a layer of emotional armor and unconscious sensitivity. Mars here operates from hidden places, driven by protective instincts and buried memories. This placement often alludes to ancestral or collective trauma, reflecting the soul's desire to act with compassion or secrecy. Mars in the 12th can indicate both concealed rage and profound spiritual strength—King's ability to portray violence and fear without glorifying it may stem from this placement, enabling him to accommodate the darker aspects of human nature without being overwhelmed by them.

Overall, Eris in the 9th house acts as a catalytic force in King's evolutionary journey, compelling him to uncover distorted beliefs, question conventional morality, and share stories that awaken readers to their own inner shadows. Her expansive fire trine with Pluto conjunct Saturn, and the Moon provides a reliable channel for this outpouring of truth, while his Libran and Scorpionic circuitry enhances and deepens the delivery. His chart reflects a soul forged in the fires of fear, transformed through emotional waters, and tasked with reshaping the collective psyche through narratives that provoke, illuminate, and endure.

Stephen King's chart reveals a soul whose evolutionary path focuses on exposing what society hides—from cultural hypocrisies to ancestral trauma—through the mediums of imagination, emotion, and mythic narrative. With Eris in the 9th house forming a rare and powerful grand trine in fire to Pluto and the Moon, his creative genius is firmly connected to a mandate of ideological disruption and emotional truth-telling. The chart reflects a seamless blend of instinctive power, emotional depth, and visionary expression. Through his writing, King fulfills an evolutionary imperative to confront collective fear, transform moral and cultural assumptions, and serve as a truth-teller from the edge of the known world—one who illuminates the shadows and brings meaning to the monstrous.

10th House ~ Consensus Reality

The 10th house, aligned with Saturn and Capricorn, embodies the yang cardinal archetype of the earth triad. It structures and defines the collective framework through which society operates, establishing the ethics, norms, and expectations that shape consensus reality. In Capricorn, Saturn crystallizes the customs and laws regulating human behavior, ensuring that a community functions within an orderly system that reflects its values and traditions. This archetype governs the institutionalization of societal authority, dictating acceptable behavior and outlining the boundaries of success, responsibility, and public recognition.

Consensus reality, as articulated through the 10th house, is constructed upon an intricate framework of rules, regulations, and hierarchical authority. Laws, ethical codes, and cultural customs serve as the scaffolding through which society sustains stability, providing a sense of predictability and order. This represents the domain of man-made law, distinct from natural law, where societal constructs determine what is considered moral, just, or acceptable. Governments, legal institutions, and social hierarchies arise as manifestations of this archetype, reinforcing a collective understanding of what defines proper conduct. The standards established within this house define status and success, rewarding those who adhere to them and reinforcing the authority of existing structures.

The philosophical and ideological foundations of a society, represented by the 9th house, find tangible expression in the 10th house as they become codified into laws, governmental systems, and institutional traditions. What begins as belief is formalized into the rules that govern the collective. This process reflects how the dominant cultural narrative establishes authority and sustains itself through nationalism, patriotism, and adherence to tradition. The natural square to the Ascendant and Aries highlights the tension between individual identity and societal expectations, revealing how social conditioning starts in early childhood. From birth, the individual is shaped by cultural norms, familial expectations, and external pressures that define success and acceptable behavior within the collective framework.

Identity formation is significantly influenced by factors such as gender, religion, socioeconomic status, geographic location, and generational context. These factors shape an individual's perception of their place within the social order, impacting their ambitions, limitations, and sense of duty. The 10th house reflects how one is recognized in the public sphere, encompassing career paths, reputation, and overall societal roles. It symbolizes the aspirations and responsibilities that define a person's contribution to the broader framework of civilization.

In the family dynamic, the 10th house is traditionally linked to the father or an authoritative parental figure who instills discipline, expectations, and a sense of duty. This parental influence acts as an early model of authority, shaping the individual's understanding of responsibility, societal roles, and success. In mundane astrology, this house corresponds to the highest levels of governance, representing leaders such as presidents, monarchs, prime ministers, and other figures who embody the collective authority of the state.

Through the 10th house, the individual navigates the expectations of the external world, balancing personal integrity with societal demands. This archetype inherently rewards achievement and penalizes failure to meet established standards. It also challenges individuals to operate within hierarchies that may either uplift or suppress personal potential. Whether one rises to prominence, struggles against imposed limitations, or works to redefine existing structures, the 10th house remains the domain where personal effort intersects with the larger framework of collective order.

Judy Garland

Judy Garland's meteoric rise and tragic fall mirrored the dazzling yet unforgiving nature of Hollywood. Her life, marked by instability from the start, reflected the heavy toll that fame can take under relentless pressure and exploitation.

Born into a troubled family, Garland's existence was uncertain from the start—her parents even considered terminating the pregnancy. Her early years were characterized by emotional neglect, but she found solace on stage, performing by the age of two. She later said, "The only time I felt wanted when I was a kid was when I was on stage."

In 1926, her family moved to California, partly to support her talent, although it did little to ease family tensions. Her father was rumored to have secret affairs with young men, while her mother, Ethel Gumm, pushed her relentlessly. Garland described her mother as "the real Wicked Witch of the West" and recalled being forced to perform even when sick. Ethel also introduced her to pills before the age of ten to keep her energized and help her sleep.

At 13, Garland signed with MGM, but rather than finding stability, the studio deepened her suffering. Louis B. Mayer ridiculed her appearance, referring to her as "my little hunchback," and subjected her to harsh scrutiny regarding her weight. She was placed on extreme diets and given amphetamines to control her appetite and keep up with grueling filming schedules.

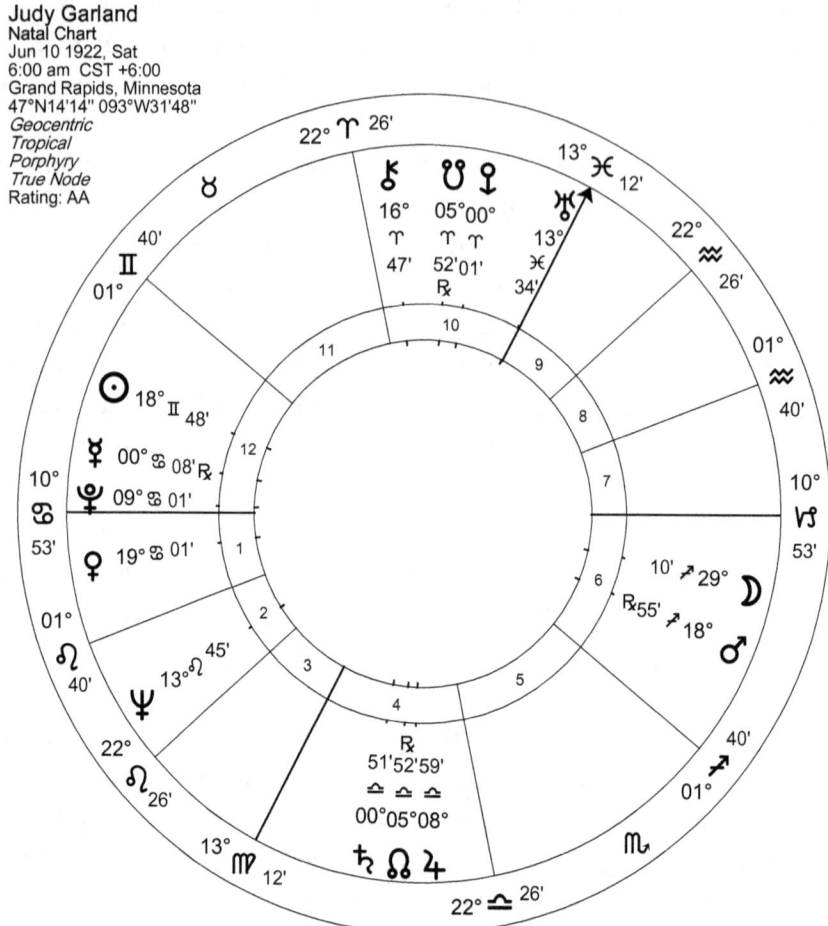

Garland once said, "From the time I was 13, there was a constant struggle... whether to eat, how much to eat, and what to eat." The physical and emotional toll trapped her in a cycle of addiction that persisted throughout her life.

Despite her brilliance, Garland struggled with unstable relationships, financial difficulties, and recurring substance abuse. Her extraordinary talent continued to captivate audiences, even while her private life unraveled.

In 1969, Garland died at just 47 from an accidental overdose. Her story serves as a powerful reminder of the hidden costs of fame—a gifted performer whose light brightened millions, even as her own world grew dim.⁶⁵

Judy Garland's 10th house Eris powerfully anchors one side of a dynamic grand cross, directly opposing her 4th house Jupiter, Saturn, and North Node in Libra. Positioned at a fully potentiated 0° Aries, Eris exactly squares her deeply intuitive and imaginative 12th house retrograde Mercury at 0° Cancer, which is widely conjunct transformative Pluto. Additionally, Eris forms an intense square to her sensitive and emotionally-charged 6th house Moon at 29° Sagittarius, situated precisely at the critical "ring-pass-not" degree, symbolizing energies that demand karmic completion.⁶⁶

This powerful configuration symbolizes the need to release and fully express vital initiatory energies on one axis, while also necessitating a profound karmic clearing and discharge of accumulated soul energies on the other. This alignment metaphorically appears as a volatile "hand grenade in a steel box," encapsulating intense internal pressure and the potential for explosive release—frequencies that have been present within Garland's auric field since birth.

Garland's Eris in the 10th house highlights a life path marked by public intensity, personal upheaval, and profound existential challenges. It consistently fueled her quest for authentic self-expression, urging her to redefine the boundaries of her professional and public life. This dynamic further underscores the revolutionary influence Garland had within her

---

65 Paraphrased from https://www.biography.com/actors/judy-garland-facts-bio
66 The phrase "Ring-Pass-Not" comes from Theosophical and esoteric teachings (you'll find it in H. P. Blavatsky, Alice Bailey, and other writers who influenced modern spiritual and astrological thought). The Ring-Pass-Not is a spiritual or energetic boundary that limits the consciousness of a being (an individual soul, a planetary logos, even the solar system). It is the outermost edge of what can be experienced, known, or expressed at a given level of evolution. For the individual soul, the Ring-Pass-Not is the karmic limit of what you can hold at your present state of evolution. You can press against it (through crisis, initiation, or awakening), but you can't dissolve it until the soul has integrated prior lessons. For humanity collectively, the Ring-Pass-Not represents the current edge of our group consciousness. Beyond it lies dimensions of awareness we haven't yet collectively embodied. In astrology, some use it poetically for Saturn — the traditional limit of the visible planets — but it can also be applied to Pluto and beyond, as thresholds of transformation that demand soul initiation.

industry, challenging established norms and embodying powerful themes of pioneering courage, rebellion, and ultimately tragic vulnerability.

Mercury in Cancer in her 12th house endowed Garland with an extraordinary ability to immerse herself emotionally in any role she undertook. Closely paired with profound Pluto, this combination consistently produced performances rich in psychological depth and raw emotional power.

Mars in Sagittarius intensified the dramatic quality of her performances and life experiences, often steering her toward self-destructive behaviors and recurring bouts of deep self-sabotage, driven by a restless search and inner turmoil.

Garland's stabilizing Saturn in Libra, positioned in her 4th house alongside Jupiter and the North Node, provided essential grounding and emotional balance. This alignment fostered the resilience and enduring strength necessary to navigate and overcome persistent personal challenges, anchoring her inner self-reliance throughout a lifelong cycle of adversity.

The tense sesquisquare aspect linking Garland's dreamy and idealistic 2nd house Neptune in Leo with her fiery 10th house Aries stellium paved an illusory path—an enticing yet dangerous escape. This aspect represents the seductive yet ultimately destructive pathway into substance dependency, which tragically contributed to the premature ending of her life.

Fidel Castro

Fidel Castro was a Marxist-Leninist revolutionary and political leader who played a central role in the Cuban Revolution, overthrowing the dictatorship of Fulgencio Batista. He served as Cuba's Prime Minister from 1959 to 1976 and as President until his resignation in 2008, making him one of the longest-serving leaders of the modern era.

> "Quality of life lies in knowledge, in culture. Values are what constitute true quality of life, the supreme quality of life, even above food, shelter and clothing. A revolution is a fight to the death between the future and the past...Condemn me, It does not matter. History will absolve me."
> —Fidel Castro *My Life: A Spoken Autobiography*

Eris Through The Houses   211

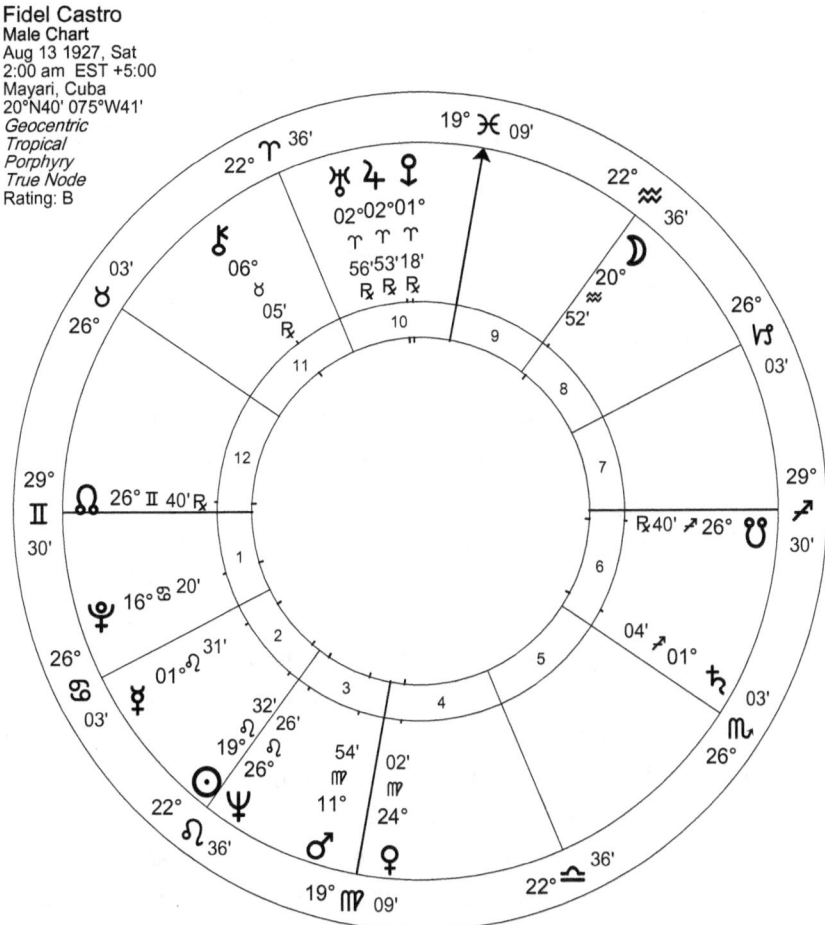

During the Cold War, Castro aligned Cuba with the Soviet Union, leading to significant global events such as the Cuban Missile Crisis in 1962, which brought the world to the brink of nuclear war. His decision to host Soviet missiles directly challenged US dominance in the region.

Under his leadership, Cuba became the first Communist state in the Americas, implementing Marxist-Leninist reforms in healthcare, education, and land ownership. These changes enhanced literacy, public health, and economic equality, though often at the price of political freedoms.

Internationally, Castro supported liberation movements and leftist causes, becoming a symbol of anti-imperialism and socialist solidarity.

While some admire him as a visionary, others condemn him as an authoritarian. Castro remains a deeply polarizing figure.

Regardless of the viewpoint, his impact on global politics, socialist ideology, and Cuba's national identity is undeniable, shaping debates on revolution, sovereignty, and governance for decades.[67]

At the core of Fidel Castro's revolutionary psyche is a fire grand trine linking Mercury at 1° Leo in the 2nd house, Saturn at 1° Sagittarius in the 6th, and the triple stellium of Eris, Jupiter, and Uranus in early Aries in the 10th house. This formation created a closed circuit of conviction, willpower, and ideological momentum—expressed through voice (Mercury), discipline (Saturn), and radical leadership (Eris–Jupiter–Uranus).

This trine begins with Mercury in Leo, the mouthpiece of self-possessed authority. In the 2nd house, Castro's mind was not just expressive—it was formative, forging personal values into public declarations. His speech was currency and command. Mercury's trine to Saturn in Sagittarius reveals an applied mind—systematic, strategic, ideologically rigorous. Saturn in the 6th house adds a pragmatic streak: revolution was not merely conceptual, it was executed with militant structure, daily routine, and tireless labor.

At the apex of the trine is Eris at 1° Aries, conjunct Jupiter and Uranus at 2°, all in the 10th house—a triple charge of revolutionary insurgency aimed at reconfiguring the collective order. Jupiter lent ideological breadth, Uranus broke from convention, and Eris injected an untamable, combative will to disrupt the status quo. In the 10th, this was not personal—it was historical. Castro didn't just speak for himself; he embodied a role, a cause, a system-defying flame projected into the architecture of power.

This grand trine gave Castro confidence, internal coherence, and visionary stamina. Yet, from an evolutionary perspective, it also made his worldview self-reinforcing. Lacking natural friction from squares or oppositions, the trine allowed Castro's rhetoric, ideology, and methods to circulate in a loop—uninterrupted by doubt, contradiction, or humility. That doesn't diminish its brilliance; it simply reveals that his power to inspire was matched by his inability to yield.

Saturn in Sagittarius carries karmic themes. It suggests past-life mastery of dogma, moral systems, and structured beliefs—now repurposed into service of a larger ideological mission in this life. The South Node at

---

[67] Paraphrased from https://en.wikipedia.org/wiki/Fidel_Castro

26° Sagittarius in the 6th house reflects a karmic residue of service through righteousness or militant belief, while the North Node at 26° Gemini in the 12th calls for a more open, diverse, and humble relationship to truth—something Castro resisted.

The grand trine in fire signs was not merely a technical feature—it was the spine of Castro's entire evolutionary path. It structured his mind, his mission, and his myth. But fire is consuming. It lights the way and burns the bridge. Castro lived by that fire—and the world was reshaped in its heat.

11th House ~ Liberation from Conditioning

The 11th house, Uranus, and Aquarius embody the yang, fixed energy of the air element, associated with revolution, insurrection, and the disruption of crystallized structures that have reached their peak in the 10th house and Capricorn. The momentum of Uranus interrupts, fractures, and deconditions, dismantling the rigidity that Saturn constructs while shattering societal expectations, personal limitations, and deeply ingrained patterns. Through this process, Uranus and Aquarius expose individuals to sudden changes, shocks, and awakenings that propel them into new ways of perceiving reality. The 11th house does not operate within the known; rather, it extends beyond, fostering awareness that transcends conditioned limitations and catalyzes new paradigms and radical shifts in consciousness.

The disruptive force of Uranus relates to the traumas experienced, endured, and revisited in the 4th house, as well as the confrontations and transformative crises that arise in the 8th. These experiences create conditions for a necessary detachment from outdated emotional imprints, karmic conditioning, and societal structures that no longer facilitate evolution. Through these disruptions, space opens for greater objectivity, allowing one to observe life and self without the distortions of subjective attachment. This process naturally cultivates a distance from conventional thinking. As detachment increases, the ability to perceive broader, unconventional, and even futuristic perspectives develops. A new worldview is emerging, prompting individuals to reject imposed societal norms and explore alternative lifestyles, ideologies, and ways of being.

Uranus is associated with the higher mind, where thoughts, impressions, and ideas flow in spontaneously, often striking like lightning and transcending logic or deliberation. These seemingly random insights catalyze the individuation process, a concept Carl Jung described as the natural unfolding of one's unique essence, distinct from collective expectations. Individuation necessitates dismantling inherited patterns—those shaped by parents, society, and past-life memories—allowing a distinct sense of self to emerge. Uranian energy disrupts the conditioned ego structure, shattering what has become calcified to enable radical reformation. With each upheaval, the conscious mind connects to something beyond the personal, linking to a broader field of knowledge, innovation, and higher awareness.

In the framework of Evolutionary Astrology, as articulated by Jeffrey Wolf Green, the 11th house corresponds to the Individuated state of evolutionary progression. In this developmental phase, the individual begins to recognize that the conditioned reality of consensus culture no longer provides profound fulfillment. The security once sought through conformity dissolves, replaced by an inner awareness that something more meaningful exists beyond mainstream definitions of success, morality, and purpose. An organic rejection emerges of artificial, man-made laws and societal structures that conflict with the deeper truth of natural law. The 11th house archetype aims to liberate the soul from these limitations, guiding it toward a more authentic self-expression. Creativity flourishes in this state, not merely as artistic expression but as a profound way of engaging with reality, whether through innovative philosophies, holistic approaches to life, or the recognition that all beings exist within a greater web of interconnection.

This archetype also speaks to community—one that is not defined by proximity, blood relations, or social obligation, but rather by resonance. The 11th house represents individuals who align with our unique perspectives, visions, and values; those with whom we share an intuitive sense of belonging, despite existing outside conventional societal structures. Through these connections, the individual finds support in forging an unconventional path, embracing a life untethered from external validation. The pursuit of security no longer hinges on societal approval or material accumulation but on a deeper sense of alignment with personal truth.

Uranus and Aquarius, through the 11th house, act as agents of deconditioning and awakening, freeing the soul from the misconception that safety exists in the predictable or socially approved. This liberation is not always comfortable, nor is it linear; it frequently appears as sudden, erratic, and sometimes unsettling disruptions that fulfill the evolutionary requirement of awakening. These disruptions remove illusions, urging individuals to perceive reality clearly, create a life that is uniquely their own, and align with the vast, infinite intelligence that flows through all things.

The 11th house is where consciousness transcends the personal and ventures into the unknown, driven by an unyielding quest for truth, freedom, and authenticity. In this domain, the individual is no longer shaped by external influences but actively engages in shaping reality itself.

Martin Luther King

Martin Luther King, Jr., born Michael Luther King, Jr. on January 15, 1929, in Atlanta, Georgia, changed his name to honor the Protestant reformer Martin Luther. Raised in a deeply religious family, he followed a long line of pastors at Ebenezer Baptist Church, co-pastoring with his father from 1960 until his assassination in 1968.

Growing up in the segregated South, King attended schools designated for black students under Jim Crow laws. A gifted student, he entered Morehouse College at 15 and earned a sociology degree in 1948. Influenced by Benjamin Mays and his theological studies, he pursued ministry, earning a divinity degree from Crozer Theological Seminary and later a Ph.D. in Systematic Theology from Boston University, where he met and married Coretta Scott.

In 1954, at the age of 25, King became the pastor of Dexter Avenue Baptist Church in Montgomery, Alabama. A year later, he gained national prominence during the Montgomery Bus Boycott, sparked by Rosa Parks' arrest. The 382-day protest led to a Supreme Court ruling against bus segregation and marked the beginning of King's civil rights leadership.

King co-founded the Southern Christian Leadership Conference (SCLC) in 1957, advocating for nonviolence inspired by Mahatma Gandhi. In the following decade, he spearheaded numerous campaigns across the US, including the Birmingham Campaign in 1963, during which he wrote

216   *Eris*

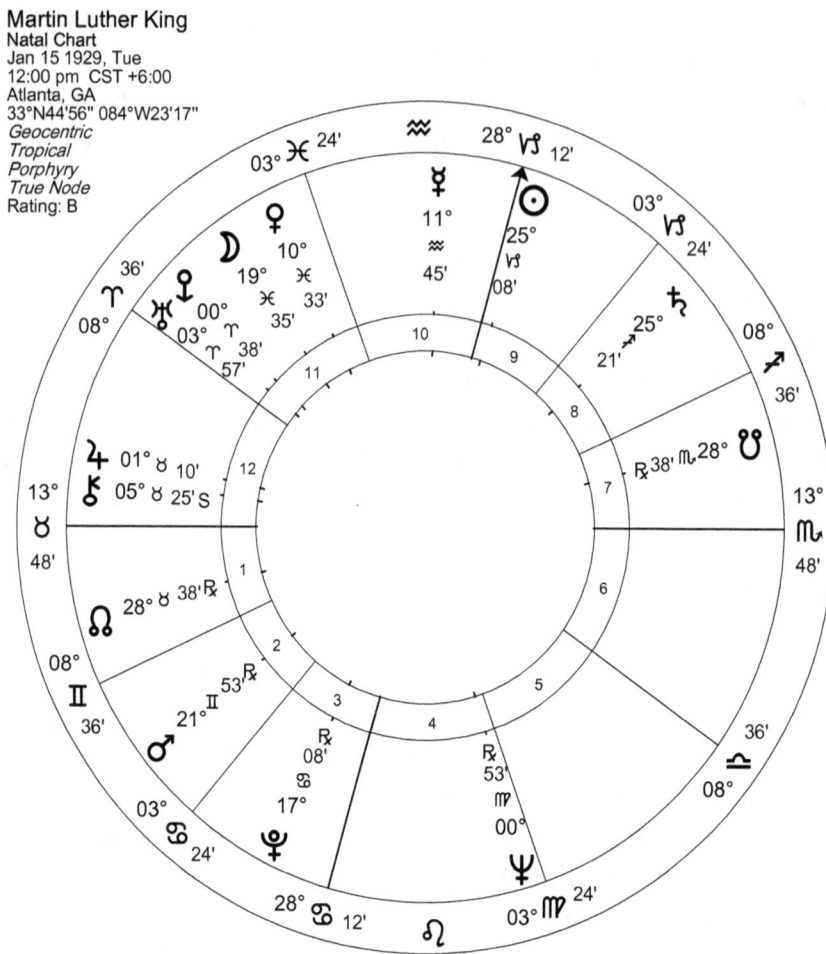

his pivotal *Letter from Birmingham Jail*. Later that year, he led the March on Washington, delivering his historic "I Have a Dream" speech to over 250,000 people.

His activism played a crucial role in the Civil Rights Act of 1964, which outlawed segregation and discrimination. That same year, he became the youngest recipient of the Nobel Peace Prize and generously donated the prize money to civil rights initiatives. In 1965, he led the Selma to Montgomery marches, which resulted in the Voting Rights Act.

Despite facing criticism—from segregationists and more radical activists—King remained dedicated to nonviolence. He broadened his focus to include poverty and opposition to the Vietnam War, which heightened tensions but affirmed his moral leadership.

On April 4, 1968, Dr. King was assassinated in Memphis while he was supporting striking sanitation workers. His death was a national tragedy, but his legacy lives on. He is celebrated worldwide as a symbol of peace, equality, and justice, honored through monuments, a U.S. national holiday, and countless tributes. His vision continues to inspire global movements for human rights and social change.[68]

Martin Luther King Jr. was born when Uranus separated from Eris in Aries in his 11th house, signifying him as a revolutionary force for collective change. With Eris at 0° Aries in the 11th house, conjunct Uranus at 3° Aries, Martin Luther King Jr.'s chart reveals a soul marked by a revolutionary imperative to expose injustice and catalyze transformation within the social, political, and racial collective. Eris in this placement acts as a fierce disruptor of group norms, cutting through false consensus and inherited ideologies with unrelenting clarity. In Aries, the call is direct and uncompromising: to awaken sovereign consciousness within the people, even when that path leads into direct confrontation with systems of oppression.

Martin Luther King Jr.'s Neptune in Virgo symbolized his soul's evolutionary intent to embody spiritual ideals through humble service and moral purification. He was called to reveal the illusions of America's false purity and guide the collective toward authentic healing and justice. His vision was not only transcendent but practical and disciplined, showing Neptune's highest expression in Virgo: the sacred work of service as a vessel of divine love. Uranus conjunct Eris in the 11th house electrifies this revolutionary theme. King wasn't just a visionary—he was an awakener. This conjunction speaks to his ability to spark change at the levels of ideology and social movements, igniting a moral uprising rooted in individual dignity and collective evolution. Eris and Uranus together in Aries cut through illusion and inertia, galvanizing the masses with the thunderclap of truth. However, that lightning also struck inward.

King's Sun at 25° Capricorn in the 9th house reflects his embodiment of moral authority, spiritual law, and disciplined leadership. He sought not only social justice but also cosmic justice—aligning himself with higher principles that transcended nation or creed. The Capricorn Sun governs

---

68 Paraphrased from https://www.nobelprize.org/prizes/peace/1964/king/biographical/

his capacity for long-term vision, while the 9th house positions him as a messenger of faith, prophecy, and higher truth. The sextile to the South Node in Scorpio in the 7th house indicates past-life mastery in the areas of power, relationships, and emotional survival—skills repurposed in this lifetime toward sacred service.

The nodal axis, with the South Node at 28° Scorpio in the 7th house and the North Node at 28° Taurus in the 1st, outlines a soul journey from karmic entanglement and shared trauma to embodied presence and personal sovereignty. The Scorpio South Node implies lifetimes characterized by intensity, betrayal, and complex relational dynamics—potentially lifetimes spent navigating underground resistance, surviving persecution, or engaging in power struggles within collective movements. Conversely, the Taurus North Node calls the soul toward groundedness, simplicity, and the reclamation of inherent worth. In this life, King's evolutionary task was to rise from the consuming fire of collective history and ground his activism in a calm, unshakeable inner center.

But Eris in the 11th house disrupted this journey, not to derail it, but to deepen it. She demanded not only self-possession (Taurus) but also collective clarity. She refuses ease or comfort if it means compromise. In King's context, Eris pressed against both ends of the nodal axis, requiring him to integrate personal value with relational responsibility in the crucible of public life.

Pluto at 17° Cancer retrograde in the 3rd house provided the evolutionary backbone of King's chart. His soul's intention involved transforming how truth is spoken, heard, and remembered—particularly through emotional, familial, and racial narratives. In the 3rd house, Pluto empowers the voice. In Cancer, it draws from deep wellsprings of ancestral memory and emotional understanding. The retrograde motion indicates that this work of reclamation was deeply internalized. King's oratory did not arise from mere intellect but from a cellular understanding that transcended his own lifetime.

In the chart, Pluto trines both Venus at 10° Pisces and the Moon at 19° Pisces, both located in the 11th house, which further emphasizes the emotional and spiritual tone of his collective mission. These Pisces placements in the house of community suggest an unshakeable commitment to empathy, unity, and transcendence—even while grappling with profound personal sorrow. His Moon in Pisces signifies sensitivity to the suffering of others, while his Venus here radiates the spiritual magnetism of unconditional love. These planets infuse the Eris-Uranus conjunction with compassion, balancing its disruptive energy with a current of grace.

Mars at 21° Gemini retrograde in the 2nd house, ruling Eris, further emphasizes the internalization of action and conflict. Mars retrograde can feel slow or blocked in outward motion but operates with fierce persistence beneath the surface. In Gemini, this Mars battled with words, ideas, and adaptability. In the 2nd house, it grappled with questions of worth, voice, and survival. King had to fight—repeatedly—to claim and reclaim his value, both as a black man in America and as a spiritual teacher challenging empire. His Mars answers to Mercury at 11° Aquarius in the 10th house, assigning him the role of public communicator, rebel thinker, and architect of a new world vision.

The Moon, Venus, Eris, and Uranus in the 11th highlight King's emotional life, values, revolutionary instincts, and spiritual love, all within the realm of collective change. The 12th house Jupiter–Chiron conjunction in Taurus reflects the spiritual pain he carried and the expansive healing he offered. Chiron in the 12th speaks to hidden wounds associated with invisibility, sacrifice, or spiritual exile. However, with Jupiter at 1° Taurus, there was also divine protection, faith, and a promise of abundance emerging from suffering.

Eris, acting through all of this, was the unrelenting presence that made it impossible to conform, to retreat, or to be silent. Her influence demanded truth. It demanded rupture. And it demanded a courage that endured beyond the end of his life.

Mick Jagger

Mick Jagger is more than just a singer and performer; he's a cultural icon whose influence on rock music spans decades. As the electrifying frontman of The Rolling Stones, Jagger helped shape the sound, style, and spirit of rock. His distinctive voice, boundless energy, and flamboyant presence made him one of the most recognizable figures in popular music. Alongside his creative partner Keith Richards, Jagger co-wrote some of rock's most enduring songs.

Mick Jagger

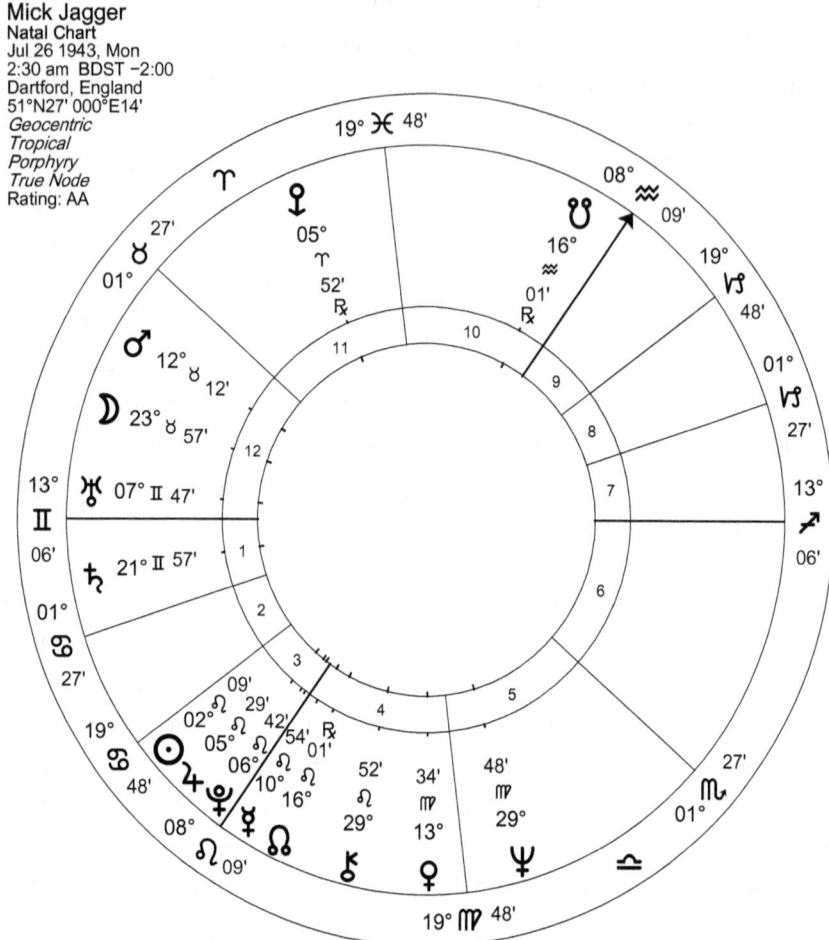

Natal Chart
Jul 26 1943, Mon
2:30 am BDST −2:00
Dartford, England
51°N27' 000°E14'
Geocentric
Tropical
Porphyry
True Node
Rating: AA

Born in Dartford, Kent, England, Jagger first met Richards as a schoolboy. They reconnected in London in 1962, the same year Jagger enrolled at the London School of Economics—though music soon took precedence. That year, along with Richards, Brian Jones, Bill Wyman, and Charlie Watts, he formed The Rolling Stones. Inspired by Chicago blues legends like Muddy Waters, their gritty sound sharply contrasted with the polished Beatles, earning them a rebellious image.

Initially covering blues and R&B classics, Jagger and Richards soon began writing original songs. Their 1965 hit *(I Can't Get No) Satisfaction* became an anthem that defined a generation. The hits that followed—*Paint It, Black, 19th Nervous Breakdown, Jumpin' Jack Flash*—showcased Jagger's raw emotional expression and provocative charisma. From 1968 to

1972, the Stones released some of rock's most influential albums: *Beggars Banquet*, *Let It Bleed*, *Sticky Fingers*, and *Exile on Main St.*

Jagger's influence extends beyond the Stones. He has embarked on solo projects and collaborated with artists like Tina Turner, David Bowie, Lenny Kravitz, and Bono. His duet on *You're So Vain* with Carly Simon remains iconic, and his song *Old Habits Die Hard* with Dave Stewart won a Golden Globe in 2005.

He has also made his mark in film, starring in *Performance* (1970) and co-producing *Enigma* (2001) and *Havana Moon* (2016), a documentary about the Stones' historic concert in Cuba that drew over 500,000 people.

Recognized globally, Jagger was inducted into the Rock and Roll Hall of Fame in 1989 and received a knighthood in 2003. Even after six decades, his vibrant stage presence and artistic evolution make him not just a rock star but a living legend whose legacy continues to inspire.[69]

Mick Jagger's 12th house Mars in Taurus governs his retrograde Eris in the 11th, influencing his individuality and groundbreaking musical journey to become a distinctive presence in the world. His leadership role within The Rolling Stones and, by extension, the broader rock and roll movement was shaped by the unwavering determination and physicality of Mars in Taurus, operating behind the scenes in the ethereal yet powerful 12th house, whose influence allowed him to harness collective energies, transforming raw instinct and sensuality into a larger-than-life persona.

Like many of his generation, Jagger's Neptune in Virgo opposes Eris, creating tension between his personal creative vision and the broader cultural and artistic shifts of his time. This dynamic fueled his ability to channel profound creative forces, making his music not only an individual expression but also a reflection of the evolving consciousness of an era. Neptune's placement in the 5th house, which governs self-expression, artistic creation, and performance, served as a direct gateway for him to produce an iconic musical legacy. This positioning dissolved boundaries, opening an endless well of inspiration and allowing him to craft a back catalog of music that solidified The Rolling Stones the most enduring rock band in history.

Jagger's 12th house Uranus in Gemini, combined with his Moon in Taurus and Neptune in the 5th, contributed to his unique musical talent,

---

69 Paraphrased from https://www.songhall.org/profile/Mick_Jagger

dramatic stage presence, and boundless creativity. Uranus, the planet of revolution and unpredictability, activated within the subconscious realm of the 12th house, endowed him with an innovative, rebellious spirit, while Gemini infused him with an agile and restless intellect, enabling him to continually reinvent his artistic style. His Taurus Moon provided grounding amid this dynamic chaos, ensuring that his sensuality and emotional depth were expressed in his visceral musical and physical performances, while Neptune in the 5th further enhanced his artistic genius, rendering his creative expressions captivating, otherworldly, and timeless.

The foundation of his creative talent, empowered self-image, vibrant musical voice, and eccentric lifestyle lies in his Leo stellium with the Sun, Jupiter and Pluto in the 3rd, with Mercury and the North Node in the 4th, all conjunct the IC. His Leo Sun radiates undeniable charisma, amplified by Jupiter and Pluto, which enhance his presence and transformational power. This stellium provides him with a voice capable of commanding, inspiring, and provoking, making him a magnetic frontman who embodies the raw energy of rock and roll. Pluto in the 3rd offers an intense and provocative style of communication, while 4th house Mercury ensures that his creative ideas are not only intellectual but also deeply rooted in an instinctive understanding of his audience and the emotional pulse of the era. His North Node highlights his evolutionary path toward self-actualization through artistic expression, affirming that he was destined to embrace a role of creative leadership and cultural influence.

Brian Wilson

Brian Wilson is a legendary musician, singer, and producer best known as the creative force behind The Beach Boys. Famous for his groundbreaking compositions and innovative studio techniques, Wilson has influenced generations of artists through his introspective lyrics and intricate harmonies.

Born in Inglewood, California, Wilson was the eldest of three brothers, with Dennis and Carl completing the trio that would form the heart of The Beach Boys. Cousin Mike Love and friend Al Jardine joined them. Gifted with a keen ear from an early age, Wilson drew inspiration from Gershwin, Chuck Berry, and The Four Freshmen, developing the lush arrangements

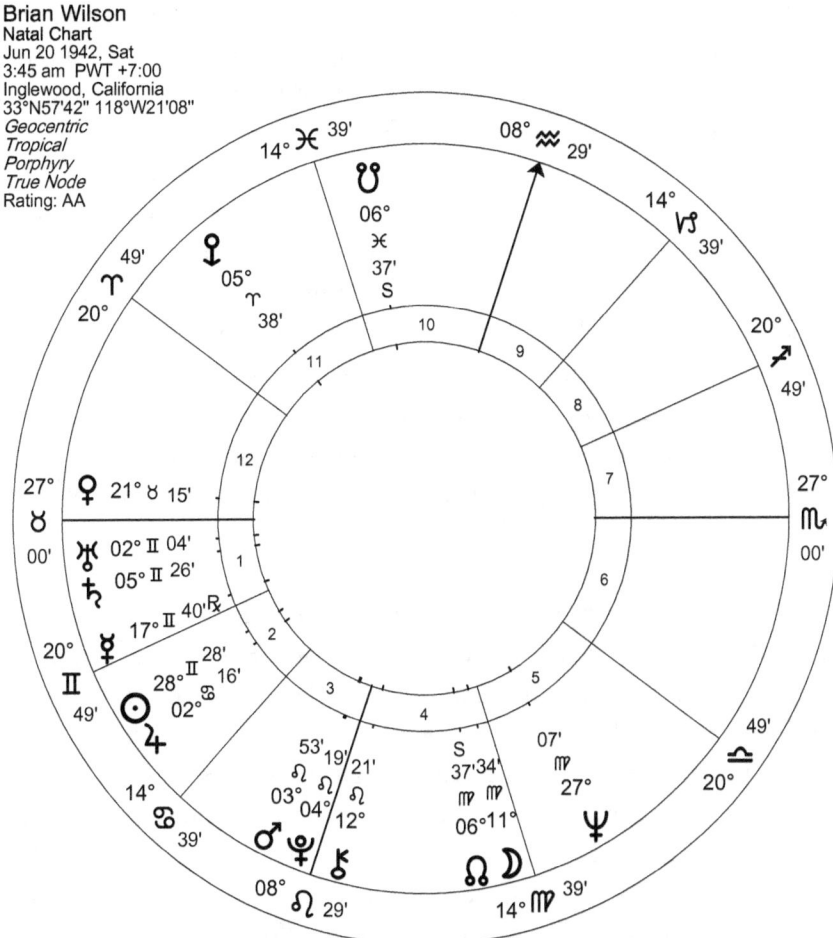

that defined the group's sound. Despite a strained relationship with his father, Murry Wilson, Brian pursued music with intensity and vision.

Wilson led the band as they rose to fame with early hits like *Surfin' U.S.A*, *I Get Around*, and *California Girls*, defining the upbeat "California sound." However, behind the scenes, the pressure of fame and artistic responsibility began to weigh on him. In the mid-1960s, Wilson retreated from touring to focus on studio work, producing the landmark album *Pet Sounds* (1966). With emotionally rich tracks like *Wouldn't It Be Nice* and *God Only Knows*, the album redefined pop music, showcasing Wilson's emotional depth and sonic experimentation.

However, Wilson's mental health deteriorated, exacerbated by drug use and a developing diagnosis of schizoaffective disorder. By the late 1960s, he became increasingly reclusive, suffering from paranoia and hallucinations. Under the care of controversial therapist Eugene Landy, Wilson endured years of manipulation until his second wife, Melinda Ledbetter, assisted him in breaking free in the late 1980s.

Despite personal turmoil, Wilson made a comeback with his 1988 solo debut. He faced further losses in 1998 with the deaths of his brother Carl and mother Audree, yet he continued to create music and gradually rebuilt his life. Over the years, he received numerous accolades, including induction into the Rock and Roll Hall of Fame and multiple Grammys.

Wilson's first marriage to Marilyn Rovell was characterized by his descent into addiction and illness. His second marriage to Ledbetter proved to be stabilizing—she became both his wife and manager, helping him regain balance and purpose. Now under conservatorship, Wilson remained engaged in music while he received the care he required until his death in 2025.

Through triumph and tragedy, Brian Wilson's story exemplifies unmatched talent, vulnerability, and resilience. His profound musical legacy continues to inspire, reminding us that even from the deepest struggles, transcendent beauty can emerge.[70]

Brian Wilson's 11th house Eris, governed by his 3rd house Mars in Leo, weaves through every aspect of his chart, forming connections with every planet and both lunar nodes. This dynamic placement intensified his experiences of disruption, individuality, and creative genius while also revealing significant challenges. With Mars in a conjunction with Pluto in Leo, both trining Eris, the force of transformation, power, and intensity flowed through his artistic expression. Pluto in conjunction with Chiron in the 4th highlighted themes of deep emotional wounding, healing, and a primal need to express his inner world through music. This Leo stellium—is also ruled by his Gemini Sun—created an immense reservoir of creativity but also carried an undeniable current of trauma.

Virgo's influence, expressed through his Moon, enabled him to translate emotional nuance into structured musical compositions, particularly through his 1st house Mercury, ruling both the Moon and North

---

70 Paraphrased from https://www.britannica.com/biography/Brian-Wilson-American-musician

Node. This mercurial dexterity is evident in his piano compositions—meticulously crafted yet infused with raw emotional depth.

His 1st house Uranus conjunct Saturn in Gemini and aligning with his Ascendant, highlights a restless and unpredictable mind characterized by both brilliance and instability. Saturn's sextile to Eris intensified his struggles with mental health, emphasizing the oppressive burden of his inner turmoil and the enduring discipline that shaped his musical legacy. The presence of Uranus on the Ascendant suggests moments of radical innovation but also the disruptive, unpredictable facets of his psyche. A quintile from Mercury to Eris provided the capacity to transform his crises into poetic, deeply evocative lyrics, turning personal chaos into art.

Relationships proved to be a battleground, as seen through his 7th house Scorpio cusp, ruled by the Mars-Pluto-Chiron stellium. The significance of this stellium extended into his interpersonal life, surfacing in difficult and often painful dynamics with his first wife, therapist, and father. His intimate relationships bore the imprint of Scorpio's intensity, manifesting as deep psychological entanglements, betrayals, and power struggles that reflected the broader themes of his life's journey.

His lunar nodes are stationed direct, an uncommon condition that heightens their karmic significance. Since the nodes are typically retrograde, their stationary motion indicates an intensified level of fate and a necessity for urgent evolution. The 10th house South Node in Pisces, now stationary, reflects unresolved karmic imprints from past lives—spiritual, artistic, and possibly sacrificial in nature. His 4th house North Node in Virgo, on the other hand, emphasized the importance of establishing personal security, meticulous craftsmanship, and emotional healing. The path of his nodes, transitioning from the 10th house (career, public image) to the 4th house (home, inner world), illustrates the profound tension between his external success and internal struggles. While his career achieved legendary heights, his personal life became a maze of wounds, influenced by the pressures of fame, family dynamics, and the relentless expectations placed upon him.

Brian Wilson's Eris in the 11th house acted as a catalyst, enhancing the unpredictable, disruptive, and revolutionary aspects of his creative and personal experiences. His ability to channel deep emotional discord into music transformed not only his own life but also the landscape of popular music. He left behind a legacy that reflects both the beauty and suffering woven into his chart.

Erica Jong

Erica Jong, the second of three daughters in a creatively gifted Jewish family, grew up on Manhattan's Upper West Side. Her father, a former Broadway percussionist, encouraged her early writing, while her mother, Eda Mirsky Mann, was a visual artist of Russian Jewish descent. Surrounded by art, Jong painted with her grandfather as he sang Russian folk songs, absorbing a rich creative legacy.

At Barnard College, Jong participated in writing workshops, edited the literary magazine, and earned Phi Beta Kappa honors. She completed a Master's in English Literature at Columbia, during which she married and quickly divorced Michael Werthman, later marrying Allan Jong, a Chinese-American psychiatrist.

Influenced by poets such as Sylvia Plath and Anne Sexton, Jong began publishing her poetry in literary journals. Her debut collection, *Fruits & Vegetables*, won the Bess Hopkins Prize from Poetry Magazine. Encouraged by an editor at Holt, she wrote *Fear of Flying*, which was based on her poetry. The novel, which fictionalized her life through the character Isadora Wing, candidly explored female desire, sexuality, and creative ambition. It faced mixed initial reviews, but praise from John Updike and Henry Miller pushed it to bestseller status. The paperback hit #1 on *The New York Times* best seller list, eventually selling over ten million copies.

The book's commercial success partly stemmed from its provocative content. Isadora's longing for a "Zipless Fuck"—a guilt-free sexual encounter—became iconic. While some critics derided it as sensational, feminists hailed the novel as a cornerstone of second-wave feminism.

Although raised in a Jewish home, Jong later acknowledged a delayed engagement with her Jewish identity, which she explored in her later novels. Her fiction combines mass-market appeal—sensationalism, clichés, graphic sexuality—with literary references and historical depth.

Despite ongoing critical debate, Jong continues to write, although her celebrity has often overshadowed the literary seriousness of her work. Her publishers have capitalized on this by printing her name larger than the book titles to emphasize her persona. Nevertheless, her writing speaks

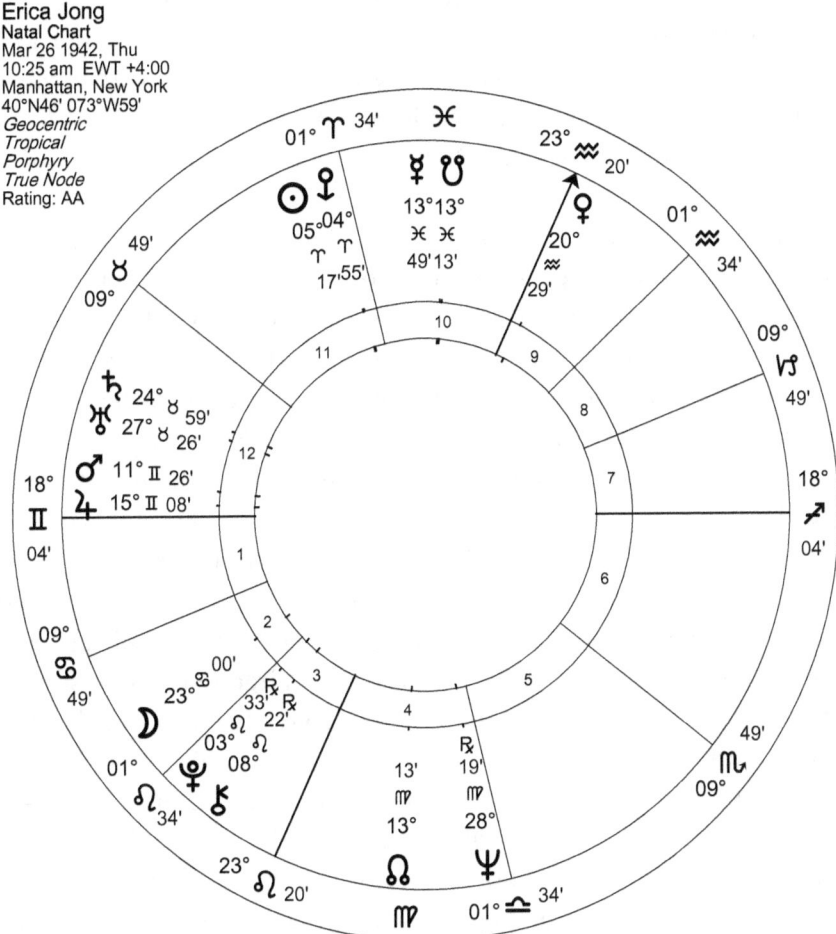

boldly about female agency, asserting that the threat of sexual violence remains a barrier to true sexual liberation for women.[71]

With Eris at 4° Aries in the 11th house, conjunct the Sun, Jong's soul entered this life with an evolutionary mandate to disrupt the collective silence surrounding female desire, identity, and truth. In Aries, Eris erupts with primal courage, stripping away social niceties in favor of instinctual honesty. In the 11th house this energy radiates outward—through culture, community, and collective awakening. Jong didn't just write about sex; she ignited a literary rebellion that shattered the psychological and sexual constraints imposed on women.

---

71 Paraphrased from https://jwa.org/encyclopedia/article/jong-erica

Her Sun–Eris conjunction shows the self fused with the disruptor archetype: her very identity compelled her to defy cultural repression and claim space for the sovereign female voice. *Fear of Flying* was not simply a confession—it was a cultural detonation.

The Moon in Cancer in the 2nd house reflects a profound emotional need to feel secure in her values, voice, and worth. This placement grounds her rebellious intellect in emotional authenticity and legacy—what she gave voice to carried weight because it originated from the soul's inner chamber. The Pluto–Chiron conjunction retrograde Leo in the 3rd house further intensifies the evolutionary task of reclaiming her voice after lifetimes of creative suppression. Her healing came through confronting shame and illuminating it with bold expression.

The Mars–Jupiter conjunction in Gemini in the 12th house forms a mutable T-square with the nodal axis. This suggests a karmic bypass of action and integration. In past lives (South Node in Pisces in the 10th), Jong may have been a mystic, artist, or public figure who drifted into visionary ideals without clear boundaries. Her current challenge is to integrate Gemini's discerning intellect with Virgo's clarity of service and precision—yet the 12th house Mars–Jupiter suggests this drive to communicate was hidden, scattered, or misapplied. In this life, she has had to consciously recover her power to name, describe, and distinguish—to give voice to what had been formless or taboo. She accomplished this by crafting vivid, articulate, and often controversial narratives that made the unconscious conscious—pulling female erotic fantasy out of the shadows and into the realm of language.

Venus in Aquarius in the 9th house reflects a love of freedom, unorthodox relationships, and philosophical inquiry. Her values were never conventional—she sought liberation through thought, belief, and the written word. Mercury in Pisces conjunct the South Node shows a karmic echo of poetic sensitivity, spiritual language, and the tendency to dissolve boundaries in communication. Her challenge was to move from this dreamy past into practical, embodied speech—not abandoning the poetry, but refining it through structure, purpose, and truth.

The Uranus–Saturn conjunction in Taurus in the 12th house speaks to a powerful, if unconscious, tension between rebellion and form. Saturn provides discipline; Uranus wants breakthrough. She channeled both in her literary form: breaking taboos with structure, not chaos. That's Eris in Aries working through an embodied, poetic, and politically relevant voice.

Phil Spector

Phil Spector achieved his first hit while still in high school with The Teddy Bears, whose song *To Know Him Is To Love Him* topped the charts in the US and UK. Born Harvey Philip Spector on December 26, 1939, in New York City, he moved to Los Angeles with his family after his father's suicide in 1953. At Fairfax High School, Spector met future bandmates and began songwriting.

Although the Teddy Bears disbanded after limited success, Spector returned to the music industry, learning from producers Lester Sill and Lee Hazlewood and collaborating with Jerry Leiber and Mike Stoller. He quickly rose to fame at Dune Records and co-founded Philles Records in 1961, scoring hits with The Crystals. By age 21, he was a millionaire with 20 consecutive hits, and developed his signature "Wall of Sound" technique, later emulated by artists such as The Beach Boys and Bruce Springsteen.

In 1966, Spector produced *River Deep, Mountain High* for Ike and Tina Turner, which did not perform well in the US, causing him to retreat from the spotlight for two years. He returned in 1969 to work on solo albums for George Harrison and John Lennon and to complete The Beatles' *Let It Be*. Although he continued producing into the 1970s, his unpredictable behavior led to professional conflicts.

Despite controversy, he was inducted into the Rock and Roll Hall of Fame in 1989. His career ended in 2003 when he was arrested for the murder of actress Lana Clarkson, who was found dead in his home. The first trial resulted in a mistrial, but in 2009, Spector was convicted of second-degree murder and sentenced to 19 years in prison. He died of natural causes on January 16, 2021.[72]

Eris conjoined with Jupiter in the 11th house signals a soul whose destiny involves disrupting collective patterns. Here, the individual becomes a lightning rod for conflict and revelation. Jupiter amplifies Eris' voice, giving it a prophetic quality—too loud to ignore, too disruptive to silence. The call isn't for conformity but for breaking open consensus reality to allow something more authentic to take hold.

---

72 Paraphrased from https://www.biography.com/musicians/phil-spector

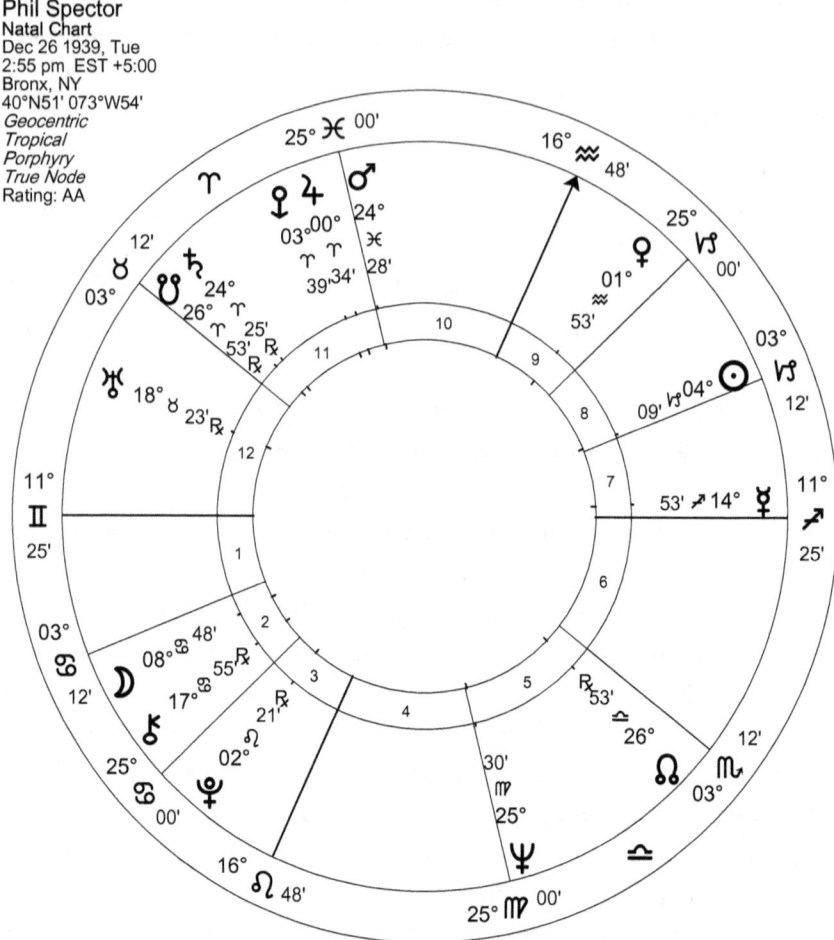

The squares to both Sun and Moon confirm that this is no simple mission. Eris disrupts the very foundations of identity and emotional security. The ego feels constantly challenged, and the instinctual life remains unsettled. This soul cannot find peace or belonging; Eris ensures that discord emerges in the most personal areas of life, forcing the individual to grow through disruption rather than stability. It is a challenging signature, as it undermines illusions of harmony, but within its chaos lies the potential for real transformation.

Mars hovers near this conjunction, a restless force that pushes Eris' discord into motion. Although the contact is out of sign and house, its impact is clear: words and actions come swiftly, often before reflection, with a hint of volatility that can spark upheaval. Yet beneath this raw energy lies the deeper current of Pluto. In a harmonious trine to Eris, Pluto stabilizes the archetype of discord, giving it an evolutionary purpose. Every disruption, every confrontation with shadow, is not just chaos but a chance for empowerment and rebirth.

The nodal axis and Saturn deepen the overall picture. A South Node conjoined with Saturn reveals a karmic history characterized by authoritarianism, repression, and control. Old lifetimes bear the imprint of rigidity and fear, relying on suppression rather than transformation. Pluto opposing Venus and squaring Saturn and the nodes amplifies this dynamic, tying the soul to evolutionary struggles related to power, authority, and relationships. The missed step here is that the soul must learn to interact with power genuinely, to release the karmic inheritance of domination, and to transform its shadow instead of repeating it.

The overall picture depicts a life not intended for an easy journey. Eris ensures conflict: the voice that interrupts, the identity that struggles to find stability, and the emotions that remain constantly stirred. However, in the Individuated State, this conflict is sacred. It becomes a vital tool for growth. This embodies the archetype of the disruptive visionary, the truth-teller who cannot accept false harmony. The soul is called to face the shadow of control and exclusion, not only within itself but also within the collective, transforming discord into a catalyst for awakening. Though life may seem broken, its purpose is complete: to awaken, to unveil, and to transform.

12th House ~ The Reconnection

The 12th house represents the yin mutable expression of the water triad, and is deeply connected to the energies of Neptune and Pisces. It serves as a vast, all-encompassing field of consciousness where boundaries dissolve, the illusion of separation is stripped away, and the soul's journey encounters its most transcendent realizations as well as its most haunting abysses. Water, by its very nature, erodes and reshapes everything it touches. A rushing torrent can obliterate obstacles in an instant, while a slow and steady drip gradually wears away stone over time. This process of dissolution, relentless and inevitable, embodies the work of Neptune, Pisces, and the 12th house in a natal chart—dismantling anything that hinders the soul's ultimate return to The-Source-of-All-That-Is.

In this realm, the subjective ego relinquishes its illusions, tightly held sense of identity, and meticulously crafted narratives of self, allowing the greater soul consciousness to emerge. However, this surrender is rarely without struggle. The 12th house is where we confront the desire to merge with something greater, the unbearable weight of isolation, the allure of fantasy, the pitfall of addiction, and the maze of self-destruction. It is where the soul grapples with the tension between divine transcendence and earthly suffering, where the urge to save and the inclination to sacrifice intertwine, and where the boundaries between martyrdom and spiritual liberation blur.

The subconscious currents of both the individual and the collective converge here, dissolving personal boundaries and revealing the raw, unfiltered truth of existence. This is the realm of ultimate reality, as it is all-encompassing. It includes the light of divine grace and the shadows of despair, the presence of guiding spirits, and the echoes of past betrayals. The 12th house calls forth the ineffable—a direct, wordless understanding that cannot be constrained by logic or language. It is the realm of dreams, symbols, and whispers from the unseen worlds, a liminal passageway between form and formlessness, life and death, beginning and end.

In the natal chart, planets in the 12th carry an imprint of energies that seek transcendence, yet may initially be shrouded in mystery, confusion, or illusion. Here, the ego often struggles to grasp the full extent of what these planets represent, as they operate beyond the realm of personal will. A 12th house Sun might experience a loss of clear identity, driven to merge into something greater, whether through service, creativity, or suffering. A 12th house Moon may retain the emotional residue of past lives, feeling deeply connected to unseen realms while also being prone to feelings of isolation or escapism. Venus in this house might pursue love that transcends the ordinary, yearning for divine or karmic unions, sometimes at the cost of discernment.

Everything in the 12th house is in motion, seeking dissolution and return. In the 4th house, through Cancer and the Moon, the soul gains self-awareness through the subjective emotional body, forming the foundation of personal identity. In the 8th house, through Scorpio and Pluto, the soul confronts its fragmented aspects, reclaiming lost parts of itself through crisis, transformation, and by merging energies with another. In the 12th house, through Pisces and Neptune, the individual self is no longer separate; it is drawn back into the infinite, like a wave returning to the ocean, completing a cycle that has never truly been broken.

The paradox of the 12th house is that, while it reveals unity, it also reminds us of the perpetual incompleteness of the human experience. Like the unfinished Enso, the hand-drawn Zen circle that remains open and imperfect, the soul continues its journey of dissolution and return, forever seeking and forever surrendering. The evolutionary intention of this house is to align with a higher order of reality, recognize the interconnectedness of all that exists, and embrace a transcendent belief system that allows for both dissolution and renewal. In this space, the personal dissolves into the universal, the known gives way to the infinite, and the longing for meaning finds its resolution not in certainty but in surrender.

John Lennon

When we think of "The Spiritual Beatle," George Harrison often comes to mind for his devotion to Hinduism and Eastern mysticism. However, John Lennon also had a rich inner life worth revisiting, as Jude Southerland Kessler, author of *The John Lennon Series*[73], suggests.

At age nine, Lennon told his Aunt Mimi, "I've just seen God," describing Him as "just sitting by the fire." She replied dryly, "I expect He was chilly." It was a quiet yet profound moment—just the first of many spiritual glimpses in Lennon's life.

During the height of Beatlemania, the band dismissed religion, identifying as agnostic or atheist. However, in 1965, while Harrison immersed himself in Hinduism, Lennon began searching for something deeper. Fame had left him disillusioned, and he started to explore life's bigger questions. Despite his distaste for organized religion—stemming from childhood rejection by Woolton Parish Church—Lennon wasn't anti-faith. His song *God* reflected a shift: *"God is a concept by which we measure our pain."* Though rejecting external idols, he acknowledged a divine presence he couldn't quite dismiss.

Lennon's mysticism surfaced again in a dream that inspired *#9 Dream*, with its haunting chant *Ah! böwakawa poussé, poussé!* The phrase meant nothing, yet it carried deep personal resonance. Similarly, *Across the Universe* emerged after a late-night argument with his wife, Cynthia.

---

73 https://www.johnlennonseries.com/

234   *Eris*

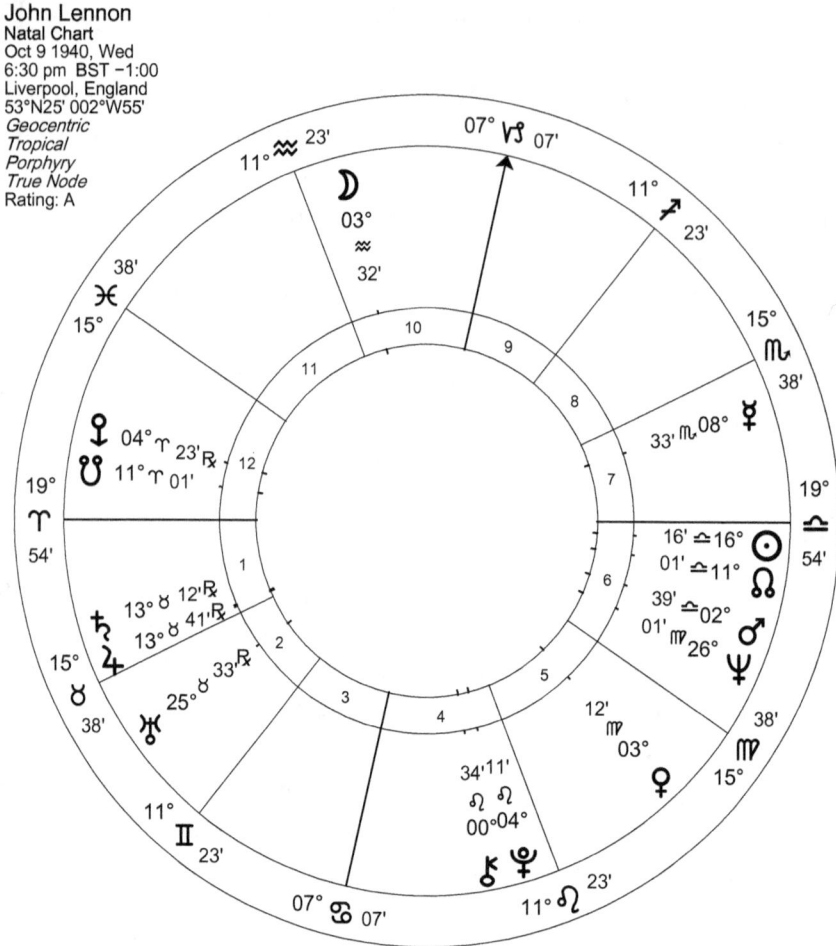

Lying in bed, words began to flow through him, and he went downstairs to capture them.

The result was a "cosmic song," filled with flowing thoughts and transcendent imagery: *"Words are flowing out like endless rain..."* The refrain, *"Jai Guru Deva Om"* ("Victory to God Divine"), served as a soothing mantra. Lennon described the song as coming through him, unbidden, a gift he didn't fully understand.

He envisioned the divine not as judgmental but as "undying love that shines around us like a million suns." Although he loved the song, he was never satisfied with any recording—perhaps because the spiritual can't always be captured in sound.

Lennon's life was marked by tragedy, rebellion, and a relentless search for meaning. He sought wisdom beyond icons like Elvis or Dylan and saw religious texts as symbolic dramas, not rules. Reflecting on his time with Maharishi Mahesh Yogi, Lennon embraced lessons from many traditions: "I'd like to be like Christ… love is a great gift… you have to protect it."

John Lennon may not be the first Beatle associated with spirituality—but he was always reaching for the sacred, in his own poetic, searching way.[74]

At the evolutionary core of John Lennon's chart is Eris retrograde at 4° Aries in the 12th house, conjunct the South Node at 11° Aries. This placement reflects past-life dynamics of isolation, rupture, and fierce individualism—where the soul acted on instinct, often in defiance of collective norms. Eris in the 12th serves as a shadow disruptor: hidden from conscious identity yet erupting in moments of soul crisis, visionary creation, or psychic exposure. Lennon's transformative impact on music, culture, and global consciousness arose from this buried evolutionary engine—where truth emerged through confrontation, and where selfhood was forged in spiritual exile.

Retrograde Eris opposes Mars at 2° Libra and the North Node at 11° Libra, both situated in the 6th house. This powerful polarity encapsulates Lennon's evolutionary tension: a karmic past marked by raw independence, now challenged to evolve into relational accountability, refined action, and service.

Mars in Libra in the 6th can struggle with indecision or misplaced aggression, yet it also carries the potential for intentional, fair action in partnership. Opposing Eris, it becomes a trigger point—revealing where Lennon's drive for peace and relational fairness clashed with unconscious rage, instinctual rebellion, or a refusal to compromise. His public contradictions—preaching love while being combative or sarcastic—reflect this unresolved dynamic.

With the North Node in conjunction with Mars, it serves as a catalyst for growth. Lennon's soul was learning how to wield power in service of others, express individuality without alienating, and channel discord into meaningful engagement with the world. This was no easy task: the

---

74 Paraphrased from https://www.culturesonar.com/john-lennon-the-spiritual-beatle/

Eris–Mars–Node axis suggests a life of confrontational service, where the very path of growth involves dismantling illusions of harmony to uncover deeper truth.

Neptune at 26° Virgo joins Mars in the 6th, creating a spiritual backdrop to this evolutionary struggle. This pairing infuses action with idealism but also introduces the risk of disillusionment, avoidance, or martyrdom. Neptune here aims to dissolve ego through service, but opposed by Eris, the lesson was clear: Lennon could not transcend conflict without first facing it directly. His music, activism, and public stances often reflected this tension—yearning to heal the world while still carrying the wound of isolation.

The Sun at 16° Libra in the 6th house represents the ego's growth path—evolving through service, refinement, and relational consciousness. The Sun is situated within a house of labor and humility. Its opposition to the 12th house with its Eris–South Node complex resonates with the larger polarity. Lennon's identity was forged through effort and confrontation: his quest for peace demanded that he view both himself and the world without illusion.

Venus at 3° Virgo in the 5th, ruling the North Node, symbolizes the need for precise, humble, and sincere love and creativity. It forms a quincunx to Eris—creating an awkward, non-negotiable evolutionary tension. Venus in Virgo seeks order, while Eris in Aries demands rupture. Lennon's artistic and romantic life reflected this: oscillating between idealization and critique, between devotion and disruption. The path was not to choose between them, but to allow Eris to reveal where integrity in love required courageous self-honesty.

The rare alignment of Saturn and Jupiter, both retrograde at 13° Taurus in the 1st house, signifies profound inner work around embodiment, security, and value. Retrograde motion internalizes both the moral compass (Jupiter) and structural authority (Saturn). In Taurus, these planets required that Lennon ground his radicalism in a stable identity—but Eris, emerging from the unconscious, continually challenged his capacity to feel at peace with himself. This conjunction doesn't aspect Eris directly, but it influences the container that struggled to contain her fire.

Uranus retrograde at 25° Taurus in the 2nd house reflects an inner revolutionary spirit—disrupting values, income, and security structures. While not in direct aspect to Eris, Uranus operates in resonance with her archetype: liberation through shock, awakening through confrontation. With Uranus ruling his Moon at 3° Aquarius in the 10th, Lennon's emotional body was attuned to shaking the system—an agent of cultural and political upheaval whose disruption of social values was both instinctive and intentional.

This Moon made Lennon emotionally connect with collective ideals and public identity. It formed a wide sextile to Eris, creating channels between his hidden rage and public persona. He deeply felt the world's expectations and responded with both visionary emotion and calculated provocation. He didn't just sing to the people—he felt through them.

Mercury at 8° Scorpio in the 7th house empowered Lennon to speak truths from the depths. Although not in direct aspect to Eris, Mercury here carries her imprint—a voice sharpened by shadow, unafraid to reveal what others have suppressed. His communication was relational, transformative, and emotionally charged, often acting as a mirror for the collective unconscious.

Pluto at 4° Leo and Chiron at 0° Leo, both in the 4th house, reveal a wounded heart and ancestral trauma. Pluto's exact trine to Eris illustrates the emotional fuel behind her fire. The Leo wound involves love, abandonment, and identity—experiences that Lennon lived through profoundly. Eris activated these unresolved issues from the shadows, erupting during times of intimacy, loss, or betrayal.

In John Lennon's chart, Eris retrograde in the 12th functions like a spiritual volcano—erupting not in his personality, but in the soul currents beneath him. Her opposition to Mars, Neptune, and the North Node places her at the heart of his evolutionary arc. She asked: "Can you fight for peace without erasing yourself? Can you serve truth without becoming its casualty?"

Venus seeks to purify Eris, Saturn and Jupiter aim to contain her, Uranus resonates with her, Mercury articulates her, and Pluto remembers her.

Eris exposed Lennon's contradictions—and through him, those of the world. In confronting the unconscious, the unjust, and the unresolved, he didn't just personally evolve—he helped us all evolve.

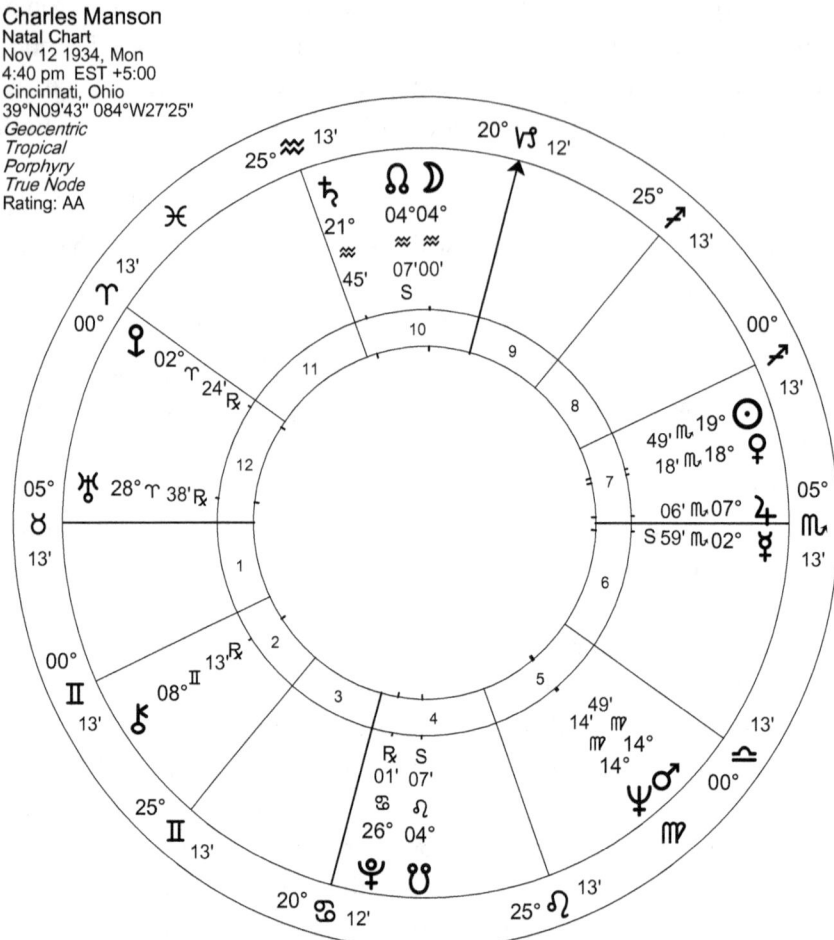

Charles Manson

Charles Manson was born Charles Milles Maddox to 16-year-old Kathleen Maddox. After a brief marriage to William Manson, the boy took his surname and kept it for life. Manson's early years were shaped by instability—his mother was an alcoholic, frequently jailed, and showed little maternal care. In one disturbing incident, she jokingly traded young Charles for a pitcher of beer, leaving him with a waitress until a relative found him.

Raised among dysfunctional relatives, Manson endured religious fanaticism, ridicule, and even a suicide in the family. By the age of nine, he was already stealing, which resulted in frequent stays in reform schools where he progressed to burglary and auto theft. At 17, he was arrested for driving a stolen car across state lines and sent to federal prison, where he accumulated assault charges before being transferred.

At 19, Manson married 17-year-old Rosalie Willis, and they moved to California in another stolen car. When she gave birth to Charles Manson Jr., he was already back in prison. She later divorced him. His second marriage to Candy Stevens, a prostitute, also ended in divorce and produced another son, Charles Luther Manson.

In 1960, Manson was sentenced to seven years for multiple crimes and served time at McNeil Island Penitentiary, where he became deeply involved in Scientology and music. Upon his release in 1967, he aimed to become a performer. In Haight-Ashbury, he attracted disillusioned youth with drugs, music, and apocalyptic visions.

One of his first followers was Mary Brunner, a librarian who left her previous life due to his influence. By using charisma and manipulation, Manson attracted more followers, claiming to be a prophet and warning of an impending race war he thought was foretold in the Beatles' song *Helter Skelter*. Aspiring for fame, Manson connected with Gary Hinman, who introduced him to Dennis Wilson of The Beach Boys. Wilson briefly supported him and introduced him to producer Terry Melcher, whom Manson thought would launch his career. When Melcher declined, Manson's resentment grew.

The group moved to Spahn Ranch, living communally and adopting Manson's ideology. When the race war failed to erupt, he decided to start one. The first murder was that of Hinman, staged to implicate the Black Panthers. Feeling encouraged, Manson sent his followers to 10050 Cielo Drive, which had once been rented by Melcher and was now the home of actress Sharon Tate and Roman Polanski. On August 9, 1969, Tate—who was eight months pregnant—was brutally murdered, along with four guests. The following night, Leno and Rosemary LaBianca were also killed.

By December 1969, Manson and several of his cult members were arrested. The trial captivated the nation, with Manson's erratic behavior and swastika tattoo becoming symbols of evil. Convicted of murder and conspiracy, he was sentenced to death, which was later commuted to life when California abolished the death penalty in 1972. He remained at Corcoran State Prison, was denied parole twelve times, and died in 2017 at the age of 83.

Despite the horror of his crimes, Manson became a grim cultural icon—his image appearing on posters and T-shirts, while his story inspired numerous books, films, and TV shows. Vincent Bugliosi's *Helter Skelter*, based on the trial, remains the definitive account. As Laurie Levenson said, "If you're going to be evil, you have to be off-the-charts evil, and Charlie Manson was off-the-charts evil." His legacy remains a symbol of manipulation, madness, and America's darkest countercultural shadows.[75]

Charles Manson's natal chart reveals a soul twisted by fragmentation, delusion, and unresolved rage. With Eris retrograde at 2° Aries in the 12th house, the evolutionary impulse to break free and assert identity lies submerged in the unconscious, emerging not as conscious rebellion but as psychic disturbance. Eris in Aries demands individuation through instinctual force; however, in the 12th house, that drive becomes entangled with shadow material, ancestral pain, and a distorted spiritual identity. For Manson, this manifested as a pathological dissolution of self into rageful archetypes—messiah, martyr, tyrant—fueled by delusion and masked as a divine mission.

The psychic distortion intensifies with Uranus retrograde at 28° Aries, also in the 12th house, electrifying the unconscious field with erratic, revolutionary surges. His inner world was charged with unpredictable, dissociative flashes of insight—mystic or manic—and combined with Eris, this blend suggests a volatile psychic mix of spiritual alienation and unintegrated rage. His need for liberation was overtaken by unconscious content too explosive to process internally.

The danger of this unprocessed psychic material is emphasized by Mercury at 2° Scorpio in the 6th house, quincunx Eris, revealing a mental structure misaligned with the deeper unconscious drives attempting to surface. His mind became a channel for manipulation and domination rather than self-understanding, fueled by paranoid survival logic and control disguised as insight.

Manson's Pluto at 26° Cancer retrograde is conjoined with the South Node at 4° Leo in the 4th house, disclosing a karmic inheritance of entanglement, manipulation, and abuse of power rooted in the emotional

---

[75] Paraphrased from Rosenberg, Jennifer. *Biography of Charles Manson, Cult Leader and Mass Murderer*. ThoughtCo, Sep. 9, 2021, thoughtco.com/charles-manson-cult-leader-serial-killer-1779365

body. The soul enters this lifetime burdened with unresolved trauma around family, belonging, and betrayal. The home itself becomes a crucible of distortion, where intimacy, instead of nurturing, was bound to control, abandonment, or exploitation. Communication and ideology are implicated, but their roots lie deeper: in a history of unmet needs and unresolved wounds of origin. This Pluto–South Node configuration speaks of past-life roles where power was exerted from a place of emotional hunger, where the need for security and recognition became twisted into dominance over others. Rather than moving beyond these dynamics, the soul carried them forward, intensifying the very patterns it was meant to outgrow.

Manson's Pluto retrograde at 26° Cancer conjoined with the South Node at 4° Leo in the 4th house discloses a karmic inheritance bound to distorted belonging, betrayal, and power struggles rooted in the emotional body. The soul enters this lifetime carrying the weight of unresolved trauma around family, home, and intimacy—places where nurturing had been fused with control and exploitation. Instead of receiving nourishment, the past-life pattern was one of manipulation, domination, or abandonment. This imprint suggests lifetimes in which power was misused from a place of emotional hunger, turning the need for security into compulsion, and the longing for belonging into control.

Uranus retrograde in Taurus in the 12th house, forming a square to the nodal axis, intensifies this karmic complex as a skipped step. The soul has been fractured by experiences of sudden loss, exclusion, and exile—traumas of belonging that left deep imprints in the unconscious. The unresolved Uranian material disrupts the soul's evolutionary axis: rather than moving toward the Aquarian North Node in the 10th, which calls for authentic responsibility and the building of community based on equality, Manson replayed the trauma compulsively. His rebellion against consensus norms was not the liberation Uranus intends, but anarchy, paranoia, and alienation. He created a "family" distorted by the very dynamics of control and betrayal that Pluto on the South Node reveals, turning the wound of belonging into a theater of domination.

Taken together, the Pluto–South Node conjunction and Uranus square the nodes describe a soul bound to unresolved karmic fractures around family, power, and individuation. The evolutionary intention was to transform the trauma of exclusion into wisdom, to use radical individuality in service of collective truth. Instead, Manson intensified the very shadows he was meant to evolve beyond. His chart discloses the archetype of a soul caught in its own skipped steps—unable to resolve the wound of belonging, unable to integrate the shocks of Uranus into authentic liberation, and thus repeating history as pathology rather than transcending it as evolution.

The Moon is positioned at 4° Aquarius conjunct the North Node in the 10th house, symbolizing a potential for emotionally grounded involvement in social evolution. However, this potential is distorted by a series of volatile aspects: the Moon squares Mars, indicating emotional reactivity and rage; it also squares Uranus, highlighting dissociation, instability, and psychic unpredictability. Rather than evolving emotionally, Manson became fragmented. His emotional body could not bear the burden of the ancestral, karmic, and psychic content seeking to emerge.

The Sun at 19° Scorpio in the 7th house, square Saturn at 21° Aquarius, reveals the ongoing conflict between personal will and the need for individuation. Saturn in Aquarius demands inner authority and accountability, but the square indicates a refusal—or inability—to mature. The tension between these two suggests a fractured ego trying to assert power in relationships while rejecting the limits and boundaries of reality. Venus at 18° Scorpio, also in the 7th, further complicates the obsessive relational entanglement and the use of charm as a means of control.

Mercury square Pluto amplifies a mental fixation on domination and secrecy, blocking the soul's intended path forward. The mind remains trapped in karmic loops. Pluto square the nodes reinforces this: his evolution requires a complete restructuring of emotional survival patterns, yet instead, the soul repeats them at an even deeper level.

All of this feeds back into Eris in the 12th—the daemonic disruptor operating behind the veil. She did not emerge in clarity or courage but through distortion, fueled by centuries of repression, rage, and displacement. Without a conscious ego capable of holding her fire, that archetypal force bled into every corner of Manson's psyche, leaving him both the carrier and the victim of an unintegrated revolution of the soul.

From Chaos to Clarity

In this era of upheaval, the children and siblings of Eris stride boldly across the world stage. As their mother sowed discord to awaken hidden truths, they too manifest in the movements, revelations, and reckonings of our time. Strife, rivalry, lawlessness, and ruin may walk alongside us, yet justice, perseverance, and the relentless call for truth also accompany us. Each figure from myth echoes through the challenges we face, their shadows falling upon institutions and hearts alike.

Yet it is not only her offspring who stir the cauldron of our age; it is Eris herself, always watchful and cunning. Her schemes are evident in the rapid unraveling of deceit and the sudden, undeniable revelation of what was once hidden. She casts the proverbial golden apple into the banquet halls of power, provoking conflict and exposing the vanity and miscreant behavior of those who rule. When the structures of our lives begin to break apart, hidden truths often emerge from the very cracks created by chaos, rising to the surface. The turbulence she incites serves a purpose: through the collapse of falsehoods, the possibility of renewal arises.

The offspring of Eris emerge from the fissures of societal fabric—whistleblowers exposing corporate deceit, activists challenging the erosion of civil liberties, and voices raised against the unchecked power of oligarchs. Strife exists in the courts and congresses, where ideological battles rage on. Rivalry thrives in competitions for resources, technology, and global dominance. Lawlessness manifests in abuses of power, the neglect of the vulnerable, and the manipulation of justice for personal gain. Ruin looms in ecological degradation and the disintegration of systems that no longer serve the whole.

Yet Eris does not stir solely to create chaos. Her influence compels the recognition of what has festered in silence. In every scandal exposed, in each demand for accountability, and within the rising movements for equity and sustainability, we find her children's presence. The fall of corrupt leaders, the breaking of generational cycles of harm, and the dismantling of exploitative structures bear witness to her catalytic power.

Consider the global uprisings against systemic injustice—voices uniting to denounce oppression, from the streets of major capitals to the digital realms where truths are unearthed and shared. The children of Eris thrive in these spaces, where courage fuels movements and hidden truths come to light. The unraveling of corporate monopolies, the resistance against environmental destruction, and the relentless pursuit of transparency all exemplify her influence. Every toppled dictator, every exposed crime of power, and every empowered community demonstrates the inevitability of her justice.

Like a serpent shedding its skin, society writhes in discomfort as the old falls away. This is the labor of collective evolution. Where injustice once reigned unchallenged, the guardians of truth arise. Eris calls upon us to look beyond the veil of illusion, confront the consequences of negligence and greed, and reclaim the dignity of shared responsibility.

Even now, the global yearning for regenerative systems reflects a mythic narrative. The rise of grassroots governance, the reimagining of economies to serve the many rather than the few, and the protection of Earth's sacred ecosystems indicate the resolution she demands. Ancient karmic debts seek balance. The echoes of colonialism, exploitation, and marginalization call for acknowledgment and restitution. It is through this reckoning that renewal takes root.

The sibling presence of Discord and Strife reminds us that conflict is not inherently destructive; rather, it is the crucible in which complacency is burned away and clarity is forged. Through discontent, we are called to examine our values and confront the forces that we have allowed to shape our lives. Rivalry, when tempered by wisdom, gives birth to innovation and resilience. Lawlessness, when observed without blinders, inspires the strengthening of genuine justice. Even Ruin, grim and unrelenting, brings clarity about what must never be repeated.

Walking the path of Eris means embracing the discomfort of transformation. The ferocity of her truth burns away illusion, leaving only what is essential. Through her children's tumult, she beckons us toward the restoration of harmony. The era we inhabit is not merely one of destruction but of rebirth—a time when we stand on the threshold of our mythic becoming. Just as the golden apple cast by Eris revealed the vanity of the gods, her presence demands that we ask ourselves: What shall we value? What truths shall we serve? And how will we write the next chapter of our shared fate?

The children of Eris remain present, urging us to articulate what has long been unspoken, dismantle what no longer serves us, and forge a future that can sustain generations to come. They embody the restless call for equilibrium, the storm before the stillness, and the challenge to rise with courage and integrity. And behind it all, we glimpse Eris herself—the silent orchestrator of change, the keeper of the mirror in which we must confront our own reflection.

To deepen this reflection, I encourage you to revisit the chart examples and case studies within this book. Examine the patterns of Eris in your astrological chart. How has her influence woven through your experiences, revealing truth through disruption? In what ways have her children played a role in your personal journey, and what lessons remain to be integrated? Through this lens, you may come to see how the myths of old resonate in the stories of our lives, urging us to embrace our part in the ongoing mythology of awakening and transformation.

In moments of distress and disappointment, the lessons of Eris guide us toward practical resilience. Embrace the truth, even when it is uncomfortable. Reflect on the patterns of conflict in your life and consider what they reveal. Lean into personal growth through radical self-honesty. Support collective healing by participating in movements for justice and renewal. Remember that from the wreckage of what was, the seeds of what will be are sown. Through self-examination, compassionate dialogue, and courageous action, we align with the transformative power of Eris and become agents of the evolution she demands.

As we cross this threshold, may we call upon her spirit not merely as a destroyer, but as the midwife of the world to come.

Afterword

"She didn't ask for a seat at the table. She threw down the apple and rewrote the rules."

I invite you to sit with the mirror that Eris holds up—not to history, but to you. Where does Eris live in you? Is she the voice you silence when truth feels dangerous? Is she the instinct you suppress to stay safe?

We've seen how Eris reveals her signature through the unmistakable force of the soul set ablaze—how she calls out truth in the voice, the body, the page, the stage. She erupts as presence, conviction, defiance, demand.

Angelou named her. With **Eris in the 8th**, she pulled truth from the underworld, transmuting trauma into testament. She didn't just speak—she testified, transforming private pain into public power.

Coltrane played her. With **Eris in the 1st**, he sounded her—each note a consecrated breath. Eris surged through him as soul-fire and sacred devotion, lifting the collective into altered states through pure vibration.

Baez sang her. With **Eris on the South Node**, she channeled ancestral rebellion, standing weaponless yet unyielding before empire. Her courage rang clear in every protest, every phrase, every stage she reclaimed as sacred ground.

Ginsberg howled her. With **Eris in the 1st**, he shattered the silence. His words weren't just poetry—they were prophecy. His howl made Eris audible to a world that had tried to forget her. Raw, embodied, uncontainable, she poured through his language as confrontation and flame.

McCartney harmonized her. With **Eris in the 7th**, he gave voice to a generation longing for something real. His music didn't merely soothe—it summoned, calling forth unity, love, and the radical re-enchantment of human connection.

And then there's **Manson**, whose **Eris in the 12th**, twisted the signal—warping truth into delusion, prophecy into manipulation. He, too, was possessed by a fire, but lacked the center to guide it. His was a shadow mirror—a warning.

Where **Ginsberg** bore the burden of awareness, **Manson** collapsed into illusion. Ginsberg turned the fire into a signal flare—lighting the way for misfits, mystics, and edgewalkers to follow.

Manson distorted it.
Warhol styled it.
Obama embodied it.
Fonda fought with it.
King died for it.
Chávez organized it.
Assange exposed it.
Temple sweetened it.
Grace carried it with elegance and edge.

So… what will *you* do with it?

Will you silence it—or listen?
Will you follow the path of concealment—or revelation?
Will you distort the truth—or let it blaze through you, wild and whole?

Because Eris doesn't ask for permission.
She asks for courage.
And she's already speaking through you.

Before we toss the apple, we must first see ourselves—not as perfect, but as whole. You've heard her story—through myth and movement, through poets and prophets.
Through silence broken and truths reclaimed.

Eris is not a threat. She is an opener. Not everything disrupted is lost.
Not every fracture is failure.
Sometimes, the break is where the light begins.

Every soul experiences a golden apple moment.
That moment when you:
Cannot keep the secret any longer.
Decline to participate
Tell the truth that shatters the silence.

Sometimes, it's public. Sometimes, it's quiet.

The golden apple moment isn't about vengeance.
It's not about creating chaos.
It's about revealing what's already broken—so healing can begin.

Ask yourself: What am I no longer willing to acknowledge?
Where is my silence betraying my soul?
What truth am I here to throw into the center of power?

Remember: You don't need permission.
You don't need a seat at the table.
You just need to listen when your soul says:

Now…toss the apple.

About the Author

Daniel Fiverson is a certified Evolutionary Astrologer, trained in the Jeffrey Wolf School of EA. He is a teacher and writer whose work combines astrology, the I Ching, Tarot, and Kabbalah to bring psychological depth, karmic insight, and archetypal precision to a multidimensional approach to counseling. His services include Evolutionary Astrology readings for natal charts, transits, solar returns, synastry, and relocations.

His astrological lineage is rooted in a diverse and influential group of teachers and thinkers, including Jeffrey Wolf Green, Dane Rudhyar, Liz Greene, Howard Sasportas, Mark Jones, Brian Clark, Jason Holley, Kim Marie Weimer, and others whose work has shaped the landscape of modern astrology.

Daniel's current work highlights Pluto and Eris as catalysts for both personal transformation and collective awakening. He regularly posts astrological commentary on his website and social media under the title *The Astrological Weather Report*. He actively participates in Kepler College Toastmasters, where he continues to enhance his skills in astrological storytelling through public speaking. He also serves as one of the lead instructors for Kepler College's Evolutionary Astrology Certification Courses.

Daniel lives in Santa Fe, New Mexico, with his partner, Susan Waller. Together, they continue to explore the symbolic threads of spirit, shadow, and the stars—honoring astrology and their connection to the Earth as a living language of the soul.

evolutionaryastrologer.net

facebook.com/evolutionaryastrology

www.ingramcontent.com/pod-product-compliance
Lightning Source LLC
Chambersburg PA
CBHW050349230426
43663CB00010B/2048